Random Destinations

Random Destinations
Escaping the Holocaust and Starting Life Anew

Lilian R. Furst

RANDOM DESTINATIONS
© Lilian R. Furst, 2005.

First published in 2005 by
PALGRAVE MACMILLAN™
175 Fifth Avenue, New York, N.Y. 10010 and
Houndmills, Basingstoke, Hampshire, England RG21 6XS
Companies and representatives throughout the world.

PALGRAVE MACMILLAN is the global academic imprint of the Palgrave Macmillan division of St. Martin's Press, LLC and of Palgrave Macmillan Ltd. Macmillan® is a registered trademark in the United States, United Kingdom and other countries. Palgrave is a registered trademark in the European Union and other countries.

ISBN 1–4039–6975–2

Library of Congress Cataloging-in-Publication Data

Furst, Lilian R.
    Random destinations : escaping the Holocaust and starting life anew / Lilian R. Furst.
        p. cm.
    Includes bibliographical references and index.
    ISBN 1–4039–6975–2 (alk. paper)
        1. English fiction—20th century—History and criticism. 2. Refugees, Jewish, in literature. 3. English-speaking countries—In literature. I. Title.

PR888.J4F87 2005
23'.914093529924—dc28   2005047208

A catalogue record for this book is available from the British Library.

Design by Newgen Imaging Systems (P) Ltd., Chennai, India.

First edition: September 2005

10 9 8 7 6 5 4 3 2 1

Printed in the United States of America.

*To the Memory of my parents, Dr. Desider Furst and
Dr. Sara Furst-Neufeld, who had the wisdom to guide me to safety,
and to all those members of the Furst family
who did not manage to escape.*

CONTENTS

INDIA

ACKNOWLEDGMENTS

It is a pleasure to express my thanks to the many people who have helped me in various ways during the course of my work on this study:

Alice Kuzniar, who started my reflections by urging me to go and see *Into the Arms of Strangers*, and who invited me to contribute to the University of North Carolina's series on German–Jewish cultural relations.

Ester Zago, as ever, whose enthusiasm for and belief in the value of the project has sustained me throughout, and who arranged at an early stage to have me address the Boulder Jewish Community Center.

Madeline G. Levine, whose stimulating suggestions prompted new ideas, and whose computer expertise was decisive in dealing with my stubbornly dyslexic software.

Marina Alexandrova, my model research assistant, who so willingly gave me help far beyond the call of duty.

Willi Goetschel, who invited me to speak at the University of Toronto.

Wolfgang Wierscheim, who sent me W.G. Sebald's *Austerlitz* in summer 2001 on its publication in Germany.

Susan Groag Bell, who arranged to have Anita Brookner's *The Next Big Thing* mailed to me from England.

Anabel Aliaga-Buchenau and Ingrid Aliaga-Weber, for giving me Stefanie Zweig's *Nirgendwo in Afrika*.

Warren A. Nord of the University of North Carolina's Program in the Humanities and Human Values, who asked me to speak at a summer seminar for middle- and high-school teachers.

Erika H. Casey, whose continuing interest and sound judgment were a lasting source of support.

Wolfgang Frank, who invited me to speak at the Institute for Social Research in Frankfurt, Germany.

Janice H. Koelb, for her great patience with my repeated stupidity at the computer.

Dr. C.F. Irons, last but by no means least, whose insights fostered a deeper understanding of the entire topic.

TO THE READER

I hope you will read this preface. Many readers apparently don't bother to do so, preferring to plunge straight into the first chapter. I would very much like you to read this preface because it explains the book's genesis, title, terminology, and methods.

Random Destinations is about a category of people who have been called "escapees," that is, those who managed to flee the European mainland in the 1930s before the full fury of the Nazi deportations and killings. They are "shards from the explosion,"[1] scattered at random through many parts of the world, where they have resettled and started life anew.

I was reminded of these escapees by the film *Into the Arms of Strangers: Stories of the "Kindertransport"* (1999) about the remarkable enterprise in late 1938 and 1939 to save European children from the impending disaster by transporting them to England, where they were brought up mainly by volunteer foster families. The children ranged in age from three to their late teens, and most of them never saw their parents again after taking leave from them at the railroad station. The vast majority of their parents perished, as the children heard after the war. The film juxtaposes black-and-white photographs, newsreel clips from the late 1930s of the persecution of the Jews, and atmospheric footage with recent color interviews of twelve of those "children" who recount how they felt, how they coped, and how their lives took shape. An Oscar-winning documentary the film has aroused great interest in Europe, especially in Germany, where it has been shown to schoolchildren as an educational tool.

I must declare my personal stake in this topic. Born in Vienna I was myself registered for such a *Kindertransport* and was to go to a family in Norwich, which had a daughter of my age. When my parents and I left Vienna in December 1938 on a train heading west I saw the first batch of those children. It was an unforgettable, indeed traumatic, sight—a whole carriage full of children sitting glum and silent, each with a number on a cardboard placard hung round his or her neck on a string. How they stared at me, the only child walking along the corridor of that train securely gripping her father's hand! This autobiographical experience together with the oral history I picked up from my parents and their friends forms the extraneous frame and the impetus to this study.

The accounts given by those interviewed as aging adults in *Into the Arms of Strangers* of the course of their subsequent lives made me wonder whether and how such individuals had been portrayed in fiction. I found a considerable number of short stories and novels, which showed them at various ages and stages of their new lives in their adopted countries. No concerted analysis has been carried out of these *literary* representations, although there are many sociohistorical studies as well as an abundance of memoirs. I am dealing only with those who escaped Central Europe before the outbreak of war in September 1939, not those who survived the concentration camps or in hiding, and exclusively with *fictions* of their post-escape lives.

My title, *Random Destinations*, is meant to capture the contingencies of their flight and the fortuitousness that governed where they ended up. "We were all," wrote my father, "victims of an unprecedented upheaval, a gigantic hurricane that lifted us out of our homes and dropped us indiscriminately all over the world. We were nobody's responsibility, and where we landed was a matter of luck."[2] "Random" is the appropriate word for the results of the whirlwind that struck European Jewry. It is defined in the *Oxford English Dictionary* as "having no specific pattern or objective; lacking causal relationships; haphazard; without definite method; unsystematically." Derived from the Middle English *randoun*, the Old French *randonner*, "to move rapidly or violently," it conveys the idea of moving hastily without particular direction. In this sense it is clearly pertinent to those who strove to leave Central Europe in the later 1930s. Apart from this normative denotation it alludes covertly to a mistake, which caused merriment in England during the worst days of the bombing. In order to avoid disclosing which places had been hit, the BBC news would simply announce that attacks had been "at random." The German monitoring service, seemingly deficient in knowledge of English, took random to be the name of a town so that the Germans were informed of frequent air raids on Random!

"Destination" is the place or point to which a person or thing is going or being sent. Etymologically it stems from the Middle English *destinen*, the Old French *destiner*, and the Latin *destinare*, to direct toward a given spot, which one aims to reach. In the context of the flight from the Nazis the word destination has an ironic ring for, as Peter Eppel has commented: "[O]nly in exceptional cases were refugees able to choose their eventual country of asylum freely and with foreknowledge of what would be awaiting them there."[3]

I have been using the term *refugees* because the new arrivals in their host countries were consistently designated as such. The description is apposite insofar as it means, according to the *Oxford English Dictionary*, "a fugitive from his own country, seeking shelter in another, especially from persecution on account of religious or political views." Derived from *refugié*, the French past participle of *refugier*, to put in a refuge, the word refers to one who, owing to religious persecution or political troubles, seeks asylum in a foreign country. First applied to the French Huguenots, who came to England after the revocation of the edict of Nantes in 1658, it then came to be used for those driven from home by war or the imminence of invasion or some other disaster. British officials resorted to it descriptively in the Boer War, in World War I, and in the course of the late 1930s and World War II. The necessity of finding protection, shelter, a haven, or sanctuary is the refugee's defining characteristic.

But how long does one remain in the limbo of refugeedom? After the passage of several years, when the refugees have acquired the language of their adoptive country along with citizenship, stable homes, and livelihoods, is it not time to discard the term? The subject has sparked heated debate recently in the monthly journal of the British Association of Jewish Refugees, founded in 1941. Had the moment not come to retire *refugee* and change the association's name in recognition of the permanently settled status of its members? While some favored the suggestion, the majority resisted, asserting that it was precisely their past as refugees from Central Europe that united the journal's readership even into the second generation, which has formed a subgroup that sponsors its own activities and still feels a certain cohesiveness stemming from their parents' common past.

This debate points to a disparity between the United States and England. In the United States, where newcomers are expected to blend in the mythical melting pot, the word *refugee* is applied only to the relatively early stages of the immigrants' lives in their new country. Bernard Malamud's short story, "The German Refugee" (1963), centers on a journalist's difficulties in acquiring English in 1939 in time for a decisive lecture, while another of his stories that refers to *refugees*, "Take Pity" (1955) also deals with the struggles of fairly recent arrivals to gain an economic foothold. In England, as the naming of the Association of Jewish Refugees shows, the term has persisted longer, certainly in the consciousness of those to whom it was once attached with a rather pejorative connotation, and who now take pride in having converted it into something of a badge of honor. Although they have made many outstanding contributions to the culture of the host country, they still maintain traces of their past, which distinguish—and separate—them from their current milieu. Terminology thus assumes more than academic significance as an indicator both of the newcomers' self-image and of their position along the spectrum of integration into or lingering distance from their adopted environment.

A cluster of related words addresses this same topic of the presence of foreigners. These other words carry differing undertones although they tend to overlap so that they resist rigorous distinctions. The overarching term for all who live outside their native lands is in the literal sense *expatriates,* but the term denotes those who do so of their own volition, often for a variety of personal reasons. They are at liberty to return home at any time if they so choose.

The situation of exiles is considerably more complex. Exile may be either an involuntary state or a partly voluntary one. Exiles may have suffered enforced banishment from their native land by authoritative decree as a punishment; alternatively they may have imposed the rupture on themselves as a protest. Exile entails an ideology—generally of a political nature. Most exiles cherish a continuing attachment to their country of origin, hoping for a return once the regime offensive to them has been overthrown. As Paul Ilie has so aptly formulated it, "exile . . . is an emptiness that awaits restoration . . . the absence that compensates itself by nostalgia and hopeful expectation."[4] The key word there is "restoration" with its prospect of a return not merely territorially to a place but just as much emotionally to a state of harmony with the homeland.

The category of *exile* is not well suited to those who fled Central Europe in the 1930s. Loyal, peaceful citizens, they had by and large not been political activists. They did feel nostalgia for the pre-Nazi days, yet they were so deeply wounded, indeed violated by their homeland's virulent rejection of them that they held none of the hopes of restoration typical of exiles.[5] The majority recognized from the outset that their move was a permanent one; even before news of the concentration camp atrocities and the gas chambers, they sensed the radical break that had occurred. They censored their criticism of their host country by constantly reminding themselves of their gratitude for the shelter they were being given. Only a very few harbored serious thoughts of a postwar return. In Manchester, where I grew up, they gathered at Austria House nurturing socialist/communist ideals—and when they did go back after the war they were rudely received and grossly disappointed.

The more open-ended, generic term, which I have also been using, *emigrant*, seems at first sight more appropriate. Emigrants are people who leave one state in order to settle in another where they are not natives. But, as English and American dictionary definitions alike make clear, to emigrate and even more so to migrate carries certain implications. Migration refers to birds who have the habit of moving periodically from one region to another in search of a different climate, or food, or for breeding. By extension of this practical purpose migrant workers are those who are compelled to emigrate in order to find work, often making seasonal moves in keeping with the agricultural calendar.

Emigrants fits quite well those East European Jews in the later nineteenth and into the twentieth century who moved partly for economic and partly for political reasons. Forbidden by law to own land or to have access to the professions, they were hard put to support their large families. An already difficult situation would be brought to a head by the politico-religious upheaval caused by the sporadic pogroms, which would trigger the decision to leave and to make a fresh start in a less hostile place. Those who left in the 1930s, on the other hand, were unwilling emigrants. They did not voluntarily seek greener pastures; on the contrary they were comfortably ensconced in their homes and communities. Although discrimination against Jews was endemic throughout Europe before the 1930s, it was not sufficiently ferocious to form an incentive to emigration. Only with the intensification of the restrictions imposed on Jews as part of the escalating persecution in the course of the 1930s did the economic factor come more to the fore; the outrages of Crystal Night no longer left any doubt as to the gravity of the threat.

Nevertheless lexical slippages so pervade this entire area that categories readily prove elusive or misleading. For example those who are emigrants from their homeland may be called refugees in the host country, or may be perceived as immigrants. Walter Hölbling asserts that the "differences connoted by terms like 'emigrant,' 'exilant,' 'refugee,' and 'immigrant' . . . refer to the individual's subjective sense of their situation as well as to their objective treatment at the hand of both their countries of origin and of destination."[6] Clearly many inner and outer variables come into play to shape people's "sense of their situation." The discrepancy between the receiving administration's perception of the new arrivals and their own is articulated by Leo Spitzer in *Hotel Bolivia* (1998): "The immigrants were after all *refugees* and not voluntary emigrés. Before their departure from Europe, each and every one of them had been identified as undesirable and stripped of citizenship and belongings" (153). Their move to Bolivia was "a consequence of oppression and expulsion" (153), not an expression of their idealistic commitment to colonization through a farming experiment. In other words they saw themselves as refugees whereas to the Bolivian authorities they were immigrants.

The ambivalences intrinsic to the terminology are succinctly expressed by the German poet Bertolt Brecht:

> Immer fand ich den Namen falsch, den man uns gab:
> Emigranten.
> Das heisst doch Auswanderer. Aber wir
> Wanderten doch nicht aus nach freiem Entschluss
> Wählend ein anderes Land. Wanderten wir doch nicht
> Ein in ein Land, dort zu bleiben, womöglich für immer.
> Sondern wir flohen, Vertriebene sind wir, Verbannte.[7]

> (I always thought the name given to us was wrong:
> Emigrants.
> After all, it refers to willing travelers. But we
> Did not travel of our own free will
> Choosing another country. And did not travel
> To a country to settle there, possibly forever.
> Instead we fled. We were the driven out, the banished.)

While Brecht gives eloquent voice to the dilemmas of apposite denomination, he can offer no viable usage. "Vertriebene" (the driven out) or "Verbannte" (the banished) are simply too cumbersome.

So is *the forcibly displaced*, although it is an accurate summary of the situation. What is more *displaced persons* is a phrase with a life of its own and a specific, limited meaning; it described postwar homeless survivors who lived in temporary holding camps until they could be more permanently resettled. Moreover the great variety of people who had to leave Europe in the 1930s (not all of them Jewish) means that "[N]o single term adequately embraces them all."[8] Because all the alternatives carry associations of various kinds I am opting for the somewhat awkward "escapees." Admittedly this is not free of other meanings either (as no word can be). Normatively an escapee is someone who has bolted from prison or made off from some criminal act. The Central European Jews' sole criminality lay in their racial heritage. However in light of the fate that would most likely have befallen them if they had not succeeded in leaving, escapee is the most fitting term for them.

Destination proved so powerful a determinant of subsequent destiny that it is no mere play on words to claim that destination was destiny. As Gulie

Ne'eman Arad points out: "How Jews fared in America depended on when they came, where they came from, and where they settled. Yet the Jewish community has often been studied with little regard for the social, ethnic, and political contexts in which the Jews found themselves."[9] This holds not just for America but equally for all the other destinations where escapees sought to build new lives. For this reason I have arranged the fictions according to the places where the escapees landed: London, the British provinces, New York, the U.S. provinces, and India. The length of the sections varies, corresponding to some extent but by no means entirely, to the number of escapees who settled at each destination. Many more gravitated to the capitals, London and New York, than to the provinces. However India, which housed only about 1,000 escapees, furnishes a memorable novel and a stellar short story, perhaps because the cultural distance between the newcomers and the locals was so great as to evoke striking works. In each case the focus is on the interplay between "where they came from, and where they settle," that is, the culture of origin and that of destination. At every location the order is by ascending age so as to ascertain to what extent age at arrival in the new country affects the capacity for acculturation: How easily is language acquisition accomplished? Into what occupations do the escapees go and how successful are they? What is their financial situation? To what degree are they integrated into the communities in which they live? Are there indications of malaise or even alienation? Do they cherish religious beliefs, and if so, more or less strongly than before their dislocation? How conflicted are their feelings toward their native lands—nostalgia or anger? Are they dogged by memories of loss or do they rejoice in their survival? What factors shape their sense of identity? Are they destabilized by the presence of absence? How prevalent is anxiety even in safety? Is gratitude toward the host country tempered by a continuing sense of strangeness? And what narrative means are used to show and explore their attitudes? From whose perspective are they seen? Are they envisaged predominantly in an elegiac, pathetic, triumphant, or an ironic mode?

The actual choice of texts has been far more problematic than I had anticipated because there were more fictions than I had expected, and additional ones kept appearing in the course of my research as the escapee became almost a popular figure. Some works were quite easy to eliminate. For instance Sara Paretsky's series of thrillers, notably *Bitter Medicine* (1987) and *Total Recall* (2001), include Lotty (Charlotte) Herschel, a physician in Chicago, originally from Vienna, but they abound in errors and anachronisms, which reveal ignorance of the historical situation. This criticism applies equally to Nicolas Delbanco's *What Remains* (2000), which is full of howlers about conditions in wartime and immediate postwar London. The crass misconceptions in these novels are an obstacle to taking their portrayals of escapees seriously. In other cases the escapee character is merely subsidiary. Allegra Goodman's short story, "Fannie Mae" in *The Family Markowitz* (1997) refers to the already dead Ben, who had become a high-school teacher of French and German in New York and whose unfinished doctoral dissertation on Thomas Mann, begun in Vienna, lies unread in a drawer. A more developed but still secondary presence is that of Esther in Margaret Drabble's *The Radiant Way* (1987). Born in Berlin Esther had come to England as a child, and in Cambridge had met Liz and Alix, the novel's central characters. As an unmarried, bisexual, professionally active Renaissance art historian, Esther, who eventually moves to Italy, stands apart from the marital and family complications of Liz's and Alix's lives.

Even where the escapee is the main protagonist the focus may be on issues other than those of resettlement. Thus in Anita Brookner's *The Next Big Thing* (2002) it is the aging and approaching death of Julius Herz, in his seventies with increasingly severe symptoms of heart disease, that is at the core of the narrative. At the opposite end of the spectrum in both life stage and date of publication, Philip Larkin's *A Girl in Winter* (1947) depicts the desolation of Katherine, a young woman from Germany, who is a librarian in a small town in the English Midlands during the war. The wintry dreariness contrasts with the romance she had enjoyed on a summer visit to an English country family. The members of the Rosendorf Quartet in Nathan Shaham's novel (1987) of that title are similarly more concerned with their personal interactions and their music making than with their adjustment to Israel, their new country. Norbert Gstrein's *Die englischen Jahre* (1999; *The English Years*) is a murder mystery in which the victim happens to be an escapee. *The Amazing Adventures of Kavalier and Clay* (2002) by Michael Chabon is an exercise in the grotesque, which begins with Josef Kavalier's escape from Prague in a coffin, disguised as a female Golem, abetted by a performing illusionist. Arriving in New York via Lithuania, Shanghai, and San Francisco he goes into the comic book business with his cousin Sam(uel) Clay(man). Granted that some tales of escape were extraordinarily weird, this one nonetheless strains credibility, one of my cardinal criteria. This preference for the realist also explains why I have passed over Isaac Bashevis Singer's short story, "A Wedding in Brownsville" (1964); it also crosses the divide into the fantastic as Dr. Solomon Margolin from Poland via Berlin (he reappears later in Singer's novel, *Shadows on the Hudson*) experiences a reunion with other escapees from his hometown—after he has just been killed in an accident on the way to the wedding.

Probably the most controversial exclusions are two recent German novels: Stefanie Zweig's *Nirgendwo in Afrika* (2000; *Nowhere in Africa*), and W.G. Sebald's *Austerlitz* (2001). Apart from their common portrayal of escapees, they are utterly different. *Nirgendwo in Afrika*, openly autobiographical in source, chronicles the adventures of a German lawyer, Walter Redlich and his wife and daughter as farmers in Kenya. The emphasis is on the exoticism of their new environment, their total lack of preparation for it, and the repeated thwarting and failure of all their efforts so that ultimately after the war they return to Germany. Its narrative techniques are simple, not to say simplistic; it is sustained merely by interest in its plot despite the absence of literary subtlety. By contrast *Austerlitz* is highly sophisticated, very complex, and given to much digression in recounting the quest of Jacques

Austerlitz, who had left Prague at age four on a *Kindertransport*, to retrieve his true identity. It is admittedly hard to justify the omission of these two works. Literary quality was one of my criteria, and this counted against *Nirgendwo in Afrika*. As for *Austerlitz*, by the time it appeared I had already decided to work on Sebald's "Max Ferber." Since the novel replicates in almost baroque form the narrative strategies of the short story, I opted to remain with it because it shows Sebald's methods and preoccupations with greater clarity than the long work, which is often overladen with cultural materials to the point of being clogged.

An overview of the historical background in the Introduction, "Shards from the Explosion," is followed by literary analyses of twelve fictions. The texts are related to the social history of the particular time and place to provide a context for the understanding of the interactions between the escapees and their new environment as well as the exploration of the psychological tensions they generated. Fiction is an imaginative reliving as well as an indirect mode of education. With the dying of the generation of escapees, as Geoffrey Hartman has emphasized, "soon education will have to replace all eyewitness transmission."[10] And, he adds, "it will require both scholarship and art to defeat an encroaching anti-memory" (44). To keep memory alive and to provide a wider understanding of the escapee experience is my dual aim.

What a good kind of revenge?

Introduction: "Shards from the Explosion"

"Scattered about the globe, all these years later, we are shards from the explosion," Robin Hirsch writes in *Last Dance at the Hotel Kempinski* (1995) (4) to account for the absence of family members at his circumcision following his birth during World War II. His parents had moved from Berlin to London; his grandfathers had died in Berlin earlier, but his grandmothers had been deported and had perished in concentration camps. His father's brother had fled with his wife to Amsterdam, where they were overtaken by the Nazis. One of his cousins survived in Israel, another in Argentina.

Hirsch's is a pretty typical Jewish family story in the aftermath of the "explosion" represented by Hitler's rise to power in the 1930s and his programmatic persecution of the Jews in all the territories under his domination. Hirsch's metaphor with its double allusion to shattering strongly suggests the violence of the disruption. Shards—literally, broken pieces of pottery and, figuratively, brittle fragments—are often remnants of precious objects such as porcelain, almost relics, in contrast to debris—things destroyed and broken to the point of worthlessness. The human shards of World War II are those, like Hirsch's parents, who were fortunate enough to get out of Europe before the cataclysm of the "Final Solution." At the beginning of 1933 some half-a-million Jews lived in Germany—about 1 percent of the population—with a further 200,000 in Austria, not to count those in Czechoslovakia and the large communities in Poland.[1] "The Great Dispersal," to cite the title of one of Laqueur's chapters in *Generation Exodus* (2001), a study of those (primarily Jews) who left Central Europe in the 1930s, traces how they were scattered to almost one hundred countries in all four corners of the earth. "The persecution in Germany," he comments, "had caused a dispersal of communities and families unprecedented in Jewish history and probably in the history of any other people."[2] So the myth of Ahasverus, the Wandering Jew, was reenacted in the twentieth century.

* * *

Why did the Jews linger in Central Europe through the 1930s instead of getting out while they still could? That question, often asked, seems logical enough, but it springs from a number of misapprehensions. First and foremost it is prompted by the superior wisdom of hindsight; no one in his or her right mind could at that time conceive of the practical implementation of the Final Solution. Scapegoating of the Jews and inflammatory political rhetoric were so ingrained in Eastern and Central European tradition as to be an accepted part of the culture. Systematic extermination was another matter, and that was not fully formulated until the Wannsee Conference in January 1942. Second, the question reflects ignorance of the prevailing bureaucratic rules not only in Germany but throughout the world in the policies aimed to control emigration and immigration, respectively. (And third and not least it discounts the role of emotions, especially in this instance denial in determining human behavior.)

The question also overlooks the fact that many did leave, some immediately in response to Hitler's accession to power, more in the later 1930s as the situation deteriorated after the promulgation of the Nuremberg laws in 1935, which stripped Jews of their citizenship and resulted in their progressive pauperization consequent to the confiscation of their property and the ban on their employment in September 1938.[3] In the first year of Nazi rule 37,000 emigrated from Germany; in 1934, 23,000; in 1935, 21,000; in 1936, 25,000; and in 1937, 23,000, as well as some 100,000 Austrians.[4] An estimated 70,000 escapees entered Great Britain, and 104,098 the United States between 1933 and 1941.[5] Those who left early were predominantly people with business or family connections and/or money abroad, which could provide a basis for their existence in a foreign land. The lack of funding and also of readily transferable qualifications in the case of doctors, lawyers, and dentists, whose degrees were not recognized outside their own countries, were significant deterrents to those professionals. In addition to financial resources and connections, enterprise and sheer luck were necessary to attempt emigration and resettlement.

For to emigrate was no simple matter even for the increasing—and increasingly desperate—number of those eager to do so. One of the major paradoxes of the Holocaust is that the Nazis wanted to be rid of the Jews, but devised more and more obstacles to their emigration as the persecution gathered momentum through the 1930s. An applicant for a German passport had to present a slew of certificates attesting that rent, sundry taxes, and charges for telephone, gas, electricity, water, etc., had all been paid. Each of these certificates was valid for only one month and so it was nearly impossible to open up a window of time to leave when all the documents were in order.[6] Those who owned property or had a relative in an institution were forbidden to emigrate so as not to impose a burden on the state. In October 1938 all Jewish passports were peremptorily withdrawn in order to have a red "J" stamped onto them at the request of the Swiss so as to make Jews identifiable at first glance.

In this respect the emigration of Jews from Europe in the 1930s differed radically from the waves of mass emigration from Eastern Europe in the late nineteenth and early twentieth centuries. Fearful for their lives following a series of pogroms, notably that in Kishinev in 1903, roughly a third of the Jewish population opted to emigrate westward. Bernard Malamud's *The Fixer* (1966) gives a haunting portrayal of the imprisonment of an insignificant Jewish workman in Kiev, shortly before World War I, on the accusation of ritual murder, that is, the slaughter of a Christian child in order to drain his blood, which was purported to be a necessary ingredient of the Passover matzos. Such incidents, based on this and similar bizarre superstitions, were not uncommon, and naturally prompted terrified flight. Provided they had the courage and the scantest of means, the East European Jews were free at that time to emigrate. No bureaucratic obstacle was put in their way to hold them captive.[7] While these immigrants with their large, poor families were hardly welcome in either England or the United States—their prime destinations—they were admitted after minimal formalities, such as health screening in the United States, because they provided a pool of cheap labor.

By contrast in the 1930s to achieve the right to legal emigration was merely one side of the problem. The other, at least as great, was to obtain a visa for entry into some other country. With the still recent memory of the unemployment during the Great Depression, few countries wanted an influx of job seekers. Bernard Wasserstein states categorically: "[T]hat the great majority of Jews failed to emigrate was primarily due to the extreme reluctance of all countries to admit them."[8] The outcome of the 1938 Evian Conference, convened at Roosevelt's instigation to address the issue of Jewish refugees, was a foregone conclusion since all the thiry-two participating nations had agreed in advance that none of them would change their existing regulations to accommodate the refugee Jews. A proposal in Britain to open up immigration for Jews was shelved in favor of the compromise to admit up to 10,000 children, who came on the *Kindertransports* and who were acceptable because they were not immediate competitors for jobs. In the United States in February 1939 the Wagner–Rogers Bill to admit 20,000 children over a period of two years was "amended to death" by including the children in the normal quotas on the grounds that it was ungodly to separate children from their parents.[9] In 1936 only 26.9 percent of the quota for immigrants from Germany was filled with the issuance of 6,978 visas; in the following year these numbers rose to 40 percent and 12,532, respectively, in the wake of a short-lived economic recovery.[10] In absolute terms the numbers admitted still fell far short during the peak years of Jewish immigration between 1899 and 1914. By the end of November 1938, after Crystal Night, 160,000 frantic Jews had filed applications for U.S. visas at the consulate in Berlin.[11]

Under these circumstances a brisk trade in dubious visas flourished. Rumors circulated daily: a Yugoslav visa would be granted to those who converted to Catholicism; the consul of a South American state had died and his secretary was dispensing visas in return for a bribe. Forged visas to Cuba were held by the majority of the passengers on the ship, the St. Louis; only those with genuine documents were allowed to land, while the rest, rejected by the United States, had to head back to Europe, where most of them perished. We got a legitimate visa to Liberia, although we had no serious intention of going there. It was in the nature of a precaution; rightly or wrongly rumor had it that holders of a valid visa were less likely to be sent to a concentration camp if detained by the police as they could argue that they were on the verge of departure. From a practical point of view, however, it was useless since we could not get the transit visas to travel to Liberia; every country feared that in "transit" we might try to hide and stay. During the Christmas of 1938 we managed to cross into Belgium on foot over a snow-covered railroad bridge, guided by a German and a Belgian in the illegal emigration business for profit.

The external obstacles to emigration were reinforced by an internalized reluctance. German Jews especially were deeply rooted in their homeland, wedded to its culture, firmly grounded as well as professionally established in their communities. "More German than the Germans [was] a common sneer" directed at those who had thrown out their faith in favor of adopting "the garb of the Fatherland."[12] Patriotic citizens, many were veterans of World War I who had served with distinction and were proud of their medals, which gave them a false sense of security. They found it extremely difficult after the *Rassenkunde* (racial edict) of 1933 to acknowledge their new status as pariahs, and consistently underestimated the seriousness of the threat posed to them by Hitler. They may also have overestimated their acceptance in Germany prior to Hitler's accession to power. While the Jews sought—and believed in—their social integration, evidence testifies to a persistent undercurrent of hostility. "We thought of ourselves as being German Jews, not Jewish Germans," asserts Ilse Wolff, who was born in Berlin in 1926 and later became librarian to the Wiener Library in London.[13] In his thoughtful assessment of the mood of Weimar culture Peter Gay concludes that the Jews "were not at the heart of public affairs; they met, cultivated, sometimes influenced insiders without really becoming insiders themselves."[14] De facto excluded from the army, government, and diplomatic posts, they gravitated perforce to the so-called independent professions such as the law, medicine, and dentistry.

The self-deceiving denial, the illusion of belonging and of safety in the face of menacing developments is exemplified by Hugo Baumgartner in Anita Desai's novel *Baumgartner's Bombay* (1988). An assimilated Jew with a pronounced consciousness of his Germanness, when confronted with the crisis of rejection because of his race, he prefers to commit suicide rather than leave his homeland. After his death the Aryan Pfuehl, who has taken over his business, roars at his widow and son in exasperation: " 'You are not illiterate, you Jews, you are not peasants—then why are your minds so closed?' " Given the opportunity to emigrate to India, they behave in his eyes " 'like obstinate mice who turned up their noses at the cheese.' " Pfuehl castigates them for being " 'so delicately brought up in the old Germany with their piano-playing and singing and reading of the classics.' " He urges them to think emigration " 'and *quick*.' "[15]

The protracted absence of profound alarm can also be attributed to the weakness and rapid changes of governments in the early twentieth century, which fostered the wishful belief that Hitler would not last long either. In the mid-1930s we would encounter German Jews in the Czech spa, Karlsbad, where they went to take the waters, as did my father. My parents would sound them out anxiously about conditions in Germany. The Nazis' bark was worse than their bite, they assured us. So extreme a regime would not be tolerated by the highly civilized nation of poets and thinkers; one had only to lie low and ride out the storm, which would surely pass. Their denial was welcome to us even though it was tinged with a repressed anxiety as they boarded the train back to Germany.

We, too, engaged in denial in the face of warnings from my father's stepbrother in South America about a terrible war that was imminent in Central Europe. We wrote off the stepbrother, himself an emigrant in the 1920s for economic reasons, as a man who had always been inclined to fanciful notions and exaggeration. My parents had had a hard struggle to get through medical school in Vienna in the 1920s; apart from the already prevalent anti-Semitism, my father grappled with poverty, while my mother encountered prejudices against women. Having succeeded in establishing their practice and home they were, like many others, averse to uprooting themselves voluntarily on the basis of what they chose to deem alarmist talk. To be driven out by petty restrictions such as not being allowed to sit on street benches, go into parks, shop on Saturdays, or use sports facilities seemed an absurd overreaction. In fact up to 1938 life in Germany had been difficult but not impossible for Jews under the Nazis. The crucial turning point came after Austria joined the *Reich* in March 1938. Eichmann, put in command of Jewish affairs in the area and ambitious to make his way, introduced more virulent persecution. Vienna, with its history of open anti-Semitism from the late nineteenth century onward in the factions headed by Karl Lueger (1844–1910) and Georg von Schönerer (1842–1921), was a good place to implement far more stringent measures.

Two further important factors are usually disregarded in considering the question why the Jews didn't run away sooner. One is the marked discrepancy between the objective and the subjective perception of the 1930s in Central Europe. To historians it is a troubled and turbulent period, still under the cloud of the previous decade's economic collapse and hyperinflation in Germany, beset by political instability, and characterized by the growth of anti-Semitism. On the other hand to those living in the major cities it seemed to partake of the best of times with its vibrant cultural activity in theater, music, and the visual arts as well as its progressiveness in the sciences and medicine. Life was in fact very pleasant provided one remained ostrich-like under the shelter of denial. At this summit of civilization who could possibly have imagined the imminent barbarity of the Final Solution? Admittedly, despite oaths of silence, word did get out about concentration camps such as Dachau, from which some prisoners were still released in those early days. Vandalism, arrests, beatings, brutal interrogations, confiscation of property, and all other kinds of humiliation became familiar. However Jews had for centuries been the victims of pogroms in Eastern Europe and had survived such persecution as communities. Industrialized mass killings in gas chambers were simply inconceivable. Before the Holocaust such acts were utterly beyond the wildest imagination in a civilized country. As Aaron Hass comments in his *Aftermath* (1995), "[h]umankind passed a Rubicon of evil fifty years ago" (56).

The shock of Crystal Night was the catalyst that forcibly jolted Jews out of the complacency of their lingering denial into a realization of the gravity and immediacy of the threat facing them. The blatant outrages of November 9–10, 1938 prompted many, like my parents, to the decision to make the move illegally if it could not be accomplished legally. But in the blunt words of the German border guard who sanctioned our leaving the country, "no one wants you." That crass dismissal summarizes the other half of the would-be emigrants' difficulties.

* * *

In their dreams and hopes most European emigrants cherished certain preferred destinations. Continental Europe was too near to the imperialist Third *Reich* for lasting safety, as the invasions of Belgium, the Netherlands, and France soon proved. England was much favored because it meant still remaining within the orbit of Europe while protected by the barrier of the Channel. The United States was even more desirable to some on account of its very distance from Europe and its traditional image as the land of golden opportunity for immigrants, an image that has been shown to be severely tarnished in regard to Jewish immigrants in the 1930s.[16] In addition English was regarded as a language relatively easy to learn, at least to a basically functional level. In practice destination turned out to be synonymous with destiny, for where the refugees landed was absolutely fundamental in determining the future course of their lives.

Exact figures for the distribution of the "shards from the explosion" will never be known, as all historians agree. Where they did/could not go is easier to ascertain. For instance few were permitted to enter Canada, Australia, or South Africa, then parts of the British Commonwealth, as these countries wished to preserve their Anglo-Saxon, Christian character.[17] Together these three took in less Central Europeans than Shanghai, "the last refuge," the only place on earth for which no visa was required.[18] Shanghai was at that time a legal vacuum, a kind of no man's land as a result of the Japanese invasion of China. It was accessible by boat from Italy until Mussolini joined the Axis and thereafter by the Trans-Siberian Railroad till Hitler's invasion of Russia in June 1941. In this remote locale 20,000 refugees found shelter. Although impoverished and living in wretched conditions, they re-created a lively European cultural life with their own newspapers, coffeehouses, delicatessens, theater, orchestra, and opera. After the war, however, nearly all of them re-emigrated.

Few destinations were quite as outlandish to Europeans as Shanghai, although some came close. In *Hotel Bolivia* (1998) Leo Spitzer evokes in vivid detail the experiences of a group of refugees who tried to found an agricultural settlement in a remote region of the Andes, which had no infrastructure of roads and other services. Not only were the language, the climate, and the terrain all unfamiliar to the colonists, what is more, predominantly professionals in Europe, they were totally unprepared for farming in this (or indeed any other) environment. Like those stranded in Shanghai they endeavored to reproduce European culture through clubs, concerts, and theatricals modeled on their previous lives. But, as Spitzer's title indicates, the continuing "bewilderment and sense of strangeness" made the Bolivian outback remain "a large version of a temporary resident 'hotel.' "[19] He cites a note written in Cochabamba in July 1941 by Dr. Heinrich Stein, who had been born in Niederhausen am Harz, Germany: "*Indianer*-Indian landscape! My new homeland! Is this my homeland?" (87). Alienation here permeates sheer wonderment.

Only slightly less estranging was Turkey, which was at that time undergoing a calculated process of modernization and westernization. To further that purpose Central European professionals and intellectuals were invited to move there. Obviously this was a welcome opportunity for Jews, although conditions proved more primitive than they had expected. Among the immigrants were the distinguished Romance philologists Erich Auerbach and Leo Spitzer,[20] who were recruited to build the university but found it utterly deficient in a library.[21]

Hardly less alien to Europeans was Palestine as it was then called. It is estimated that some 50,000–60,000 German Jews, about 1 in 10 emigrants went there.[22] Immigration to Palestine was strictly limited by the British government, which had controlled the area since the mandate granted by the League of Nations in 1922. Illegal immigration in the 1930s and later was stopped by all possible means.[23] Most of those who did obtain permits were married professionals in their early thirties, who encountered major problems both in learning the language and in adapting to the collectivist mentality. While some formed kibbutzim and farming villages, the majority assumed they would be able to lead lives much as before, only in a different locale. They brought with them mahogany furniture, grand pianos, electric refrigerators, crystal and china, linens and laces, heavy tailored suits, gadgets to slice the tips off cigars, to pit cherries, to weigh letters, wick-snipping scissors, miniature brushes and pans to sweep crumbs off the table, not to mention entire libraries of German literature. Not surprisingly the "jekkes," as they were nicknamed because of their insistence on wearing jackets despite the summer heat, were widely disliked and derided, although eventually, as they became an increasingly powerful political pressure group, they were instrumental in improving educational, social, and urban facilities.

The would-be emigrants were thus torn between conflicting needs and desires. On the one hand it became ever more imperative to leave Central Europe as the persecution gathered momentum. On the other hand they hoped to find refuge in places that resembled, as far as possible, those where they had been at home before. They knew that they would have to learn a new language, but were hardly able to foresee the full extent of the adjustments that would be demanded of them. Yet the shock of their expulsion played a role in their will to adjust to their new lives; since their former culture had so violated their very right to existence, they had perforce to adopt and adapt to their host environments. In practice most of them had no

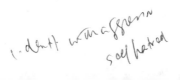

choice; they went wherever they could. So they were scattered in every known country in the west and some in the east, including about 1,000 in India. Their destinations were random.

*   *   *

The lives of the escapees after their arrival at their random destinations and the often painful processes of resettlement long drew little attention. They were, after all, the lucky ones who had got away with their lives and in some instances with a remnant of their possessions. Mostly they had not been tortured or even imprisoned more than briefly. Understandably concentration camp survivors, who had to overcome immense physical and emotional traumas on their liberation, were the subject of far more intense scrutiny than those who had been spared the labor-unto-death or concentration camps. For some fifteen years or more after the literally unbelievable images of skeletal survivors with their sunken eyes peered out from newsreels and newspaper pictures in 1945, the Holocaust faded from public consciousness. This evasion can be seen as a form of self-protection, a natural instinct, in the current psychological jargon, to move on. The majority of survivors themselves, ashamed of the bestialities to which they had been subjected, recoiled from the memory, often refusing to speak of their past to their children. In survivor families the Holocaust was like the proverbial elephant in the drawing room—everyone was aware of it, but no one talked about it. If pressed to speak, survivors frequently encountered sheer incredulity.[24]

The convention of silence was first broken by the Eichmann trial in Israel in 1961–1962. However a further twenty years were to elapse before the Holocaust emerged into open discussion as a result of media and public events. The television docudrama aired in 1978, though considerably sanitized, aroused the awareness of the rising generation and sparked horrified talk about what had happened. Steven Spielberg's *Schindler's List* (1993) attracted an incomparably larger audience than the 1982 novel of the same name by Thomas Keneally on which it was based. The film, which made a tremendous splash through its dramatic scenes of violence, startling images, and sound effects, was certainly instrumental in making the public conscious of the Holocaust. Spielberg devoted the profits from the movie to the monumental project of videotaping the memories of Holocaust survivors throughout the world so as to form an oral history resource.

The fiftieth anniversary of the end of World War II in 1995 prompted an outburst of reminiscences and memorials. The Holocaust Memorial Museum in Washington, D.C., established by a Presidential Commission in 1986 and opened in 1995, is the largest and most prominent of several similar institutions (e.g., Dallas, Tampa Bay, Rhode Island, etc.) dedicated to education as well as to remembrance and the preservation and exhibition of materials. Jewish museums and memorials of various kinds have either been erected or are under construction in many other locations. Their design has not infrequently provoked vehement arguments about the appropriateness of the proposed structure. Details of wartime atrocities were disseminated too through such highly publicized trials as that of the collaborators Klaus Barbie in 1987 and Maurice Papon in 1997 in France. The resurgence of extreme right-wing political movements, especially in France and Germany, and the claims of Holocaust deniers have fuelled anxieties about future dangers. The notorious German historians' controversy (*Historikerstreit*), occasioned by an article in one of Germany's leading newspapers, the *Frankfurter Allgemeine Zeitung*, by the historian Ernst Nolte in the summer of 1986, has been the starting point of a long and heated debate. The realization that the witnessing generation is dying out has intensified the urgency of collecting documentation.

This, briefly, is the context for the torrent of various types of writing about the Holocaust in the past twenty years or so. The volume has been so great as to have elicited misgivings: "the study of the war against the Jews has become an industry,"[25] or "a fashionable subject, good to impress or shock."[26] But before the writings became a flood Lawrence Langer in his landmark work *The Holocaust and the Literary Imagination* (1976) forcefully raised the question whether the Holocaust could or indeed should be represented. Was it not literally beyond the reach of words, so unspeakable as to have to remain unspoken? This ethical dilemma, still unresolved, has been a matter of much agonized reflection over the past quarter of a century.[27] This question does not impinge on my topic; although concentration camps are named and deportations and deaths recalled, often in the protagonists' unvoiced thoughts, no actual atrocities are directly depicted. On the contrary one of the advantages of this project is that instead of incurring the "danger of fetishizing, or erecting a cult of the dead,"[28] it throws the spotlight onto the living in order to examine how they, too, were affected by the Holocaust.

The impact of the escapees' unexpected and unwanted move from their native lands has been analyzed in a number of sociohistorical studies, which chronicle their lives in their adopted countries. These studies offer much interesting factual information, for instance, about the routes and processes of emigration, the political and economic factors that precipitated the decision to leave, and the connections abroad that facilitated the successful implementation of that decision. They focus above all on the contributions—a key word and concept—that the escapees made to their host countries, the number of Nobel Prizes they won, their achievements in many fields, especially artistic and scholarly, the innovations they introduced; in short, the benefits accrued from their presence.

Characteristic of this genre is Ambrose's *Hitler's Loss: What Britain and America Gained from Europe's Cultural Exiles* (2001). Its title immediately announces its program: to catalog the distinguished contributions made by escapees in diverse areas. Ambrose surveys the cinema, art, literature, theater, music, opera, architecture, art history, and the sciences, and through biographical accounts traces the interactions between the new arrivals and the national traditions onto which they were grafted. Ambrose's list sparkles with eminent names: Billy Wilder, Oskar Kokoschka, Arthur Koestler, Kurt Weill, the Amadeus quartet, Walter Gropius, Ernst Gombrich, Albert Einstein, Max Perutz, Ernst Chain, Hans Krebs, Enrico Fermi, and Edward Teller, to cite just a few. While the book seems just a lengthy, rather superficial list, ultimately Ambrose does, nonetheless, make his point that Hitler's loss was Britain's and America's gain.

Much more subtly probing are two anthologies devoted to the United States and Great Britain, respectively: *The Intellectual Migration: Europe and America, 1930–1960* (1969) and *Second Chance: Two Centuries of German-Speaking Jews in the United Kingdom* (1991). The latter, an outgrowth of a 1988 conference on the history of German-speaking Jews in Britain, takes a longer view temporally, but still underscores in the majority of its thirty-six essays the contributions made by these German speakers to the fine arts, music, the theater, psychology and psychoanalysis, German Studies, industry in depressed regions, politics, political science, publishing, physics, orthodox and reform Judaism, Judaic Studies, banking, engineering, medicine, historiography, etc. By far the most extensive of its three sections is, significantly, the middle one, "Social and Cultural Impact" (97–462), for this collection, too, centers on the multiple, signal contributions made to British life by immigrants. Although certain difficulties, for example, in acculturation, the "disgraceful attitude" of the medical profession, and "the internment episode" (xii), are mentioned glancingly in the preface (by Lord Claus Moser), the bulk of the volume is positive in tone, and its final section is titled "Paths to Acceptance."

Its American predecessor, *The Intellectual Migration*, consists of fourteen longer essays, which seek to explore the "unique characteristics of this migration" (3), particularly the reciprocal effect on the immigrants and the host country of the physical relocation to the new environment. Its purpose is to identify the escapees' impact on intellectual life in the United States in the natural sciences, the social sciences, and the humanities. The consequences of their presence, the role of their personalities, the importance of direct contacts, notably in cooperative research teams, are the primary targets of this investigation of the "interstitial situation" (8). Dealing with those who had received their training in Europe, the articles single out their high educational level and creative powers. Physicists, psychologists, architects, historians, and art historians are praised for altering the development of the next generation of Americans. The United States is presented as an essentially "receptive climate," a "fostering environment" (8) despite "the resistance of the American academic establishment to penetration by these sophisticated newcomers" (9). This shortcoming is related to the economic restraints still prevalent in the early 1930s, restraints that slowly loosened in the latter years of the decade. Though far more scholarly in manner than Ambrose's journalistic *Hitler's Loss*, the underlying message of *The Intellectual Migration* and *Second Chance* is the same. The escapees' stories are success stories in the careers they built as well as in the enrichment they gave.

This is also the predominant theme of Laqueur's *Generation Exodus*, a study of those born between 1914 and 1928 who escaped from Central Europe.

The recital of their achievements rises to extraordinary, at times quite bizarre heights:

> A student from Cologne (Ruth Prawer) in later life became a well-known writer and the author of some of the best known Indian films. Another girl from Frankfurt named Ruth became America's most famed sexologist. . . . Eva Siao, the Chinese photographer, was born Eva Sandberg in Breslau . . . A young Jew born in Fürth, Bavaria, became secretary of state of the United States; a boy from Chemnitz (I. Foighel) became minister of taxation in Denmark, while a third boy, born in Cologne, represented South Africa as its ambassador in Washington. Yet another became editor of the *New York Times*. Pupus (Günther) Gordau ended his days in a Beuron monastery, having attained the top position in the order of Benedictines, serving as editor of their leading journal and their representative to the Vatican. A lady from Breslau . . . achieved even more elevated status: a martyr to the church, she was eventually beatified and canonized. . . . A young Jew who had reached Nigeria became one of the chief experts on and promoters of Yoruba art and also an honorary tribal chief. One initiated the official Bolivian encyclopedia, and a postage stamp now commemorates the achievement of Señor Werner Guttentag Tichauer. A young man [after many adventures] settled in Nepal and headed a small Buddhist institute dedicated to meditation (27–8).

The veracity of each of these facts is not in doubt; yet they add up to a skewed picture of the escapees' lives. Most of them resettled into fairly ordinary existences, trying to replicate as far as conditions permitted their former lives. Some, such as lawyers whose degrees were worthless in a different legal system, went through long struggles before attaining a modicum of economic and social stability. Physicians, too, had to submit to a full course of study and examinations in a foreign language in Great Britain; faced with these demands some never managed to resume their profession.

Through their predilection for the remarkable, not to say exceptional, cases the sociohistorical studies tend to distort the overall picture of the average escapee's difficulties, efforts, and occasional failures in the process of resettlement. In *The Refugee Intellectual* (1953), a survey of immigrant professionals in the United States conducted in 1947, Kent concedes that "most of the unsuccessful ones do not answer questionnaires. As a result most of the questionnaires are greatly biased."[29] Nevertheless he, too, concentrates on the success stories, adding that some managed to convert former hobbies such as photography and dressmaking into lucrative livelihoods. Immersion in work carried many benefits—psychological as well as practical. It brought financial security, often provided a new identity, and was definitely a stabilizing factor in psychic life as a distraction from the past in favor of the present. Many escapees also engaged in charities, especially for Israel, wanting to help others in situations similar to what their own had been. Having themselves escaped extermination, often as if by chance, they were dogged by an inner need to earn their lives, to justify their continued existence by purposeful and meaningful activity. So they were more likely than the average to become workaholics and high achievers. The image of success, which frequently emerges from the sociohistorical studies, though tendentious, is not unfounded. As Malet and Grenville conclude from their interviews with thirty-four escapees analyzed in *Changing Countries* (2002): "[T]hey are remarkable for their strength in surmounting traumas of persecution and exile, as well as for their achievements in their adopted homeland, which was and continues to be greatly enriched by their presence" (vii).

But the difficulties were ubiquitous even for the already famous. The fate of some of them is traced by Anthony Heilbut in his *Exiled in Paradise: German Refugee Artists and Intellectuals in America from the 1930s to the 1960s* (1984), which represents the opposite pole to the cheerleading works. Its title is distinctly ironic; America was far from paradise for those about whom Heilbut writes. But his sample is small and slanted in a negative direction through the left-wing political agenda of its subjects in an essentially conservative society. In contrast to the bias of most sociohistorical studies toward positive achievements, Heilbut dwells on negativities. Brecht was branded "not a nice guy" (175); the Bauhaus style of architecture was representative "of an outmoded fashion" (145); Adorno dismissed American academics as "office bosses" (161); Thomas Mann suffered from "loneliness" (298–321)—in the midst of the active German artistic community in Pacific Palisades; Hannah Arendt felt she didn't "fit in" (393); the Frankfurt School resisted assimilation, refusing offers of hospitality from Columbia University's Bureau of Applied Social Research (90). *Exiled in Paradise*, while a salutary corrective to the buoyancy of the majority of sociohistorical studies, tilts too far in the other direction into a sequence of grumpy negatives.

More equitable assessments of escapees' situation have also appeared. While Daniel Snowman in *The Hitler Emigrés* (2002) categorically denies his intention of just cataloging the "contributions" his subjects made, he does insist on their "distinctive contributions to British cultural history" (xii). Yet he also heeds "the pain of having to live in a land, language and culture not their own" (xviii). Even more balanced are Marion Berghahn's *German–Jewish Refugees in England* (1983) and Doris Bader Whitman's *The Uprooted: A Hitler Legacy* (1993). These studies differ from most of the other sociological works in their focus on ordinary rather than exceptional individuals. They also use a different method in their preference for a series of personal statements from which they cumulatively deduce certain trends. Berghahn and Whitman see most of the escapees as ultimately attaining reasonably satisfactory resettlement, but such success comes in small increments and generally only after phases of hardship. The subtitle of Berghahn's book is "Ambiguities of Assimilation," ambiguities that she locates above all in the problem of what she calls "ethnic identification." Whitman, who is most concerned with the practical and emotional aftereffects of uprooting, devotes the greatest space to "The Years of Resettlement" (205–370) during which regular sources of income had to be found and homes reestablished.

Their conclusions are sober, somewhat muted, free of the exuberance of those studies that ignore the problems of forced relocation.

The emphasis on success is characteristic, too, of the large number of memoirs produced by the escapees themselves beginning in the 1970s and 1980s. As they have aged, finished bringing up their children, and retired, they have had the leisure to look back on their lives and to record their often strange stories. While the concentration camp survivors have tended to focus on that segment of their lives, the escapees have written not only of their lucky escapes but also of the new existences they built at their random destinations. Some have done so in their mother tongue, others in their second language.[30] The memoirs stem in part from a wish on the writers' part to know their past more fully as a path to better self-understanding. Such a desire was the starting-point for *Into the Arms of Strangers* (2002). Deborah Oppenheimer, one of its directors, describes in an addendum to the book version, "In memory of Sylvia Avramovici Oppenheimer" (261–72), her mother's refusal to speak of her past so as to spare her daughter pain, and her own quest after her mother's death to find out more about it, a quest that led eventually to the making of the documentary. A similar urge to recuperate the past has prompted many reunions: the *Kindertransportees* in London in 1989 and 1999 and in Jerusalem in 1994, those from Nuremberg and Furth in the Catskills in 1999, and the younger Shanghaiers' meetings almost every year in New York, Philadelphia, Los Angeles, Las Vegas, and Israel. The search for roots and ethnicity from the 1970s and 1980s onward has impelled many who had deliberately or fortuitously moved away from their heritage to return and investigate it.[31]

Like the sociohistorical studies the memoirs express pride in overcoming obstacles and often gratitude to the host country. Their tone is generally affirmative in their acceptance of the trials and tribulations that history had inflicted on them in the necessity to reshape their lives. Consciously or unconsciously these (like all) memoirs are edited and to some extent buffed, skating over setbacks and underscoring progression in the stages of resettlement. For instance in the memoir left by my father, a very honest man not given to self-aggrandizement, I noticed one setback that he had omitted: of the forty Austrian dentists admitted to do six months' training in a British dental school and then to take the final exams, all forty passed the practical exam (they were experienced practitioners) and all failed the writtens the first time round. Their command of the language was simply too scant to handle a written exam in a limited time period and without a dictionary. Ashamed of this, his only ever failure in an exam, which was a severe blow to us since our financial resources were as limited as his English, my father left it out. Of course I don't blame him. However the recognition of possible partiality either toward the host country by painting things better than they were out of gratitude, or self-protectively through deliberate or unwitting forgetting of problems along the way must foster a certain skepticism toward memoirs. Fictions, by contrast, are not constrained by such considerations of obligation or discretion; fictitious characters can fail as often as the situation warrants. This potential for the more open confrontation of shortcomings in fictions should be borne in mind when comparing them to memoirs.

*   *   *

Fictions about escapees were slow to emerge. At first, as in sociohistory and psychology, attention was directed to those who had survived in concentration camps or in hiding as well as their offspring.[32] The opus of Elie Wiesel and Aharon Appelfeld, both survivors themselves, is foremost among fictions about survivors, who somewhat later appear in American works as well. Cynthia Ozick's striking pair of stories, "The Shawl" and "Rosa" (1983), depict a woman brutalized in the camps and deeply disturbed thereafter. Her novel *The Cannibal Galaxy* (1983) is about a man who survived in hiding, as are Isaac Bashevis Singer's *Enemies: A Love Story* (1966), Saul Bellow's *Mr. Sammler's Planet* (1969), Louis Begley's *The Man Who Was Late* (1992), and Anne Michaels's lyrical *Fugitive Pieces* (1996). The greatest impact, however, was made by William Styron's *Sophie's Choice* (1976), a bestseller that, like *Schindler's List*, enjoyed further wide diffusion through the film version. It owes its popularity largely to its exploitation of the romance potential of the Holocaust for shocking and sentimental purposes. The children of concentration camp survivors have themselves also authored several novels, which explore the problems of the second generation.[33] Some literary–critical studies of such fictions have appeared too: Dorothy Seidman Bilik's *Immigrant–Survivors: Post-Holocaust Consciousness in Recent Jewish–American Fiction* (1981), and two books by Alan Berger: *Crisis and Covenant* (1985), which extracts the theological beliefs implicit in Holocaust fiction, and *Children of Job* (1997), which examines the images of the second generation.

Gradually escapees too have surfaced more in fiction. A pronounced change in demography has gone hand in hand with the growing incidence of both historical analyses and popular awareness of the Holocaust over the past twenty or so years. During the phase of relative silence fiction offered virtually no portraits of escapees. Gottfried Rosenbaum, the Austrian composer in Randall Jarrell's *Pictures from an Institution* (1954), is the first image, one that differs notably from the majority in being ironic, not to say grotesque. The earliest serious portraits come in the 1960s with Bernard Malamud's story "The German Refugee" (1963), and two stories by Ruth Prawer Jhabvala— "A Birthday in London" (1963) and "The Indian Citizen" (1968). The veritable spate of fictions about escapees does not occur until the late 1980s, continuing through the 1990s into the present century as a by-product of the public happenings that brought the Holocaust out of the closet, as it were, and made it a subject of open discussion. This greater openness not only to the events of the Holocaust but also to its side- and aftereffects forms the context for the surge of fictions about escapees in the past fifteen years or so.

These fictions offer a rather different take on the escapees than either the sociohistorical studies or the memoirs. They deal with average individuals and families, not the particularly distinguished. This is important because the vast majority of the escapees were simple, ordinary people, mainly middle class. According to Claus Moser's estimate, "of the 50,000 refugees who settled permanently in Great Britain, 500 to 1,000 reached exceptional eminence; most of the rest were pleased to make more modest contributions and a few never fully adjusted to emigré life."[34] To dwell solely on the few outstanding ones is, therefore, to give a skewed picture of the entire situation. By portraying the run-of-the-mill the fictions give a fairer total image; paradoxically, perhaps, fiction proves truer than sociology. Also paradoxically the fictions are more prosaic in addressing the practical difficulties of starting life anew in a strange environment: learning the language, trying to cope with the customs of the host country, to understand the prevailing attitudes, let alone to come to terms with the prejudices. Even so down-to-earth a matter as the ubiquitous dearth of heating in Great Britain at that time, and the more serious issue of racial segregation in the United States were a source of great discomfort to the newcomers—physically and morally, respectively. The overarching predicament is that of achieving a workable degree of adaptation and eventually of assimilation despite the escapees' intrinsic foreignness, which often persisted long after their arrival. Max Perutz, himself a Nobel Prize winner, is cited as having commented that "[O]ne reads about Jews who turned their emigration into an opportunity, but there were also many who never ceased to look backwards. They only moved in circles of their acquaintances from Vienna or Prague, and remained foreigners all their lives."[35] The extent of the escapees' acculturation in their new locations and/or the degree of their problems in social adjustment form the major focus of this study.

The tensions implicit in escapees' lives are open to exploration in fiction through its capacity to move within the protagonists' minds by means of such techniques as free indirect discourse and stream-of-consciousness. These narrative ploys facilitate the probing of the inner conflicts, which may continue to simmer even when the escapee is apparently functioning well outwardly. Indirect discourse occurs widely and frequently in fictions about escapees, often as a way to uncover the disparity between overt behaviors and private feelings. Thus fiction is much more apt than the sociohistorical studies to get under the characters' skin, so to speak, to evoke a subjective, inner sense of the escapee experience. Fiction can also manipulate time, switching in flashbacks from the protagonists' present lives to memories of their past. In such moments of remembrance the past can be revealed as shaping or intruding on the current situation, sometimes to the point of disturbing the homeostasis. Through this ready access to the characters' interior world and memories, literature is privileged as a vehicle both for the analysis of barely conscious states of existence and as an imaginative window onto history, which can foster deeper insight and understanding. By assuming the escapee's viewpoint fictions can convey what it *feels* like to be in this betwixt-and-between situation.

A statement such as this raises a problem, which has long preoccupied scholars and critics, namely, the relationship of literature to history. Marianne

Hirsch has argued that debates about truth, fact, history, and fiction, which might have come to seem rather dated in theoretical circles, have been brought to the fore again with great urgency in the wake of revisionist histories of the Holocaust.[36] Nor is revisionism the only source of controversy about the interpenetration of fact and fiction. The degree of veracity not merely of Holocaust fictions but also of survivors' memoirs is open to challenge, especially in light of the recent scandal about Binjamin Wilkomirski's *Fragments: Memories of a Wartime Childhood* (1996), which has been unmasked as a fabrication by the Swiss-born clarinet maker, Bruno Doesseker. Quite apart from such deliberate misrepresentation the essentially subjective nature of memory and its subconscious selectivity justifies questioning the extent of the reliability of even eyewitness testimony, which aspires to scrupulous fidelity to experience. But precisely because the experiences recorded are those of a suffering, brutalized individual, they are open to the suspicion of unintentional distortion.

For this reason writing about the Holocaust presents heightened difficulties for critics. Whatever their theoretical orientation they concur that Holocaust literature hovers in "an intermediate realm between ambiguity and clarity."[37] However even the most insistent and persuasive voice at the formalist pole of the spectrum, Dorrit Cohn, who emphasizes the "*uniqueness* and *differentiation*" of fiction as denoting "non-referential narration," concedes that "historical and novelistic narratives that center on a life plot [are] the generic region where factual and fictional narratives come into the closest proximity, the territory that presents the greatest potential for overlap."[38] What Cohn cautiously designates as a "potential for overlap" is often expressed in more emphatic terms as an inseparable interface in Holocaust literature between "historical fact and imaginative truth."[39]

The thorniest question, that of authenticity, does not arise in as acute a form in regard to fictions as to eyewitness testimony. Fictions consist of imaginative truths, which purport to be historical truths by mimicking them without, however, laying claim to absolute fidelity to anterior facts extraneous to the aesthetic construct. Thus literal truth, especially in realist narratives, is supplemented by a *pretense* at truthfulness, which underlies all fiction.[40] Such conflation of the historical and the imaginative is unavoidable in fictions relating to the Holocaust, and in this respect they differ from, say, nineteenth-century narratives. Whereas the names of the provincial towns and villages in the novels of Balzac or Flaubert are very unlikely to mean much to most twenty-first-century readers, those of the major concentration and death camps (Auschwitz, Treblinka, Terezin) are not only immediately recognizable as referring to actual places, but also carry automatic associations to gruesome violations. Hence Langer's assertion that "in the literature of atrocity, no fiction can ever be completely that—a fiction."[41] Although such narratives are "ballasted with the freight of fiction" (83), for instance, in their scenic organization, their characterization by means of dialogue, their periodic climaxes, historical fact and imaginative truth are inextricably wedded. The montage of the fictional realms onto the historical is clearly apparent in the references to such known happenings as the deportations to the East, the disappearance of people without trace, as well as the naming of sites infamous in the annals of the Holocaust. In these examples what Cohn calls the potential for overlap is strongly evident. Or, as Schwarz so cogently summarizes it, "the narratives draw upon history and recast it in narrative form."[42]

The fictions about escapees are prime examples of such duality. The characters in these narratives are obviously fictitious, yet they correspond to an actual group of persons the course of whose lives was directly dependent on the political constellation of the time and place where they happened to have been born. The routes they follow to their random destinations are wholly in consonance with ascertainable facts. The escapees' stories stand on the margins of the Holocaust, a tangential sideshow, as it were, to the central drama on the main stage in Europe. Although they do not command the status of social history in the strict sense, they can and should be read as credible adjuncts to history, which afford a glimpse of a curiously disregarded facet of the Holocaust.

This argument is taken a step further by Bernard-Donals in his article "Beyond the Question of Authenticity" (2001). His consideration of Wilkomirski's inauthentic *Fragments* leads him to the blunt question: "can fiction serve effectively as a vehicle for memory?"[43] He answers it in the affirmative by reference to a "rhetorical tradition that pays attention to what resides behind the language of the discourse rather than in the speaker's integrity or the degree to which this discourse can be squared with a state of affairs. The extent to which a discourse has authority depends on its ability to move an audience to 'see' an issue or an event that exceeds language's ability to narrate it" (1305). Citing Shoshana Felman's psychoanalytic approach, Bernard-Donals envisages the reception of Holocaust literature as devolving from "a kind of transference" in which the reader "sees not the experience described but something that stands beyond or before it" (1308). This is a powerful suggestion, which extends the force of readers' vicarious response to Holocaust literature.

Bernard-Donals's invocation of the concept of transference proves useful beyond the sphere of psychoanalytic relationships, for transference comprises feelings that are simultaneously—and genuinely—real and unreal. As are fictions about escapees. They are real in the literal sense in their source in the historical situation to which reference is frequently made either explicitly or in hints. At the same time they are unreal as creations of the writer's imagination. But just as the feelings involved in psychological transference meld indistinguishably those based on outer circumstances with those stemming from within, so in fictions about escapees established historical facts and imaginative interpretations are interdependent. These works stand on the cusp between history and fiction, resting on well-known facts, recast into invented plots and characters.

All the fictions that I have chosen share this characteristic substratum of historical truthfulness. This feature is important in endowing the imaginative, that is, fictitious aspect with credibility through its montage onto verifiable situations. For this reason, as I explained in "To the Reader," I do not include works that flagrantly transgress historical accuracy. While details may seem incidental to the larger course of a person's or a family's fortunes, a series of peripheral infringements of truth adversely affects belief in the construction of the plot and the feelings attributed to the various protagonists. So the transference becomes negative as the factual inaccuracy damages the emotional viability of the fiction. It all comes to seem somehow phony.

On the other hand when the fiction is mounted onto a valid historical base, it derives credence from the firmness of its foundation. The fictitious characters' stories are buttressed by connection to the known facts of history. The escapees' stories to be analyzed in the following chapters remain, of course, fictions, but their grounding in history endows them with the standing of hypothetical case studies.

Excellent info!

LONDON

1

"Twin Souls"

Anita Brookner, *The Latecomers*

(1990)

"Hartmann and Fibich [were] metaphorically and almost physically twin souls" (8–9): in this phrase Brookner offers a key to the dual central figures in *Latecomers*. Their twinship is symbolized in their shared first name, Thomas, a name none too common among German Jews in the 1930s so that this co-incidence appears as more than a mere coincidence. Both had escaped to England before the war, Hartmann coming from Munich at age twelve to his aunt Marie who was married to an Englishman, while Fibich had arrived from Berlin at age seven on a *Kindertransport*. Both hear after the war that their parents had perished in the Holocaust. The two are "paired" (6) at the boarding school to which they are sent. Forbidden to speak German, Hartmann felt "doomed," "doubly, even trebly an outsider," saved only by the accident of being paired with Fibich, which gave him "the knowledge that someone else's experience reflected his own reality" (6). From the very outset they recognize their affinity and are instinctively drawn to each other. This fortunate meeting at school initiates their bonding, which is based on a profound sense of kinship stemming from their parallel uprooting from home and family, and the necessity of coping alone in an alien environment and with a foreign language from an early age onward.

Hartmann's and Fibich's friendship at school is the beginning of a lifelong intimacy. From school Fibich goes to live with Hartmann's aunt in Compayne Gardens, a street in Northwest London favored by escapees. After Hartmann's service in the British army they become business partners, going first into printing, then greetings cards, and finally into copying. They prosper, get married, each have one child, and take vacations together. Hartmann, the older as well as the more enterprising, always takes the initiative in both business and personal ventures, even precipitating Fibich's marriage. He acts as the guiding older brother to the more timorous Fibich, who mostly follows Hartmann's lead without much demur. Hartmann insists that Fibich and his wife move to Ashley Gardens, where the Hartmanns reside. So they remain in close proximity throughout their lives. *Latecomers* chronicles their course, beginning when they are already in mid-life, retrospectively tracing their early hardships and struggles, and then returning to the present after the birth of their children. There is little dramatic action; the emphasis is on the ordinariness of their lives except for the one departure from the norm: that they are "latecomers" who "had a bad start," as Hartmann explains to Fibich (145). But Brookner shows how this one fundamental deviation of being escapees has significant ramifications, which become manifest in every facet of their lifestyles, attitudes, and responses.

Although Hartmann and Fibich are "twin souls," they are not identical twins. On the contrary the doubleness in their history as escapees exposes the radical polarity in their personalities: "their temperaments were diametrically opposed and they rarely thought alike on any matter" (7). In this dialectic they exemplify some of the potential divergences in the mentality and posture of escapees toward themselves, their past, and their present. In playing off the differences between these twin souls *Latecomers* is a study in the patterns of contrast and similarity among those resettled in a new country, particularly between looking forward and looking back.

Hartmann is the optimist, the extrovert, whose view of his and Fibich's situation invariably stresses the positive. The German meaning of his name, "tough man," indicates his resilience and determination in the face of difficulties, which he takes in stride with cheerful self-confidence. The adjectives applied to him are "deliberately euphoric" (3), "ebullient" (5), "blithe" (10), and "sunny and insouciant" (42). He "absorbed anxiety by not noticing it" (156). To Fibich it seems that Hartmann has an easy life because he "had the gift of being able to enjoy everything, every change in the climate, every prospect of a new turn" (229). He concludes that Hartmann's "robustness" and "carefreeness" originate in his having been "the loved child" (146). Adaptable and something of a hedonist, Hartmann has the capacity to extract pleasure from each daily experience. His character is rapidly and brilliantly delineated in the novel's opening words:

> Hartmann, a voluptuary, lowered a spoonful of brown sugar crystals into his coffee cup, then placed a square of bitter chocolate on his tongue, and, while it was dissolving, lit his first cigarette. The ensuing mélange of tastes and aromas pleased him profoundly, as did the blue tracery of smoke above the white linen tablecloth, the spray of yellow carnations in the silver vase, and his manicured hand (1).

The somewhat unusual word "voluptuary" is used here as a compliment to Hartmann to denote his talent for "the perfecting of simple pleasures, mainly of a physical or domestic nature" (2). To select and buy a cheese at the exactly optimal stage of ripeness is to him "another treat, another exercise in worth" (2). Brookner selects and records such telling details to characterize Hartmann with utmost economy and vividness. The choice of a cheese satisfies at once his pronounced gourmet proclivities and his insatiable need for self-confirmation.

Fibich is the antithesis of Hartmann: a pessimist and introvert with an "anxious mournful temperament" (39), fearful of decisions, fearful indeed of taking any steps because he lacks self-esteem. The adjectives to describe him are "gloomy" (4), "guilty" (4), "melancholy" (42), and "troubled and hesitant" (195). His name, Fibich, rhymes with the Yiddish word "nebich," a term for a pathetic, pitiful creature. In Fibich "the habit of caution, of self-effacement was too deeply ingrained to be entirely vanquished" (43) even under Hartmann's incessant persuasion and encouraging support. In allowing himself to be managed by Hartmann Fibich leads "a protracted adolescence" (53). Essentially passive Fibich feels defeated from the outset, musing that "perhaps death was the only resolution he would ever be permitted for insoluble lifelong problems" (198–9). His constant gloom, anxiety, and thoughts of death mark him as chronically dysphoric, whereas Hartmann inclines to the manic. In keeping with his depressed mood Fibich suffers from what appear to be psychosomatic disorders in his migraines and particularly in the stomachaches that plague him.

The dichotomy in their attitudes toward food summarizes the distance between Hartmann and Fibich at once, literally and figuratively. While eating ranks high for Hartmann in the hierarchy of his pleasures, for Fibich it is a source of worry and fear. Miserably ashamed of his tormenting appetite he smuggles peanut butter and packets of cupcakes into his room at aunt Marie's; nonetheless his hunger stays physically and emotionally unassuaged. Yet though Fibich "for all his adult life had been laughably, cadaverously thin" (32), he grows "immensely tall and handsome," a condition of which he is not aware (39). Despite his continuing "existential anxiety" (54) and his "habitual anguish" (60) he is even "oddly glamorous with his long legs and dark hair" (45), and in later years his "expensively rearranged teeth" (13). Because he is more introspective than Hartmann, Fibich is the more direct and transparent of the two. Brookner exposes his thoughts by habitually penetrating his mind in indirect discourse. Hartmann, by contrast, is given primarily to acting out his desire to create the utmost comfort in the present.

It is in their perceptions of the present and above all of the past that Hartmann and Fibich differ most deeply. Hartmann is "ruthless in dispensing with the past, since every minute of the present must be valued. And, after all, he had survived: that was all that mattered in any life" (4). For this escapee then, as for Lumbik in Jhabvala's "A Birthday in London," (1963) survival itself is *the* success story. So Hartmann basks "in the sunshine of his deliverance," cultivating "sybaritic comfort" (7) in such small rituals as the exquisite lunch to which he treats himself daily. In the crucial conversation between Hartmann and Fibich at the center of the novel Hartmann elaborates his philosophy of life: " 'The present is my secret. Living in the present . . . And if I got here by an unorthodox route I rejoice all the more that I got here at all. That I *am* here' " (145–6). Reduced to a comic level living in the present means not only having a good lunch and selecting the perfect piece of Brie or Cantal and a fine pineapple for the evening meal, but also watching television "because it was so good at keeping one in the present" (14), especially the American soap operas and most of all the operations that are infallibly successful. Why, Hartmann asks rhetorically, " 'dwell on the past, particularly when the past was so uncongenial?' " (14). " 'Today,' " he argues, " 'was another blessed day' " (15). "Look! We have come through! was a permanent thought in Hartmann's mind" (117). Hartmann elicits both admiration for his systematic joie de vivre and implicit criticism of the super-ficiality of his ideal. His rejection of Fibich's self-description as a "survivor" and his preference for the euphemistic "latecomers" (145) amounts almost to a willful banishment of his past. "Subjecting his early life to an extreme form of censorship" (20), Hartmann "would say, simply, 'It is over' " (8).

But it is not in fact quite so simple (nor so wholly over). Hartmann vaguely remembers various pleasant episodes from his childhood, such as walking with his nurse in the *Englische Garten* in Munich or playing hide-and-seek at Nymphenburg. His memory is patently selective, consciously or subconsciously. The years between the age of twelve, when he was sent to London "as a frightened boy" (6) and the start of his adult prosperity "he had decided to overlook or to forget" (5). However he is not able to do so completely. Even as he proclaims " '[I]t is over,' " his body language speaks to the contrary: "[O]n his face, when he spoke these words, there would pass, unknown to himself, an air of great weariness that was at odds with his dismissal of times long gone" (8). Nor can he fully carry out his policy of "damage limitation" by "screening out the undesirable, the inadvertent" (3). The very mention of damage limitation concedes that there is some damage; his program of systematic forgetting is most dangerously threatened by his dreams:

> There were in fact certain memories that Hartmann had consigned to the dust, or to that repository that can only be approached in dreams. For this reason, Hartmann took a sedative every night and ensured untroubled sleep. He defended this practice, as he defended all his habits, as sensible: his own glossy head was his best justification: "I eat well, I sleep well," he was in the habit of saying, when asked how he did. "What else is there?" He knew there was more, but thought that wisdom consisted in reducing the purchase of such nebulous matters or indeed of any imponderables that might darken his own impeccable consciousness (3).

That final phrase, "his own impeccable consciousness" is undoubtedly ironic since his dreams point to a troubled subconscious. Is taking a sedative a "sensible" or an evasive way of dealing with a problem that Hartmann does not *want* to acknowledge, let alone face? He does his best to avoid the fact that he is an escapee by designating himself a "latecomer."

Fibich, on the other hand, is obsessed by his inability to recall his past. Five years younger than Hartmann when he left Germany, he has scant recall of his early life. The chapter introducing him begins with: "He remembered. He remembered Aunt Marie" but "the years before his arrival were lost" (31). This loss sends him to a psychoanalyst, but "no momentous retrieval had taken place, nothing that he thought might at last supply him with an identity" (31). Fibich is driven by an intense desire to recall, and frustrated—and depressed—by his total inability to do so. He knows

> in an unrealized way, that his true life lay elsewhere, that it remained undiscovered, that his task was to reclaim it, to repossess it, and that for as long as it remained hidden from him he would be a sleepwalker, doomed to pass through a life designed for him by others, with no place he recognized as home (128).

Unlike Hartmann he acknowledges that "he was only alive by the skin of his teeth" but the price he has paid is the irrevocable erasure of his "lineage," the essential part of his past that, he feels, "would have explained his character" (33) and provided him with an identity. This sense of loss may explain his relative passivity "as if the task of discovering himself required all his best energies" (44). His lack of an identity, which encompasses his past, may also account for his dependence on Hartmann. For Fibich that unknown, apparently undiscoverable, past overshadows the present: "the past still worked actively in Fibich, seemed from time to time almost to take him over" (8). In trying to articulate his situation to Hartmann he describes himself as being " 'like a survivor. As if I arrived where I am by accident. After a shipwreck, or some sort of disaster that blacked out my memory' " (145). His gauntness makes him appear like a wraith or a puppet moving through life at Hartmann's directives, so fixated on his lost past that it seems the sole reality to him. In extreme form Hartmann and Fibich embody the dilemma of escapees in the tension to fulfill the simultaneous need to forget and to remember.

That same tension is reiterated to an attenuated degree in Hartmann's and Fibich's wives. They, too, are twin souls in one important respect: both have had a disturbed childhood without the security of a normal home. Hartmann's wife, Yvette, is of French parentage, and had come to England at a tender age when her mother married an Englishman after her first husband's death. Only late in the narrative does Yvette learn that her father had been assassinated for his activities as a collaborator during the Occupation. Mother and child have undergone considerable financial and some emotional hardship even after the second marriage, for the rather unattractive Englishman was more of an escape from exigency than a voluntary choice. So Yvette's early life, like Hartmann's and Fibich's, had been disrupted by historical forces. Yvette herself, being of a buoyant, unreflective disposition, "was not aware of having entered her life by the back door, so to speak" (117). She "had not consciously remembered, or perhaps had genuinely forgotten the penumbra of sensations that had settled around her" after her father's disappearance (116). Only the material deprivations of her childhood affect her deeply, breeding a longing for safety, comfort, even luxury. Thus Yvette is a fitting match for Hartmann, who is attracted above all by her "splendid body" as well as her "assurance" and her "bustling fastidiousness" (26). When he discovers that the splendid body is merely for self-gratifying exhibition and that Yvette has no talent for lovemaking, he characteristically compensates for his disappointment by taking a mistress. Nevertheless, despite her increasing narcissism, Yvette is a good enough wife and mother: "her interior was lavish and yet comfortable; her cooking elaborate, rich, and reassuring" (119). Like her husband she puts the hardships of her childhood out of her mind, concentrating instead on present delights.

Just as Fibich is a foil to Hartmann, so is his wife, Christine, to Yvette. She, too, had had a difficult childhood. Her mother died soon after her birth, and she grows up to the sound of her father's and stepmother's pointless quarrels in darkened rooms. She leaves their "tragic flat" (45) for aunt Marie's, to whom she is distantly related. There she feels more "at home" (46), and there she meets Hartmann and Fibich. After Marie's death she takes on the housekeeping, "her only act of independence" (48). Christine is described as "a modest girl," "self-effacing," "trained to keep silent" (48), and "timidly aware of being an anachronism" (49). Her stepmother undermines her already low self-esteem by telling her that she must earn her living because " '[I]t's not as if you had looks on your side' " (49). After the death of Christine's father the stepmother is even more brutal: " '[B]uy yourself some new clothes or something . . . You look awful. And take that expression off your face. Men hate a misery' " (51). This emotional abuse leaves Christine lacking in self-confidence, yet also curiously toughened and tolerant of Fibich's moods and anxieties. In the same way as Hartmann guides Fibich, Yvette becomes Christine's mentor, "a woman of style and confidence who might hand down vital information" (54). For Hartmann's and Yvette's wedding Christine buys her first more attractive and a little more daring dress. Her own marriage is a surprise and a source of wonder to a girl conditioned to feel unwanted. She takes to lovemaking "with unexpected ease and delight" (53), but as the years pass, "her contentment became thin, brittle, and then began to vanish altogether" because "Fibich remained distant, self-absorbed, and his self-absorption took him away from her" (57). Their sole "inalienable but unwelcome bond" stems from the fact that "they had been deprived of their childhood through the involuntary absence of adults" (129). This bond is inhibiting, indeed incapacitating, at least until the birth of their son seven years into their marriage.

Yvette and Christine function largely as accessories and echoes of Hartmann and Fibich. Both have had bitter childhoods deficient in loving warmth and continuing security. Both seek to forget this unhappy past, Yvette more successfully than Christine. However their adult personalities have inevitably been formed in decisive ways by their early experience: in Yvette's case in her extravagant thirst for luxury, in Christine's in her retreat into silence. Neither is in the specific sense an escapee, although Yvette was directly affected by the events of World War II, which led eventually to her leaving her homeland. Christine, while remaining in her native land, has by unfortunate circumstances been robbed of home and affection. In their common experience of uprooting, albeit in varied guise, as well as in their temperaments, Yvette and Christine are counterparts and appropriate wives to Hartmann and Fibich.

From another angle, however, they are inappropriate for neither is Jewish. Religion is noticeably absent in *Latecomers*. Hartmann and Fibich were, of course, born into Jewish families, but like many German Jews their parents were probably quite assimilated. As they have no consciousness of being Jewish it is not surprising that they marry out. The two families, living in the same set of flats, are so self-contained that they do not have any friends or community involvement. In this Hartmann and Fibich differ from most escapees who reached out to each other in subcommunities. Brookner chooses to focus on the interaction of just the two families. The only hint of any connection to Judaism—and it is a slight one—is in their business employees, Roger Myers, the accountant who marries the Hartmanns' daughter, and John Goodman, the company secretary. Myers and Goodman are possibly Jewish names, but Roger and John are solidly English.

Myers and Goodman participate in the coffee sessions morning and afternoon in the office, which is "got up to look like a flat, for domesticity was important to both Hartmann and Fibich" (5). A "family atmosphere" is maintained in the business; "their typists were encouraged to take time off for shopping" (5). Brookner spells out the reason for this somewhat unusual practice: Hartmann and Fibich "simply preferred to feel themselves at home, for the idea of home was central to their lives" (5).

So right at the outset one of the major themes of *Latecomers* is articulated: the veritable cult of home by those who have in one way or another lost their original homes. This longing for home forms a subterranean bond between all four main characters. And a primary feature of their homes is the "almost tropical heat" (13) on which they insist. Throughout *Latecomers* warmth carries a metaphorical connotation besides its literal meaning. Most escapees to England have dire memories of the frigidity of British homes, where single rooms were heated by smoking, dirty coal fires or, as at aunt Marie's, by a small electric fire while the rest of the house remained icy. The physical cold of aunt Marie's flat is linked forever in Fibich's mind to the absence of "that instinctive warmth" (34) that he craved and that the childless woman was unable to give. The translucence of the emotional in the physical is evident in the notation that "aunt had not felt the cold, and the single bar of the electric fire was not switched on until evening, and then only reluctantly" (35–6). Walks, which she encouraged, were a poor substitute for heating and affection. Yvette's mother, too, on coming to London, "wonders if she could ever be warm again" (23). Here the bodily sensation of coldness implies also her sense of disappointment in her second marriage.

This figurative craving for warmth as emotional comfort is externalized by Hartmann in his frank "love of luxury" (12). The air in his home "was soothed by scents of cigars, lavender polish, and rich cooking that never entirely dispersed. He vaguely remembered such scents from the parental home, which he otherwise did not remember at all or did not try to" (13). Perhaps that last phrase should be read as "tried not to," for such total amnesia in a boy of twelve is hard to believe unless it is psychologically motivated. That Hartmann remembers solely the good scents is in consonance with his optimism and sensuousness. He projects this inner need outward onto his body by becoming "a devotee of his morning toilet," filling his bathroom "with scented essences, with rose-flavoured mouth-wash, and with colognes which he would pat on his skin" (12). This dandified pampering is, like his beautifully tailored suits and his voluptuous (but sparing) meals, a further manifestation of his belief in enjoying the present to the utmost in compensation for past adversities as if magical thinking could remove them from his life. Yvette adopts a similar stance; when she feels "adrift in her life" (116) after her daughter's marriage, she takes to redecorating the flat, shopping with the same compulsive fervor that Hartmann gives to his morning toilet. Like him she finds emotional consolation in physical comfort.

There is no equally easy solution for Fibich to the problem that he identifies as "a kind of homesickness" (18). He knows that he cannot go home, that he has "no place he recognizes as home" (128). His recollections of that home are tantalizingly fleeting and fragmentary:

> He had, for example, an image of himself as a very small, very plump boy, engulfed in a large wing chair which he knew to be called a Voltaire, feeling lazy, replete, and secure in the dying light of a winter afternoon. He deduced that he must have been put there to rest after a family meal, perhaps a Sunday lunch, but he could not reach back and discover who had been present, nor could he remember the room or rooms in which these activities had taken place (31–2).

Given his later extraordinary thinness and persistent anxiety it is highly significant that he sees a "very plump boy" who is "replete and secure" in a way that he never was able to be after his losing that home.

His home with Christine does not radiate the harmonious self-satisfaction of the Hartmanns' place. Christine does not have their gift for nestmaking, perhaps because her father's and stepmother's home, where she had spent her formative years, is the epitome of dreariness and neglect:

> No flower graced the interior of his [her father's] gloomy apartment, which was decorated in shades of brown and illuminated by the weakest of lights. Government restrictions were seized on by him as an excuse not to replace the heavy walnut furniture, which seemed to be covered by a fine spray of dust and cigarette ash. The fringes of the Turkey carpet were swollen with dirt, and stood up like the epaulettes on the uniform of a Napoleonic soldier. Brown velvet curtains hung lifelessly at every window and when pulled for the blackout released more dust into the stagnant air. Windows were never, or rarely, opened (46).

Despite her best efforts Christine reproduces something of that sterile dinginess in her and Fibich's home:

> Sitting on her sofa in the somehow unresolved furnishings of her drawing-room she would wonder, for the thousandth time, why her surroundings did not please her. Thinking out of the way her old blue velvet curtains and her pinkish carpet, reflecting yet again that the pink cushions did not really enliven

the inert blue velvet chairs, she would wonder uninterestedly if she should change everything. If she changed the chairs she would have to change the curtains, for everything dishearteningly matched everything else . . . Her drawing-room exasperated her by being too insistently blue, an antagonistic colour without a hint of warmth. For this reason she kept the heating on at full strength, so that the room smelled permanently dry. This she attempted to palliate with bowls of pot-pourri, which added their own faded aroma to the iron stillness (58).

The elements of a pleasant home are there, but they are all perverted into negativities. The furnishings are "old," "inert," "disheartening," "faded," "antagonistic," do not "enliven," and are "without a hint of warmth." The essential spark is missing, as in Christine's and Fibich's marriage; the furnishings are the tangible emblems of the "unresolved" nature of their lives.

Homes thus function in *Latecomers* as objective correlatives of the aspirations of those who live in them. The meticulous profusion that reigns in the Hartmanns' establishment reflects their dual aim of control and enjoyment. The Fibichs are more confused about what they want and how to achieve it. They are surrounded by an ill-assorted medley of worn, featureless objects, which do not coalesce into an engaging whole. The dissonances between the various pieces and colors suggest the underlying unease and lack of direction in their ménage. The hideousness of the decor in which Christine's father and stepmother conduct their quarrels shows them as having given up on any hopes they might have had.

The practice of using homes as a means of characterization extends to the next generation too. The Hartmanns have one daughter, Marianne (a name as much German and French as English), and the Fibichs have one son, Thomas, known as Toto. Marianne is the perfect child, in accordance with the Hartmanns' ideals: beautiful, docile, the darling of her father and of the Fibichs. She grows up to be immaculately groomed, "attractive and polite and manageable" though "fatally deficient in animation" in her mother's eyes (96). She marries Roger Myers, whose positive qualities of blameless decency, patience, and scrupulousness have an inverse side in his slowness, quietness, and solemnity. His kindness, too, turns into uxoriousness "to the point of suffocation" (161). After bearing two children Marianne lapses into a "peasant-like immobility" (163) with her looks and appeal fading, to Yvette's distress. "These days Marianne tended to appear in trousers, even dungarees, and her swollen figure, which had not retained its earlier narrow elegance, gave her a mildly embarrassing appearance, too fecund, too exaggerated" (163–4). Marianne's defection from her parents' world is symbolized by her move to the house in Richmond, that is, a suburban area, which had been in Roger's possession. It

still bore the faintly depressing imprint of Roger's self-effacing but nevertheless rigorous personality. Green, it was, pale green, with a large desk rather too prominent in the half of the long room that was the drawing-room, and a table and chairs in the half that was the dining-room. There was space at that table,

Hartmann gloomily reflected, for quite a large family. Dusty displays of dried flowers fanned out in the empty grates. It was never quite warm enough in that house (171–2).

The dowdiness of this house, and particularly its insufficient heating sharply distinguish this home from the Hartmanns' realm; the dried flowers are as faded as Marianne's looks. Brought up to obey someone else's bidding Marianne compliantly sinks into this house and into dungarees. The Hartmanns' grandson is "a pale inert baby" (161) with chilly white cheeks (lack of warmth again) who seems "mouse-like" (160), and who grows up to be "a miniature version of his father" (244). Marianne's passive adjustment to the environment imposed on her goes against the Hartmanns' determination to shape their own milieu to their personal satisfaction. Through the weakness of her character, abetted by her early conditioning, she is a disappointment and loss to her parents, of which they never speak openly.

The Fibichs' son is the diametric opposite. From his infancy Toto is lusty, "rough," "occasionally raucous, testing his strength," and with "a laugh that was hurtful, obscurely insulting" (68). It is a relief to Fibich when Toto goes upstairs to play with Hartmann who revels in him as the Fibichs do in Marianne; Toto also has a firm relationship with Yvette. In an inexplicable chiasmus each couple has the child appropriate to the other. In comparison with Marianne, "Toto represented something crueler: the life force perhaps" (71). Intimidated by "his lack of inhibition" (72), Fibich feels him "to be a foundling, a visitant" (73) as well as an enigma. As he grows up, looking "extremely English" (79), he is headstrong to an extent frightening to his ever cautious father who believes that "in the important matters of life—always excepting the matter of survival—his son had already far outstripped him" (80). The intercalated "always excepting the matter of survival" is important for revealing that Fibich for all his diffidence does recognize his superior capacity as an escapee for survival. Toto leaves Oxford with a poor degree but refuses to go into the family business, preferring the more adventurous though, as Hartmann points out, "difficult professions" (86) of journalism or the theater. Toto insists on moving into a flat, which he shares with a couple of friends; his father puts up the money while Christine screens its suitability:

> The flat was not terrible: it was large, and light, and had the extremely empty air of a recent conversion. Dusty French windows, with an ironwork grille in front of them, opened, finally, on to a rain-drenched garden in which sun flashed tormentedly on to unkempt grass. Grey clouds bowled in from the west, darkening the high-ceilinged rooms. But it was quite a solid conversion, Christine noticed, and the kitchen and bathroom were newly installed, which would save considerably on the outlay. It had been painted magnolia, which took on a shadowy aspect under the rapidly changing sky (184).

The changing play of clouds and sun suggests Toto's own mercurial temperament. The flat is "extremely empty," like Toto's career, but basically solid.

Toto paints his room himself an artsy dark green, which looks quite handsome, especially after Christine supplies green and white striped curtains. So Toto gets a place of his own, albeit only thanks to his parents' financial and practical help. Like Marianne's home Toto's is green, though its gusto contrasts with the staleness of Roger's house.

This chiasmus between Marianne and Toto is one of the many instances of twinning in *Latecomers*: Hartmann and Fibich, Yvette and Christine, Hartmann and Yvette, Fibich and Christine, Marianne and the Fibichs, Toto and the Hartmanns. These pairings organize the novel into a clear, coherent structure. Readers' awareness of possessing a complete overview and understanding of the dynamics among these characters is fostered by the narrator's omniscience and insight into the minds of the four main protagonists. Full life histories are given for Yvette and Christine, reaching back far before their appearance as major figures in the action. Readers' knowledge of the women's past sets off the gaps in the men's—and our—command of their early years. While Yvette and Christine prefer on the whole, like Hartmann, not to recall the traumas of their childhood, at least readers are told of the forces that have shaped them. Their desire to forget, especially strong in Yvette's case, does not impinge on readers' ability to decipher them, for the narrator provides all the necessary information. Hartmann and Fibich remain more shadowy, but again this is a deliberate tactic on the part of the narrator who chooses to show them in this way, in the penumbra between forgetting and remembering. The degree of our intimacy with the characters is controlled by the use of indirect discourse, which gives access to their thoughts, though far more to Fibich's than to Hartmann's, and in a parallel manner more to Christine's than to Yvette's since hers is not a personality inclined to self-scrutiny. Marianne and Toto on the other hand are seen only from the outside, mainly through the eyes of their parents, to whom they are, as it were, appendages.

The reiterated pairings and crossovers have the effect of making *Latecomers* a satisfying novel, which readers are readily able to grasp. Its predominant transparency serves too to throw the spotlight onto the mystery of Fibich's amnesia. However this repeated pattern of twinnings is not without its drawbacks, notably when its symmetries come to verge on the schematic. *Latecomers* is like a ballet or a game of chess in which the figures make largely predictable moves in accordance with their characters as delineated in the extensive exposition on which the narrative opens. The sense of expectations fulfilled is reinforced by the recurrence of certain leitmotifs, which carry literal and figurative meanings. The most prominent are those already mentioned: warmth, food, and homes, all of which are, not coincidentally, metaphors for security. Fibich's hunger, for example, is as much a matter of his feelings as of his appetite just as his lasting thinness denotes his inability to meet his own inner needs. Brookner is highly adept at injecting a symbolical dimension into realistic details, as the descriptions of the various homes show. Together with the symmetries this narrative strategy contributes further to the characteristic translucence of *Latecomers*. Through the pervasive interplay of dualities and polarities the narrative mirrors the underlying psychological stasis it portrays. Marianne and Toto grow up and develop in unexpected directions but the four main figures, especially Fibich, are trapped in compulsive behavioral repetitions, which reflect the means they have devised to cope with their past.

The only dramatic action occurs in the last two of the novel's fourteen sections when Fibich visits Berlin. He makes it seem quite a casual decision, maybe a short business trip so that even Christine has no inkling of its significance to him. For Fibich has come to the conclusion that only "illumination would render him whole" (199) and give him the identity he craves. And that crucial "illumination" can be attained, he believes, solely by his reconnecting with that small plump boy he had once been; he seeks to close the chasm between that child and the adult self who feels bewildered and, as it were, amputated from the core of his being. " 'I sometimes think it has all been a dream,' " he confides to Hartmann, " 'that it has all happened to somebody else. And I have no understanding of that person—not myself—to whom it has all happened' " (146). Fibich is pained by this dissociation, haunted by a thirst for self-knowledge. In this respect again the twin souls Hartmann and Fibich are opposites. In light of his mantra " 'Look! We have come through!' " it would be "indecent, unthinkable," indeed nothing short of "an act of treachery and of cowardice" to spoil Hartmann's pleasure by reminding him of his losses (147). Fibich realizes this as well as the fundamental difference between Hartmann and himself: "for himself these losses had coloured his entire life, like ink dropped in water" (147). This simple but striking image brilliantly captures Fibich's insuperable dejection and its causes.

His visit to Berlin is a quest for a cure, an alternative to the psychoanalysis that had produced so little. He longs to bridge the gap between his pre- and his post-emigration self, to be "assuaged by fact, by circumstantial detail, by a history, a geography" (147). The word "assuage" suggests both the therapeutic dimension of the journey and the modesty of his expectations; while acknowledging that his losses cannot "be made good," he is nonetheless dogged by "a longing, a yearning" for specific memories. Throughout these reflections the words attributed to Fibich are very revealing: things "cannot be made good," at best his suffering can be "assuaged." But the venture itself is fraught with risk. Fibich sees "the slow sad opening of the abyss into which he thought momentarily he might vanish" (198). The metaphor of the abyss is one that many escapees invoke in thinking about the threat emanating from their precarious past. This sense of danger is translated into graphic domestic terms when Christine notices how Fibich prepares for the trip by reaching out "for the biscuits until he had finished them, storing up sugar again for the terrible adventure ahead" (197). Once more food serves as a cipher for unspoken feelings. The "terrible adventure" is an "experiment . . . one more effort" to give himself "roots, a family, an inheritance" (199–200).

The experiment appears initially to be a failure. Fibich wanders round Berlin for several days, guidebook in hand, like an "anonymous tourist" (206), hoping for elusive connections: "he courted recognition, but nothing came" (206). "But nothing came" is repeated; "he recognized nothing of what he saw" (206). Yet even if the outer scene awakens no resonances in him, at some subconscious level change is taking place. He falls swiftly into "a calm sleep of extraordinary depth" (206) such as he cannot achieve in London. He feels as if he "were undergoing some test which, incredibly, he was managing to survive" (206); simply "to survive" is the crucial achievement. As a result his self-esteem begins to rise; for the first time he compares himself favorably to Hartmann: "his was and always had been the harder part" (206). He judges his progress by the waning of the homesickness that has so long beset him, and though he doesn't recognize locations in Berlin as he had hoped, he understands "the homesickness itself as the luxury that had replaced the raw and fundamental terror that had powered him from one country to another all those years ago" (207). Squeezing through the narrow doorway to the train back from East Berlin he can actually laugh at this experience of "a symbolic birth" (208).

So Fibich does not elicit in Berlin the personal memories he had sought. Instead he stumbles on a far more precious "illumination": a psychological liberation from his fears "because he had passed a test he had set himself" (208). He has dared to look back and unlike Lot's wife he has not perished. He can think of his last glimpse of his parents and wonder how much longer they had remained alive. He absolves himself of the guilt of having left them. Thus he enables himself to turn to the present, to thoughts of his wife, his son, and the "amity" with Hartmann (209) in a sober acceptance still far removed from Hartmann's determined exuberance. A "great peace" comes over him as he realizes "at last that his purpose in life had been not to find his own father but to be a father himself" (210). This insight amounts to an epiphany, which accomplishes his reorientation from past to present and indeed future. He does ultimately become a "twin soul" to Hartmann, albeit in a totally different style. Perhaps Fibich's path has really been the harder one for he has had to wrestle with the long shadow of the past whereas Hartmann has rather glibly dismissed it in order to "bask in the sunshine of his deliverance" (7). On the flight back to London, high above the clouds, Fibich experiences "an enormous sense of joy" as "sunshine flooded the cabin, signalling to him his release from stress" (212). The image of sun and warmth continues as he decides to take up Hartmann's suggestion that they buy vacation homes in the South of France. Fibich can now look forward because he acquiesces in the fact that "not everything is capable of being resolved in this life" (212). "Resolved" echoes the unresolved furnishings of the Fibich flat. Through the use of indirect discourse and symbolical detail *Latecomers* largely dispenses with narratorial comment so that readers experience the vicissitudes of the protagonists' lives vicariously alongside them. This is a source of the novel's power.

To let *Latecomers* end on Fibich's move into the sunshine would be too facile a conclusion as well as a diminishment of the genuine existential anguish he has suffered. Brookner adds a surprising twist, a sight at London airport that does, after all quite unexpectedly, trigger Fibich's recall:

> He inched slowly ahead in a queue, longing to be free, to be home. The crowd grew denser, and he was aware of a commotion behind him. "Keep still," cried a voice. "Don't push. A woman has fainted." Fibich, hampered by his parcels, felt the stirrings of the old panic. As he knew he must, he turned, in time to see the figure of a woman, collapsed into the arms of her husband, who bent over her to lay her on the ground. Together they formed a mourning group, ageless, timeless, without nationality. His mouth dry, his heart beating, Fibich pushed on, stumbling now, his peace and calm destroyed, on and on, somehow, until he reached Hartmann and fell into his arms (213).

This archetypal "mourning group" brings to the forefront of Fibich's mind his last glimpse of his mother fainting into his father's arms on the railroad platform as their child's train pulls out. The mature Fibich has a bulwark against the "panic" he then felt and now reexperiences it by himself falling into Hartmann's arms. The density of *Latecomers* becomes apparent in such echoes backward and forward, which mimic the movements of memory itself.

As he relives that parting trauma Fibich goes into an acute depression. He loses interest in work and food, clings to home, and has a revival of guilt. Hartmann becomes his de facto therapist. In a long conversation over a lunch, which is a counterpart to that in the middle of the novel, Fibich tells Hartmann how the episode at the airport had prompted memories of his parting from his parents. Torn between anger and pity at Fibich's collapse Hartmann reassures him: " '[Y]ou are safe. You are here. Try to eat. You have such a good appetite. Make the effort' " (224). At this point Hartmann reveals a deeper understanding of Fibich—and of himself—than ever before: " '[Y]ou did what you had to do, faced facts, did your grieving. Perhaps it is over for you now. I was lucky,' he went on, wiping the moisture from his eyes, 'I dismissed it all' " (226). In Hartmann's tears emotion he had thus far repressed surfaces. So do memories: the name of the family's housekeeper in Munich was Frau Dimke. " 'I have just remembered it. And my nurse was Frau Zarzicki' " (231). Now it is Fibich who waves a hand at him

> as if to say, "That life is over. Leave it alone. It has no place here. Remember not to remember, or you will be like me." And Hartmann nodded, as if he understood what Fibich did not need to put into words, so present was it in both their minds (231).

In this role reversal between Hartmann and Fibich the circle is completed. The two souls are truly twinned, each complementing the other as each internalizes components of the other.

Latecomers closes on the letter Fibich writes to his son. He is thereby carrying out his resolution to *be* a father rather than to look for his own father. The letter discloses that Fibich has finally recuperated memories of his family, found roots and a heritage, which he now passes on to Toto. He names his parents and signs himself Thomas Manfred Fibich, thereby significantly including his father's name and placing himself in a continuous lineage. To the letter he appends a notebook, a memoir such as many escapees have written. This low-key ending is not only psychologically convincing but also once more anchors Brookner's fiction in reality.

Latecomers hinges on a perennial and ubiquitous problem of escapees: the tension between remembering and forgetting, between recalling the previous life in the native land and accepting the current one in the adopted host country. How to accommodate the past in the present is a recurrent dilemma to which there is no definitive solution. Each escapee has to negotiate his or her own peace. In *Latecomers*, rather unusually, Hartmann's and Fibich's attitude to remembering/forgetting is not determined by the events of the Holocaust, which are noticeably absent from the novel except for the bland statement that their parents perished. They seem already reconciled to this fact by the time they hear the news so that it does not cause them grievous distress. Unlike most escapees they do not mourn the disappearance of their families. Hartmann's program of forgetting is not shaped by the self-preserving necessity of banishing thoughts of concentration camp horrors from his consciousness.

Hartmann and Fibich represent the two extremes: one has fashioned a creed of almost totally obliterating the past in order more fully to enjoy the present, while the other devalues the present because he remains obsessively fixated on a past he is unable to recall. In the divergent reactions of the twin souls to their parallel situation personality plays a large part. Hartmann's cheerful, almost manic temperament is conducive to his cult of pleasure and love of luxury, whereas Fibich's gloomy, depressive disposition leads to anguish and anxiety. But this still does not wholly account for the dichotomy of their respective forgetting/wanting to remember. Since he came to England at age twelve Hartmann must surely have brought a more coherent set of memories than Fibich who had been merely seven. Perhaps it is this very incompleteness, a fragmentation of self, a lack of identity that so profoundly troubles Fibich.

Having begun their second lives at an early age in Fibich's case and relatively early in Hartmann's both could be expected to make the transition fairly easily. Naturally the younger the escapees were on their arrival in their new environment, the more readily and effortlessly they adapted, casting off their past as if it were a burden (as it often was). The absence of closer family cuts two ways: on the one hand it intensifies the loss, the amputation of the first life, but on the other it fosters adaptation by immersing the escapee into the new world without the buffer of family members with whom to share difficulties. The acquisition of the local language is, of course, a crucial factor in the process of acculturation. Forbidden at school to speak German, Hartmann and Fibich mastered English, although Fibich on his visit to Berlin can still manage in German. But unlike most fictions about escapees *Latecomers* never mentions that Hartmann and Fibich have foreign accents or linguistic peculiarities. They are at a distinct advantage too in not yet having embarked on higher education, let alone careers, so that they do not have to deal with the interruption of their professional path. Because of this they do not hanker back to their former positions of respect in their communities, as do the characters in Jhabvala's "A Birthday in London," who are well into middle age. In addition to school Hartmann has "an unexpected introduction to conviviality" during his National Service when he is sent "to mind stores in Wiltshire" and finds himself "much in demand as a source of supplies" (11). This familiarizes him with British mores—sufficiently to make him grasp that "they would never know enough to be insiders" (11). For this reason he rejects Fibich's idea of their going into publishing, a field in which being an "insider" and having the right connections are essential. Financed by reparation payments from Germany and an inheritance from Fibich's parents, secreted in a Swiss bank, they follow the traditional Jewish route of going into independent business. Materially they prosper so that they can afford to establish comfortable homes. The preconditions for integration into the host country—knowledge of the language and economic security—are more than adequately fulfilled.

And yet—do they ever truly assimilate to British life? Not by coincidence both Hartmann and Fibich marry women who are not "insiders" either, one by virtue of being a foreigner, the other marginalized by her background of misfortunes. By choosing as their partners those who are, mutatis mutandis, outsiders, like themselves, they form a cohesive island of otherness rather than integrating into the mainstream. Their business is a small, very personal one with few employees, one of whom is annexed into the family by marriage. Their detachment from the community is indicated by their lack of friends or associates. The location of their homes, one above the other in the same building, and their reciprocal attachment to each other's offspring further reinforces their interdependence (the Fibichs move to Ashley Gardens at Hartmann's insistence). Through their physical and emotional closeness as well as their cultivation of home they create a preserve that is at once protective and disjunctive in effect. By contrast, probably in rejection of this engulfing, restrictive enclosure, Marianne and Toto, that is, the second generation, remove themselves from their parents' orbit. They do assimilate in the fundamental sense of becoming more like, more absorbed into, the wider world beyond the Ashley Gardens enclave. Marianne goes to live in Roger's house in Richmond and abandons her mother's recherché elegance in favor of grungy dungarees, while Toto goes in for a Bohemian lifestyle. Hartmann and Fibich never really integrate into British life; from their schooldays onward they remain joined to each other rather than entering the mainstream. Their decision, as retirement approaches, to buy homes in the South of France has multiple implications. On one level it reflects their continuing longing for warmth, but it also suggests a wish for occasional distance from their host country and perhaps a certain latent yearning to connect again with their Continental origins.

2

"THE HIDDEN ABYSS"

Gillian Tindall, *To the City* (1987)

"As the plane landed with the smallest of bumps, he was already travelling rapidly in his mind across vast snowscapes, probing the contours obsessionally and inconclusively, seeking the hidden abyss" (27). Joe Beech's plane is landing in Zurich from London. He is going on a skiing vacation in Austria with his wife, Caroline, his son, David, David's girlfriend, Lisette, and family friends, Tom and Mary Lovell and their son, Jerome. On his way to a midwinter break, as in previous years, Joe would be expected to be full of joyous anticipation. Instead his mind dwells "obsessionally and inconclusively" on "the hidden abyss." The ominous closing sentence of the first chapter of *To the City* and especially its final words arouse readers' curiosity. What "hidden abyss" does Joe fear and why?

On a skiing vacation the hidden abyss may simply have a literal meaning of a crevasse covered by loose snow into which a skier may fall. This overt denotation is a real possibility; some of Joe's party are experienced skiers, others are not; however good skiers may be more tempted to take risks and be as vulnerable to accidents as beginners. So the reader's first thought is that it is an accident of some sort, which preys on Joe's mind as "this awful Thing that is going to happen" (27). One of the group, Jerome, does have an accident, but is fortunate enough to get away with a broken collarbone. The potential for serious, even fatal injury is evoked by the long covered stretchers that the ski patrol uses to bring hurt skiers down the mountain and, which look " 'so horribly coffin-like' " to Mary (139). When David and Lisette fail to return at dusk one day Joe becomes terribly anxious and scours the entire village for them. He imagines them "having a nasty fall. Or, realizing they had gone hopelessly wrong, trying with an awful intrepid folly to make their way down . . . to the edge of a dark precipice" (96; *sic.*). His forebodings are mistaken; they had heedlessly gone for another run late in the day, and when Joe gives up the search and returns to the chalet they are already there, "talking and laughing with the others and demolishing the last of the cake" (97). The incident is significant not only as a reminder of the dangers lurking in the background of the jolly vacation but as an indication of Joe's pronounced tendency to be nervous and apprehensive.

Joe himself has a narrow escape when he goes high up a remote part of the mountain in order to get away from other people. He disregards the onset of snow and the warning that this area is "Nur für erfahrene Schifahrer" (125; only for experienced skiers), and before long is in considerable difficulties. The episode is strongly reminiscent of Hans Castorp's dangerous adventure in the snow in Thomas Mann's *The Magic Mountain* (1925). For Joe as for Hans the experience is one of near death. For a while, when he believes he will die, he sees this as a fulfillment of his dread: "Well, he had expected it all along" (129). The vocabulary is closely related to the image of the hidden abyss as Joe surveys "this landscape of ice and invisible precipices" and is aware of a "crater" that he manages "by pure good luck" to avoid by "a perilous and unmapped detour . . . stumbling upon another way down" (130).

In negotiating this treacherous terrain Joe reminds himself that he is "a survivor" (130). Once before he has by pure good luck and a perilous and unmapped detour got away with his life when he evaded the Holocaust by coming to England from Vienna in June 1939 on a *Kindertransport*. Metaphorically his whole life is poised, as it were, over a hidden abyss. He has apparently weathered this early dislocation without bad memories. On the contrary he recalls the journey as a "happy" one, singing and playing games with the other children (20), believing that this would be a short visit. He deems himself "lucky" to have been fostered by a really nice, kind, good couple to whom he became attached (20) and who even bought him a dog to replace the one he missed from Vienna. Significantly mention is made of his missing the dog, not his parents or his sister. When the war broke out he was told that he would "have to stay on a bit longer" (21). By the end of the war he had become "an English grammar school boy. German gone all rusty" (21), intent on girls and the cricket team. Because he was young (just under eight) when he came to England, well cared for, educated in an English school and then at Oxford, he seems to be fully acculturated to his new home. He has, of course, at that early age had no trouble at all in acquiring the language; his intimacy with English is shown in his familiarity with and love for English poetry.

Only after the war does he come to understand that his parents had passed up the opportunity to escape:

> Some semi-relations in America were prepared to sponsor them. But it would have meant leaving everything and going in the clothes they stood up in. They didn't think they could do that. They were quite comfortably off. To leave my father's business, their savings, the apartment, the furniture—it went right against the faith they had lived by. I think, in the end, they were lost really because they couldn't abandon their bloody furniture (21).

Joe here seems to be misinterpreting his parents' motivations through his ignorance of conditions in Vienna in 1938–1939. Jewish businesses and savings were confiscated, and even furniture became Nazi property although it could be bought back by its original owners (the Nazi party needed money).

But like many assimilated Jews, Joe's parents likely believed they were not seriously threatened precisely because they had assimilated. The perils of assimilation can thus be seen as one form of the hidden abyss. Failing to grasp the situation Joe is angered at what he perceives as his parents' folly as well as at Mary's "articulateness" in unearthing this subject. His own hidden abyss is being exposed, and he resents and flinches from this airing of his buried past.

Although Joe has made no secret of his origins, he has to a very large extent transmuted himself into a regular Englishman, as his summation of his current position makes clear:

> I am Joe Beech, a good English-sounding name, joint director of a prosperous publishing firm I helped to found in easier times than these, with a degree from Oxford, married to a Protestant English woman for nearly twenty-five years (can it be?) and father of two agnostic English children (24–5).

The change of name is emblematic of the change of identity. He had been born Josef Buchsbaum into an "assimilated" Jewish family, which was "Viennese first, they thought, their Jewishness reduced to a small mystery, just something *there*" (25). His parents had conformed to a trend characteristic of Viennese Jews in the late nineteenth and early twentieth century by breaking away from the traditional world of Galician Jewry from which his grandparents had emerged. In assuming his present identity Joe is therefore continuing and completing the family's pattern of deviating from an inherited identity to one more in consonance with—and more acceptable to—the environment of the moment. Chameleon-like adaptability? A sound instinct for self-preservation? Or self-betrayal out of sheer convenience?

Joe's marriage to Caroline is motivated by the same desire to belong:

> I was lonely, I think. My life was going well on the surface, but I wanted to belong somewhere. . . . I believe I wanted to attach myself to the whole way of life that Caroline and her kind represented: all those people living in Shropshire and Dorset . . . and being country solicitors and magistrates, GPs and landowners—full of knowledge about this and that and also knowing nothing, nothing. That fact that they knew nothing about people like me and my background was just an added benefit. That being so, I could insinuate myself among them incognito (47).

The belief in his "incognito" is a self-deception for in his heart of hearts Joe knows and admits to himself how Caroline's family perceives him:

> No, I didn't exactly fear that they would think me "a common little man" though such phrases were part of the natural intimate vocabulary of Caroline's mother: after all, I did have my Oxford degree to protect me, and a social veneer acquired there and as a National Service officer in a rather smart regiment living beyond my means. But I guess they would think—I know—that in spite of this good camouflage I was really a rootless person, landless and essentially homeless, a frequenter of cities—Typical Jew (45).

In applying the words "camouflage" and "veneer" to his identity as Joe Beech, Joe is conceding the duality innate to his existence. For beneath Joe Beech lurks the former persona: "I am also, or was, Josef Buchsbaum" (19). The order of the tenses here, with the present preceding the past, suggests the immanence of Josef Buchsbaum within Joe Beech. The change of name has resulted in an apparent change of identity, but beneath the surface the earlier other remains hidden, like an abyss. Despite his escape from persecution Joe exhibits a trait common among concentration camp survivors, as noted by the psychologist Aaron Hass: that they lead "double lives," maintaining a semblance of normality, acting as if their life were ordinary, yet haunted by an inner life that reflects the magnetism of their past."[1]

This doubling of the outer and inner existence, of the literal and metaphorical meanings of the hidden abyss finds appropriate form in the twin modes of narration in *To the City*. In the forefront is the realistic chronicle of the vacation: the minor happenings on the journey, the arrival, the distribution of rooms in the chalet, the other guests, the activities, the tensions and disagreements among the group. An omniscient third-person narrator and dialogue between the characters carry this aspect of the novel, which deals with the present-day doings of the person who calls himself Joe Beech. But just as Joe Beech had insinuated himself into Caroline's milieu, into fatherhood, and into publishing, so now in midlife vestiges of Josef Buchsbaum in turn insinuate themselves into Joe's façade. The vacation gives Joe the time for reflection, and the location, his native Austria, further encourages the resurgence of his memories. This facet of *To the City* surfaces in the extensive use of interior monologue, which gives insight into Joe's mind as well as into the dreams that uncover his subconscious. In a sense Joe's excavation of his memories, the return of the repressed, amounts to a descent into the abyss he has been trying to circumvent as he does the menacing crater on his exploration of the mountain heights.

Joe has sought to avoid this cluster of memories. His preference for avoiding the unpleasant is hinted early on in his reason for going on vacation at the turn of the year: "we are avoiding the more equivocal echoes produced by the New Year at home, and the first empty, uncertain days of January" (7). But avoidance and banishment cannot be controlled by conscious acts of will, as Joe discovers when he begins to learn German in high school and is surprised to find that this childhood language, "sunk deep into my own memory bank . . . was already there" (92). The subterranean presence of German is one indication that Joe Beech has not succeeded in one of his primary aims: "the disappearance for ever of little Josef Buchsbaum. His annihilation not by cyanide and fire but by assimilation" (49). For years after his marriage to Caroline Joe had felt "safe from discovery" above all because "she deeply did not understand by life what Joe meant" (49). Joe here expresses escapees' frequent alienation even from those closest to them on the grounds that they cannot grasp the radical insecurity, the awareness of the instability of any kind of order engendered by their own experiences. Caroline's world is one in which people "feel it is tasteless to refer to unpleasant things, or even to think about them, who like to believe that reports of atrocities or even natural disasters are 'much exaggerated' " (46). So Caroline is even upset when the children are told a version of the Garden of Eden story, that is, of humankind's fall from grace. In this context of programmatic denial Joe finds safety not only from discovery by others of his origins but also from his own confrontation of his past. Joe himself nurtures the pretense that little Josef Buchsbaum has been annihilated by "attempting to edit memory" (25). But, as he ruefully puts it, even God "cannot undo the past" (14). Ultimately Joe Beech comes apart not as a result of any crassly dramatic exposure of his Continental Jewish background, but because "the banked fires of alien subversion began to burn" (49). His own need to reconnect with his roots leads him "to plunge into memory" (124) on his lone outings during this vacation, although he intuits "the silent abysses beneath the fragile, clanking lifts" (26). The literal meaning of "abyss" here coalesces with the metaphoric one.

The immediate trigger to his memories is his upcoming visit to Vienna, the novel's titular city. At the end of the week, when his family and friends return to England, Joe is to go to Vienna partly on business but mainly to meet his longstanding lover, Anna. While strongly attracted to his birthplace, Joe has no illusions about Vienna's ambiguous history:

> Freud's city. Wittgenstein's city. Also Viktor Adler's and Schoenberg's and Mahler's and Schnitzler's and Stefan Zweig's and Klimt's and Kokoschka's and Egon Schiele's. And Theodore Herzl's. Also Karl Lueger's—Lueger who "decided who was a Jew." Also, for a significant while, Adolf Hitler's. Also Eichmann's. "The streets of Vienna are paved with culture," said Karl Kraus, when it was still the city of liberated Jews, that famous all-pervasive cosmopolitan intelligentsia. And yet a city that was fundamentally Catholic, provincial, philistine, nationalistic—anti-Semitic. The city where Freud exalted the importance of the individual to the status of a cult was also the place where Hitler in his years of house-painting obscurity, incubated the ideas that were to destroy the individual, in millions, almost without protest (23–4).

"Not only a city of dreams but of doom" (24), Joe concludes, "a whole way of thought and social organization," "a belief," indeed "a cult" for assimilated Jews like his parents, who were "so horribly disappointed," "betrayed," and had "their identity broken" by what befell them at the hands of the Viennese (74). For Vienna itself from the late nineteenth century to 1938 represented a kind of hidden abyss for Jews. They were prominent and highly successful in many fields: the arts, journalism, medicine, law, business, yet they were at the same time the object of a virulent racial and political anti-Semitism propagated by Hitler's predecessors, Karl Lueger (1844–1910) and Georg Schönerer (1842–1921). In the initial stages of the Final Solution too Vienna played a sinister part in the persecutions devised by Eichmann. While the Jewish elite could up to 1938 lead comfortable lives amidst the city's cultural attractions, the hidden abyss was already there, preparing to swallow them up. Joe actually uses the word abyss to denote their disappearance: "Just as if, that day in June 1939, the whole lot had fallen through a trap door into an abyss" (69).

Vienna is the scene of Joe's dreams. They begin as he dozes on the plane with a brief fragment when he sees his uncle's and aunt's large house at Türkenschantzplatz, a square named to commemorate the Turkish invasion of Vienna. The mention of that unique name allows for immediate identification of the as yet unnamed city. Already in this early dream Joe feels that his "automatic happiness was being overtaken by dread" (18). For Joe's feelings about Vienna are as bifurcated as his contradictory image of the city. On the one hand there is a kind of nostalgia: "And this Vienna is my city of dreams, the one I like to think was my natural inheritance, the one where my true cultural roots lie and where I would have taken my proper place, had the patterns of European fate gone differently" (24). On the other hand, however, it is now associated for him with "doom" and "dread" because of the betrayal of its Jews—and of his kin. This most recent perception of the city overlays his earlier thoughts of belonging there by making him recognize the abyss that yawned beneath those illusions. In this conflicted response to his place of origin Joe is typical of many escapees who are torn between nostalgia for the happiness that was once theirs in that former place and revulsion at the irrational, unmotivated rejection inflicted on them. Joe exemplifies a characteristic love/hate relationship to the native land.

The majority of Joe's dreams are blurred because they are distant recollections of childhood dreams he had had after coming to England. He recalls having dreamt of Mitzi, the dog that he missed, and vaguely of "my home" (69). Although Vienna continues often to be the backcloth to his dreams it loses its specificity, becoming rather "a grainy black-and-white vision, like a prewar film" (70). The faded quality of Joe's dream pictures is a sign of his increasing and perhaps partly deliberate removal from the reality of his past, certainly on the conscious level.

His memories are stimulated less by his dreams than aroused by a process that Marianne Hirsch has dubbed "postmemory." Hirsch coined the word to apply to those, like herself, who "grow up dominated by narratives that preceded their birth, whose own belated stories are evacuated by stories of the previous generation shaped by traumatic events that can be neither understood nor recreated."[2] Although Hirsch's profile fits the second generation more, the children of survivors, Joe, as the intermediate generation, experiences a kind of postmemory, especially on this vacation in Austria. Austrians, he notes, "behave as if history had never been" (32); when a waiter openly voices his anti-Semitism at "that little Yid slobbering over her; it's sickening" (81), the phrase is highlighted by the inclusion of the German in parentheses: "(jener kleiner Jud, der über sie so sabbert. Es ist zum Kotzen)." In the presence of elements both disagreeable and agreeable (*Gemütlichkeit*) from his past he has difficulty integrating them into his life as Joe Beech, yet his insistent need is, as Hirsch describes the impact of postmemory, to "re-member, to re-build, to re-incarnate, to replace and to repair."[3]

For Hirsch family photographs are a powerful vehicle of postmemory. Joe possesses two photographs in oval frames of his father and his mother, "looking uninvolved, benign, and overdressed" (71). These are his sole access to his parents whose appearance he cannot recall and who, significantly, do not feature in his dreams. He has eradicated them (more successfully than Josef Buchsbaum), perhaps as a concomitant of his anger at their foolishness in refusing the opportunity to escape. Joe is afraid even to look at those pictures because they remind him that they are "gone, all gone": besides his parents, his sister, two grandparents, seven uncles and aunts, five of them with spouses, at least ten first cousins, and a much larger number of distant cousins who "fuelled the ovens at Auschwitz or were, briefly, a pall of smoke over Majdanek or Treblinka. Or Bergen Belsen. Or maybe Buchenwald. Because I shall never know, the exact *where* and *when*" (46). The images of concentration camps Joe saw in film clips at age twelve are to him "hieroglyphs of horror" (70). This is where he looks straight into the abyss, which terrifies him but at the same time has a tantalizing draw for him.

In the depths of the abyss is his sister, Anna, whose appearance he does remember. He tells her story in strikingly blunt, laconic phrases, which hint through their bleakness at the pain this memory arouses:

> My sister, Anna Buchsbaum, was picked up in the street in Vienna, some time in May 1942. That, by a chance testimony, I happen to know, though in all the circumstances of it I would rather not . . . She would have been just seventeen. I do not know the place or date of her ultimate destination (84; *sic.*).

The connection between his sister and his lover is quite obvious. She, too, is an Anna—Anna Morley, married to a professor, resident in "a cold house . . . in a beastly, alien place, Manchester" (56), but born Anna Sieger not far from Vienna. Joe's ardent ties to this Anna can be read as a displaced reiteration of his love for his sister, the manifestation of an unconscious urge to reconnect with her.

Anna Morley occupies a central position in Joe's emotional life; his yearning for her is an expression of his ties to the past. He frets that this year she cannot join the skiing vacation because of her husband's acute attack of flu. He keeps hoping that she will nonetheless still come, and agonizes whether she will meet him in Vienna as planned. Their relationship goes far beyond a mere sexual infatuation; its lasting basis is the understanding that Anna, herself an escapee, can extend to Joe. In this cardinal respect Anna is the antithesis to Caroline. Initially the very remoteness of Caroline's milieu from his had been a source of Joe's attraction to her insofar as she seemed to represent safety. Over the years, however, the gulf between them had proved detrimental to the marriage. Joe's much more intimate rapport with Anna is more a symptom than a cause of the marital rift. "Sometimes, these days," Joe admits to himself, "I want to detach myself from all this [the marriage and family] just as passionately as ever I wanted to belong" (50). He fantasizes briefly about the death of Anna's husband, "and afterwards I would freely take Anna by the hand and we would walk off together into a brand new life" (64). But Joe immediately scuttles such hopes with the irony of his maturity: "ah, the mirage of the New Life, shining and simple and easy," for he knows that "in reality there are no such get-outs, no completely new lives" (64–5). This insight is as valid retrospectively for his transformation from Josef Buchsbaum to Joe Beech as for his longing for another new start with Anna. There can be no more than a series of snatched meetings in hotel rooms—temporary abodes of passage such as escapees often inhabited in the transitional phases of their moves when they lacked the permanence and security of a home.

The meeting with Anna after the week of skiing signifies for Joe a return "to our joint origins" (66). He muses that they had never before met in Vienna, although they had done so in Frankfurt, Munich, Paris (twice), New York, Philadelphia, Nice, and Athens. However eagerly he looks forward to the meeting, it also fills him with "dread" (66). For it must involve a confrontation with the past, which exerts an ever greater hold over him as his children grow up and he himself moves into middle age. After endeavoring for decades to avoid it, he now acknowledges "the pain that just *is there*" (64). If not directly of that pain, at least of his lost family he is willing to speak more openly to Lisette Mandel than to others in the party. Lisette is Jewish, and although Joe has had no Jewish upbringing, he feels an affinity with her based on the intuition that her attitude to the Holocaust will not be like that of Caroline's set. As part of his reckoning with the past Joe wonders whether he should have married Naomi, the daughter of Ted Litvak, an old London friend of his also from Vienna. Naomi, a social worker, not pretty but gentle and with a gift for sympathy, would have been a more congruent match than Caroline—albeit a better match for Josef Buchsbaum than for Joe Beech, who quickly dismisses the idea as "sentimentality" (118).

Nevertheless, like Hartmann in Brookner's *Latecomers* (1988), Joe cannot control a residue of anxiety beneath his successful exterior. His nervousness (incidentally the opposite of the traditional British stiff upper lip) is another pointer to the hidden abyss he is all the time skirting. That constant need for avoidance would itself result in tensions. Trying to imitate British stoicism Joe is ashamed of his weakness; before boarding the plane "he had already taken (these days such was his strategy) two tranquillizers wheedled from a doctor friend: pride and secrecy created a powerful resistance in him to going and asking his own GP for such a thing" (17). While Hartmann regularly takes sedatives to assure sound sleep, Joe resorts to tranquilizers only occasionally. It is travel above all that mobilizes what he himself designates as "his familiar panic" (14). No psychoanalysis is required to trace this "personal journey angst" (15) back to his childhood experience of the *Kindertransport* notwithstanding his overt assertion that he remembers that journey as a happy one (20). The evidence of a lasting trauma is strong: "The same sense of irrational fear and despair could be produced in him by boarding a long distance train, especially one where he must sleep overnight, as if the claustrophobic hours stretched out on a bunk put an impassable barrier between one life and another" (14)—the "impassable barrier" that separated him forever from his parents. The jolting effect of his abrupt transportation is confirmed when he supplements his comment that it was as if his parents had fallen through a trap door into an abyss in June 1939 with the observation: "Though perhaps it was rather *I* who had fallen through the trap door, like Alice falling down the rabbit hole, and had emerged into another country" (69). The tragic outcome of his parents' descent into an abyss is contrasted here with the comic adventure, in an English children's classic, of tumbling down a rabbit hole into another country, as he had done. It may be such unexpected consequences that make him hate "journeys in general" (19), and this one, as Mary points out, must be particularly stressful since he is going back to Austria, "the same trip in mirror image" (26).

Joe's angst at the prospect of travel is rooted in his association of a journey with death. From the outset he envisages the journey as "a rehearsal for death" (4), entering in his Notebook a passage from a poem by John Mansfield: "we press / Westward in search, to death, to nothingness." "Why 'westwards' specifically?" he wonders, "Why not 'eastwards' " (1). Westward was the direction of his journey in June 1939 from Austria to England, while eastward is that to the ski resort and on to Vienna. But eastward is also the path to the concentration camps where his family met their end. The "foreboding" and "angst" (4) provoked in Joe therefore reaches beyond his *Kindertransport* experience toward the abyss into which his family disappeared. And falling into an abyss is tantamount to dying.

An awareness of death pervades *To the City* even at the resort, Heiligenhof (hallowed house). Apart from the possibility of injury—and death—on the ski slopes it lowers in apparently casually interspersed details: the death by drowning of Mary's goddaughter at age seventeen, the grotesqueness of Anna's microcephalic child, the severely handicapped son of the elderly couple at the chalet, Joe's sense of loss as his children grow up and move away "almost as if they died" (153). Death is "like some bloody great scythe ripping through the whole fabric of life, calling everything into question, making a nonsense of it all" (143). In an attack of survivor guilt Joe identifies his circling round death as a "fear" of "*Retribution*": "isn't that what I really fear? Retribution for my saved life, all my good fortune and the hubris and carelessness it has begotten. Retribution for not having gone into that abyss where the others went, where my father went at the age I am now" (145).

The link in Joe's mind between retribution, journey, and death is elaborated in his blank statement: "I have no map for the rest of my life" (76). The image of the map recurs later in *To the City* when Joe escapes death on the mountain by taking an "unmapped detour round that crater" (131). This route parallels his earlier escape on the *Kindertransport*, also an "unmapped detour" away from an abyss. The sense of an ending, of an approaching "ultimate destination" (54), which obsesses Joe, is fostered by the "stalemated, fixed" state of his relationship with Anna (91), and especially by the coincidence of his current age with that of his father at the time of his death no later than 1944 and possibly earlier. Invoking the metaphor of the map

Joe realizes that

> all these years, it seems, I have been carrying, unknowingly, my father's map,
> aware of course that it was for another country but mindlessly imagining that
> the terrain was about right all the same: a route winding upwards via hard work,
> ambition and assimilation, marriage, two children (the older a girl), friends, the
> pleasant, sunlit plateaux of what is called success and security (76).

The model of his father is a potent and frightening one because

> in my father's map, a giant scar across the landscape, a scar called the
> Holocaust, inescapable whichever way you approach it, whatever skilled
> manoeuvre you adopt: a landslide, a precipice such as no skier can avoid, the
> map itself torn in two (76–7).

Here the Holocaust is categorically named as the hidden abyss, which had
abruptly cut across his father's map and life.

At this juncture in the very middle of the novel two contrasting positions
in regard to the Holocaust are put to Joe. Mary, the Englishwoman from a
background similar to Caroline's, urges: " 'Oh, give over, Joe, for Christ's
sake!' " (77). The exhortation is laden with irony since as a Jew Joe is unlikely
to respond to an appeal to Christ, even though it is just a cliché, as indeed is
the thought it expresses. " 'I *can't* give over. I can't. I wish I could,' " Joe
replies. Not Mary but Ted, also an escapee, "has got it right" in Joe's opinion
when he tells him:

> People like you and me, Joe, we can't hate the Holocaust—we don't even have
> the option of being bored by it. Because it is part of us. We have internalized it.
> There is no escape. It is just there (77).

It is the scar, the pain that permeates the escapee's life.

The figure of Ted becomes increasingly pivotal in the plot of *To the City*
and eventually is instrumental in its denouement. Ted fits into the recurrent
pattern of doubling that underpins the novel: the literal and figurative meanings of abyss, the present happenings of the ski vacation and the recall of Joe's
history, Anna Buchsbaum and Anna Morley, the marriage and the affair, Joe's
secret of his meetings with Anna and Jerome's secret of his homosexuality,
the surface normality of Joe's life and his underlying fears, his status as an
assimilated insider, Joe Beech, and the repressed specter of Josef Buchsbaum,
Joe's position vis-à-vis Vienna, his birthplace, "from which he was nevertheless, ultimately and always, an outsider" (178). In this pattern of doubles Ted
has a crucial role as "the only father" Joe had ever known in his adult years.

The news of Ted's sudden death in London of a heart attack precipitates
the major crisis in the novel. In accordance with Jewish convention he is to
be buried as soon as possible; Naomi asks Joe to deliver the eulogy. To do so
would entail sacrifice of his planned meeting with Anna in Vienna on the very
same day. As ever Joe tries avoidance by pleading that he doubts whether he

counts as a Jew, having not set foot in a synagogue since he was a small child and not having had a bar mitzvah. "A Jew is a Jew for ever, you know that perfectly well, however far his life or his scepticism carry him into alien paths," Naomi responds (115). Her stance places Joe firmly back in his original context despite his intermarriage and his assimilation, figurative deviations into "alien paths." It emphasizes that escapees, much as they wish to shed their ethnicity or turn their backs on it, cannot disown it. It is the fundamental reason for the dislocation that has shaped their lives, and while they may not practice their Judaism as a religious faith, it nonetheless remains a characterizing identity. Joe's special affinity to Lisette confirms his instinctive closeness to Jews.

Joe's refusal to change his plans in order to go to Ted's funeral severely aggravates the guilt he had already been feeling. "*Unfaithful.* Not only an unfaithful husband but also an unfaithful friend. And, worst, in this case something close to an unfaithful son as well" (116 *sic*), he berates himself. His betrayal and abandonment of Ted conjure up memories of having left his family in 1939. On the rational level the parallel does not hold because he was passive in that decision made by his parents to send him away. But like Fibich in Brookner's *Latecomers*, he has a quite irrational bad conscience for having been singled out for survival. That guilt is now compounded by shame, pity for Naomi, and anger at himself. It is as though this crisis makes Joe fully aware of the split within himself between his commitment to his present life and his allegiance to his past. He comprehends—and judges—his own behavior without being able to amend it. It is as if he were a double, Joe Beech still interlocked with Josef Buchsbaum. This is the point where he makes his life-threatening trek into the mountains.

His overnight journey to Vienna and first few hours there have a phantasmagoric quality. As he moves "backwards not only in space but also in time" (171), the narrative moves inward into his mind. The focalization is blurry: Joe is exhausted and dizzy from the long journey, feels vaguely lost in the city, and terribly anxious whether Anna will finally come. In this befogged state he thinks, no, he is sure he sees Ted boarding a tram across the street. He rushes toward him as the traffic signals are changing and is hit by a car. The whole incident is told exclusively through Joe's sensations of being suddenly struck by a car radiator and falling down into the dark: "Down into death, or life. A new life, beyond the abyss" (181).

3

A "SUCCESS STORY"

Ruth Prawer Jhabvala, "A Birthday in London" (1963)

" 'Sometimes I say to myself, what have you achieved in your life? And then I answer myself I have survived, I am still alive, and this is already a success story' " (138). This is the conclusion of Karl Lumbik, one of the three guests at Sonia Wolff's birthday party in Swiss Cottage, a pleasant area of London where many of the better-off escapees lived. Instead of settling in the traditional Jewish enclaves in the East End of London, they gravitated to the more attractive parts of the city, notably St. John's Wood, Hampstead, and Swiss Cottage. The time is left open, probably the later 1950s when most of the former "refugees" were well established in their new environment, spoke English fluently, and had become British citizens. Theirs are success stories. Another of the guests, Mrs. Gottlob (whose name means "Praise God"), echoes Lumbik: " 'here we all are, no bones broken' " (128), and later points out that they are all " 'healthy and alive' " (138). " 'What else matters?' " she asks. This is the positive reading of these escapees' situation; however it defines success in modest, even minimal terms, which suggests how the escapees' view of themselves and of the world may depart from the norm that would be likely to project rather higher expectations for success.

"A Birthday in London," which originally appeared in the *New Yorker* and was included in Jhabvala's first collection of short stories, *Like Birds, Like Fishes*, is indeed a celebration: of a birthday and of success in the sense defined by Lumbik, but it also exposes other issues beyond mere survival, which concern escapees. Apart from Sonia, whose birthday is the occasion for the gathering, two of the three guests have special cause to celebrate. Lumbik has just been granted British citizenship, while Else has had word that she is to receive 10,000 Marks in compensation from Germany. Such events mark milestones in escapees' resettlement. For Sonia "the thrill had worn off" (124) as she has been a citizen for ten years already, and is "a rich woman again" (129), living "in a luxury flat, with central heating and a lift" (131). Citizenship and an assured income are the twin foundations for the stabilization of life after a phase of insecurity and financial exigency. Jhabvala would know this from her own experience; she came to England from Germany in

1939 (a year after Sonia) at age twelve, was naturalized in 1949, and took an M.A. in English literature at Queen's College, London, in 1951 with a thesis on "The Short Story in England, 1700–1750." That same year, on her marriage to an Indian architect, she moved to India. "A Birthday in London" is the only one of her stories set in England.

The sixteen-page story spans just the two–three hours of the birthday party, but even as they celebrate their present well-being, hostess and guests alike constantly recall their past both individually and collectively so that a long temporal vista is opened up. For "A Birthday in London" shows these middle-aged escapees shuttling in their thoughts and conversations between now and then. Everything is liable to evoke memories. For instance the large and ornate box of chocolates, tied with a blue satin ribbon, that Mrs. Gottlob brings Sonia "was just like the ones Otto [her husband] had so often brought for her in Berlin" (125). She remembers the scene vividly: "He used to come tiptoeing into what they called the morning-room, where she would be sitting at her escritoire writing letters or answering invitations; and smiling and pleased, the box held roguishly behind his back, he would say, 'Let us see now what nice surprise there is for us today.' And she would jump up, all large and graceful and girlish: 'Oh Otto!' " (125–6). This is a characteristic example of Jhabvala's method: the passage begins with a description of the box of chocolates in the narrator's voice ("large and ornate," etc.). As the narrator's perception overlaps with Sonia's, the drift into her thoughts in indirect discourse ("It was like the ones Otto had so often brought for her in Berlin") is completed seamlessly. So the transition from the present to the past is rapidly effected. Sonia's memories of a reiterated scene back in Germany are so acute that narration gives way to a graphic dialogic scene emanating from her mind. With Mrs. Gottlob's question, " 'So how does it feel to be twenty-five?' " there is a sudden return to the current time of the birthday party. This tactic of shuttling from the here-and-now to the then-and-there is repeated throughout the story, and it enables Jhabvala to present simultaneously the present and former existences of the four characters in the story as the narratorial voice melds with theirs in their conversations, their views of each other, and their recall of their memories. Thus the life history of each one of them can be reconstructed in outline from just a few deft strokes.

The most detailed and complex picture is that of Sonia. Née Rothenstein, Sonia was, as her son puts it, the " 'well-bred, well brought-up' " (134) daughter of an affluent family. We can also deduce this from the fact that her parents spent their honeymoon in Biarritz, an expensive playground for the elite. The other places mentioned where the family went on vacation in summer and winter fall into the same category: St. Moritz, Karlsbad, Marienbad, Bad Ems, the recreational spas favored by the rich between the two world wars. In Marienbad, at age seventeen, Sonia had met Otto Wolff, then thirty-six, "dapper and neat, in his well-cut suit made of the best English cloth, spats over his hand-made shoes and smelling of gentleman's eau-de-cologne" (128). He owned a factory and after their marriage they lived in a villa in

Charlottenburg, an exclusive part of Berlin, until their emigration to England in 1938. The Rothensteins and the Wolffs represent prosperous German Jewry enjoying lives of ease before Hitler.

The radical transformation of their lives in the early years in London is one memory that Sonia "would have preferred to forget . . .: the bed sitting-room where Otto had shivered over the gas-fire and the noise of the other refugee lodgers quarrelling over whose turn it was next to use the bathroom" (133). Otto, "so sensitive," Sonia explains—and so accustomed to his comforts—found it "difficult to adjust" (128). He is a virtual fifth person at the birthday party, a shadow presence. His decline is vividly conveyed by the image of him in Lumbik's mind: "He remembered Otto Wolff as a small, bald, shrinking man, very tired, very sick, very old, in an expensive German dressing-gown which had grown too big for him" (127). In his final years he had been "only a poor refugee who couldn't speak English and had no work" (127). Although Sonia had done her best to raise his spirits, " 'Otto had always taken everything very tragically' " (124). Obviously fallen into a state of depression, he couldn't believe that the sun would shine again: " 'no,' he said, 'it's all finished.' 'He didn't want to live any more,' " Sonia admits (131). Otto's reactions illustrate those of some elderly, previously very cosseted escapees who lacked the faith and inner resilience to meet the challenges of a foreign language, physical discomforts, the loss of prestige, and consequently of hope. Ironically the extent of Otto's success in Germany exacerbates his sense of failure in England. Women in any case proved more adaptable than men in their willingness to accept menial work and in their capacity to support their families morally as well as practically.[1]

Otto's despondency is set off against the optimism of Lumbik, a younger man (he is 56 at the time of the birthday party), a Viennese of far more modest origins than the Wolffs. He had never gone on holiday from Vienna, and none of the hotels where he had stayed "ever had a red plush carpet" like those of Sonia's youth (134). His lower expectations in life have given him the buoyancy the pampered Otto lacks. He is also less introspective, less inclined to reminisce, and perhaps because of his hard past, pleased to accept his modest but settled present as a British citizen. Both visas and citizenship had been very difficult to obtain in Great Britain. When refugees were allowed to enter in the 1930s it was the government's intention that their stay should be temporary; they were considered to be in transit, and were expected to re-emigrate.[2] In 1945 certain factions in the government advocated repatriation out of xenophobia and fear of anti-Semitism. Only Churchill's decisive opposition to this proposal tipped the scales.[3]

Lumbik has clearly had an adventurous time in reaching England. Even though he didn't take vacations from Vienna he declares " 'I'm a much travelled man—Budapest, Prague, Shanghai, Bombay, London' " (135). These are patently the stages of his escape. When Mrs. Gottlob dismisses his travels as " 'only tramping,' " he agrees that he had not traveled for pleasure, " 'for kicks,' " but because he had been " 'kicked' " (135). He delights in being " 'very English' " by making puns. Lumbik is the consummate survivor because he takes things as they come, without much thought or regret for his life in Vienna with his friends, his girlfriends, the coffeehouses, chess, and the opera. It sounds a richer life than what he has in London, yet his sanguine, cheerful nature prevents him from mourning. Through his positive attitude Lumbik indeed makes his life a success story—or at least that is how he sees it.

The other two guests at the party are more scantily sketched. Mrs. Gottlob with her "overfed body" (128) and occasionally sharp tongue is the least appealing of the four. She is the widow of a butcher in Gelsenkirchen; his fate is not elucidated, we only hear that he had the finest liver sausage in town. Mrs. Gottlob's tendency to grossness is suggested in her association with excesses in food; throughout the story she is stuffing her mouth, and it is she who brings the big box of chocolates. She is also the lowest in the class hierarchy. Lower-class Jews were proportionately less successful in escaping than the middle and upper classes partly because they did not have the necessary connections or money and partly because they could not cope with all the paperwork. In Berlin Sonia would not have socialized with a butcher's wife, but their common lot as escapees has forged a link that overrides class.

The last guest to arrive is tiny, short, plump Else, who bustles in with her coat half open, her gray bun drooping out of its pins, and an enormous old leather handbag tucked under her arm. Untidy and inelegant though she is in appearance, she has a certain refinement lacking in Mrs. Gottlob. Her handbag, for instance, is leather, and her gift to Sonia three lace-edged hankies. Else is fully conscious of coming from a respectable family. Her father, Emil Levy, a high-school teacher, had been a leading citizen of Schweinfurt and an ardently patriotic German who had kept a picture of the Kaiser and his family in the drawing room. The ironies are evident here: that a man named Levy should be such a committed German, and that he should reside in Schweinfurt (Pigford). Again the motif of travel serves to define the Levy family's financial standing. Every summer Emil Levy took his six children to the mountains where they stayed in the Pension Katz. "Pension" denotes a level beneath that of the hotels patronized by the Rothsteins and the Wolffs, while "Katz" suggests it was Jewish in ownership. Despite their patriotism were the Levys less assimilated than they themselves believed? If so why did they opt to stay in a Jewish pension? The force of anti-Semitism in Germany is never articulated in the story. Yet it is, of course, the reason why these residents of London had been forced to emigrate. Anti-Semitism is therefore quite fundamentally implicit in "A Birthday in London" even if Sonia and her friends prefer to overlook it in their idealization of the old days.

The redress of those earlier injustices is symbolized in the compensation that Else is about to start receiving. This means that her story too, after a long difficult phase, will finally become one of at least material success. In her fifties, more than twenty years after her arrival in England, she still works as an alteration hand for a Mrs. Davis, who treats her meanly, keeping her after hours so that she arrives late for the celebration. Having lost her parents and sisters Else is subject to attacks of depression when she falls prey to survivor guilt and even contemplates suicide. The compensation money changes her position; full of glee she immediately thinks of taking "a nice holiday in Switzerland in a good hotel" (130). This would be quite a step up from the Pension Katz of her childhood. Paradoxically being an escapee affects Else economically in contrary directions successively: at first she is considerably worse off, but in the long run she rises above the level into which she had been born. Presumably the compensation money will let her give up working for Mrs. Davis.

Mrs. Davis is the only British person mentioned in "A Birthday in London." All Sonia's guests are escapees; though of diverse background and social class they cluster together in a subcommunity linked by the shared experience of displacement and the imperative of adjustment in order to survive, let alone succeed. In Swiss Cottage Sonia and her friends live in an insulated European capsule. All the vacation places they speak of are European as is their food, *apfelstrudel* and coffee. Certain foods, particularly strong coffee, are emblematic of a European way of life throughout Jhabvala's work. Other details in the story also serve as reminders of the characters' past: Lumbik kisses Sonia's hand on arriving, and in speaking reveals a glimpse of a gold tooth. Sonia herself is repeatedly called "the birthday child," a translation of *Geburtstagskind*, and several German words such as *Mutti* (mummy) and *Tante* (aunt) are freely used. This European aura distinguishes the escapees, simultaneously uniting them as a group and separating them from the inhabitants of their new environment. Their European usages and terms indicate, too, how their former existence continues to permeate their present.

How each of them managed to get to London is not explained within the limits of this short story, but it is quite possible to extrapolate from the known facts. Otto Wolff, an experienced and wealthy industrialist, would likely have been admitted to England as a capitalist, a potential asset to the country's economy in creating new jobs, certainly far from the financial burden refugees were feared to be. Those distinguished in the arts or sciences, the elite and the wealthy were exceptions to the stringent control of immigration to Great Britain in the 1930s. The restrictions were cumbersome, often ambiguous in including discretionary powers, and shifting—in short designed to keep as many applicants as possible out.[4] One of the very few exemptions to this policy of exclusion was the admission of some 20,000 Central European women as domestic servants to fill a growing shortage of British servants.[5] It is probable that Mrs. Gottlob and Else were permitted to immigrate in this category. Lumbik's immigration, apparently after the war, is the most enigmatic since few visas were granted then, generally to close relatives of those already well established who guaranteed financial support. As the survivor *par excellence*, Lumbik no doubt was able to work round these regulations, and this too may contribute to his exuberance.

Having come to England in adulthood, the now middle-aged escapees in "A Birthday in London" have all kinds of difficulties in adjusting. Foremost among them is the tension between memories of the " 'beautiful times' " (133), as Sonia calls them, and the recognition, emotionally as well as intellectually, that they are gone forever, and that success and happiness must nowadays be measured in terms of survival and health. Symptomatic of this tension is the ambivalence between the temptation to yield to depression and the need for optimism. Otto and Else are not the only ones to have dark days. Even Lumbik asks rhetorically: " 'Who hasn't?' " (133). Phases of discouragement to the verge of despair are seen as a normal part of escapees' profiles (especially the older ones) as they wrestle with and often resist accepting that the past is past. Nevertheless Lumbik's ingrained optimism makes him insist that eventually, with sufficient effort, everything becomes "well again" (132). For the aged and infirm Otto things never become well again, nor can Else's compensation truly compensate her for the loss of her family. Even more than the others Sonia, despite the restoration of her physical comfort, cannot overcome her nostalgia for the bygone world of yesterday.

Tension is also innate to the question of their identity. By acquiring British citizenship do they become "one of us"? That phrase and the underlying dilemma punctuate the story. Otto takes a negative view. " 'Yes, our passports they have given us . . . but what else have we got?' " (124). At the opposite extreme Lumbik is elated, envisaging himself as "a very small member of the very large British Commonwealth" (124). The word "citizenship," used throughout "A Birthday in London," is normative in the United States; it denotes an important legal landmark conferring the right to unlimited residency along with other privileges and duties. In Britain at that time the customary term was "naturalization," which suggests a process of absorption into the new nationality and its mores. But are the four consuming *apfelstrudel* and coffee in Sonia's centrally heated Swiss Cottage flat on the way to being "naturalized," that is, integrated beyond the legal meaning?

Compared to Lumbik, still excited by his new status, the others are more blasé. To Sonia it is a matter of indifference since she has already been a British citizen for ten years. However when Mrs. Gottlob says to Lumbik: " 'you are also one of us now' " (130), the phrase has a distinctly ironic ring, coming as it does from the former German citizen of Gelsenkirchen. Insofar as any of the four is a member of a group, it is that of escapees, whatever passport they carry at the moment. Else, on becoming a British citizen, had actually taken offense at being greeted by Mrs. Davis with the identical phrase: " 'So you are one of us now' " (130). The repetition of the phrase turns it from a statement into an irony and finally into a parody, which points to its hollowness. None of the figures has assimilated to the British way of life; they remain within a distinctive, marginal subcommunity.

Else's anger is connected to another facet of the tensions faced by escapees. Although Mrs. Davis is her employer, she feels contempt for her lack of culture. " 'If you say to her Beethoven, she will think you have said a bad word' " (131). Sonia concurs: " 'English Jews are all so uncultured, they are not like we were in Germany' " (131). This remark is all the more telling coming from Sonia who generally thinks the best of people. Her criticism of an imputed lack of culture was in fact a covert source of friction between Anglo-Jewry and those more recently arrived from Central Europe. The vast majority of British (and American) Jews had come from Eastern Europe round the turn of the century in an emigration prompted by a series of pogroms as well as by economic need. In Britain as in the United States they managed to gain a foothold and to work their way up the economic ladder. But culturally they remained far behind the European Jews who had mostly had much less of a financial struggle and who had been able to participate fully in a rich artistic life up to Hitler's advent to power. They had shed Yiddish in favor of German, and had adopted the German ideal of *Bildung*, venerating liberal, humanistic traditions as the secular mainstay of their lives. If education was for British Jews the path to upward mobility and prosperity, for Central European Jews it was a precondition for self-respect and access to culture.[6] The escapees considered the British Jews to be clannish and unwelcoming, while the British Jews regarded the new arrivals as arrogant. Organized contacts with established Anglo-Jewry, whether social or institutional (through clubs, synagogues, etc.), were virtually absent. The escapees founded their own synagogue in Belsize Square in Swiss Cottage. The adverserial attitude to Mrs. Davis in "A Birthday in London" is therefore in keeping with the history of mistrust and resentment between the two communities.[7] The newcomers were at first generally poorer than the members of the indigenous community, but in their cultural heritage they were superior. This superiority in turn made British Jews fear an increase in anti-Semitism. The presence of some 1,000 escapees in Hampstead during the war did in fact fuel additional anti-Semitism, which was vented in a petition signed by over 2,000 residents of the area in October 1945 and handed to the Member of Parliament for Hampstead, urging the expulsion of the German refugees in order to make way for returning service men and women and evacuees.[8] This petition reinforced the British Jews' resentment of the escapees by strengthening their own persistent "diasporic identity."[9]

The cultural gulf between the native and the Central European Jews was certainly a factor in fostering the latter's tendency to cluster into separate enclaves. "A Birthday in London" shows how escapees who had been of quite divergent social standing back in Europe converge through their instinctive understanding of each other as a result of the trauma they have all undergone and that now forms a bond between them. They have a common language in their ready appropriation of German words into their speech; they have common tastes in food; they have common values and prejudices, for instance, against Mrs. Davis and the likes of her. While they are not "one of us" except on paper, so to speak, they are sustained by their strong sense of belonging with each other. They define themselves negatively through detachment from, if not opposition to, the environment in which they have landed. " 'We know who we are' " (137), Sonia declares with a certain defiance.

In the same sentence she voices her anxieties about her children: " 'but what does my Werner know, and my Lilo?' " (137). Sonia's two adult children represent the future, the second generation, which has scant personal roots in their parents' European heritage. Werner was four when the Wolffs came to England, and we don't know how old Lilo had been. She appears in "A Birthday in London" only in her mother's thoughts and in a letter that has arrived from Israel that very day. Sonia shows her guests the photo enclosed with the letter from Lilo and her husband, "sun-burnt stocky farm-workers with open collars and rolled-up sleeves—and their blond naked baby" (127). The contrast implicit in this photo between Lilo's present life and that led by the Wolffs in the past is stark. The clothes themselves are highly reveal-ing in the contrast between the casualness of Israelis and the formality of the prewar diaspora. Yet there is a continuity too as Sonia discerns a resemblance between the baby and its grandfather and even its great-grandfather, her own father, "a large, healthy, handsome man, who had loved good living and had died at Auschwitz" (127). This, the sole overt reference to the Holocaust, is introduced in an apparent aside in a succinct formulation, which summa-rizes the tragedy of German Jews in the unmediated juxtaposition of Mr. Rothenstein's love of good living and his death in Auschwitz.

Although a static figure, present only in the photo, Lilo nonetheless plays an important role in the story. Why and when she emigrated to Israel is not revealed, likely after World War II in the outburst of Zionist enthusiasm for the newly founded state. Was her re-emigration motivated by idealism, or also a feeling of not quite belonging in England, not being truly "one of us"? The photo of the happy family with baby, firmly planted on the ground, as it were, suggests that Lilo is well assimilated in Israel. This is not the positive light in which Sonia reads the photo. Recalling her own girlhood of "such lovely dresses and always parties and dancing classes and the Konservatorium in Berlin for my piano playing," her voice breaks as she begins to weep at the thought of her daughter's life: "she has had only hard work in the Kibbutz, hard work with her hands, and those horrible white blouses and shorts" (137). Sonia is incapable of grasping the difference between the superficial frivolities of her own girlhood and the deeper satisfaction Lilo can derive from her pro-ductive hard work. Whereas her mother witnessed the collapse of the old world, Lilo is engaged in the constructive effort to build a new nation. Hers may be the biggest success story in "A Birthday in London."

Sonia's son, Werner, is a more problematic character than Lilo. At age twenty-six, he is described as "a handsome boy with thick brown hair and an elegant air" (132). The handsomeness harks back to the Rothenstein grand-father, the elegance to his father. But he is still "a boy," living with his mother, whose birthday he has completely forgotten, in contrast to his sister so far away. Werner thus seems rather self-absorbed, and his attitude toward his mother reflects badly on him. He kisses her on the cheek "with a slightly condescending affection" (132), interrupts her reminiscences "with mock solemnity" (134), and rudely crowns her memories of "big hotels" by finish-ing her sentence for her: " 'With red plush carpets and a winter garden and five o'clock tea à l'anglaise' " (134). He has obviously heard this litany before, and doesn't bother to conceal his exasperated, cynical boredom. Sonia for her part ignores his irreverence, but at a deeper level she resents his want of seriousness. With his mother's ample wealth at his disposal Werner leads the life of a playboy, at best a dilettante. He is packing his bags to go on another trip, this time to Rome where he will do the same as in London: " 'a little film-work here, a little photography there, a lot of parties, a lot of girl-friends' " (136). Meanwhile Sonia muses on what might—should—have been: "Otto would have retired by now and Werner would be running the factory. He would be Werner Wolff, Director of SIGBO, everybody would know and respect him" (137). As over Lilo, though with better reason, Sonia sheds tears for Werner into one of her lace-trimmed hankies.

"A Birthday in London" is a masterpiece in miniature. It has the density and economy that are the hallmarks of the finest short stories. Every detail counts, obliquely inviting readers to make inferences about the characters' attitudes and social position without narratorial comment. For instance the description of Lumbik in the opening sentence as wearing a tweed jacket with leather buttons and carrying a big bunch of flowers in tissue paper indicates at once his Anglophilia and his continuing adherence to European usage. Lumbik's tweed jacket is one example of the often symbolic function of clothes. The contrast between Otto's elegance in Berlin and the too big, old, but expensive dressing gown he wears in London represents the extent of his decline. Similarly the collocation of Lilo's garb of white blouse and shorts, almost the uniform of the Kibbutz, with her mother's abundance of pretty dresses in her youth acts as a shorthand notation of the gulf between their respective lifestyles. Werner's tendency to dandyism emerges from his gesture of "hitching up his well-creased trousers and crossing one leg over the other to display elegant socks" (133). The red plush carpet in high-class hotels is another eloquent detail, as is the food that has already been mentioned. It is as if the narrator herself were a hidden onlooker of this birthday celebration who turns readers into spectators and by extension participants through her practice of showing more than telling.

This sense of our being there is corroborated by the very widespread recourse to dialogue. Alternatively indirect discourse is used to give readers access to the characters' minds and thoughts so that we see things from their perspective. On the other hand actual description is surprisingly scant and abbreviated. Mrs. Gottlob is fat, Else "tiny . . . as plump as she was short" (128), Werner handsome.

The most striking gap is the complete absence of any description of Sonia's physical appearance. While she stands at the center of the story the "birthday child" remains curiously disembodied. This absence of corporeal reality seems connected to her insistent return to her past as if she lived more fully then than now (hence perhaps also the denomination birthday child as if she were in some way arrested in her past). On her age, too, there is a tact-ful silence, although she is probably in her mid-fifties, like Else and Lumbik, whose exact age is specified. Mrs. Gottlob and Lumbik indulge in some good-natured banter about how it feels to be twenty-five, but Sonia skillfully sidesteps the issue by responding that her son is already twenty-six. Sonia is patently more engaged with her past than with the present, preferring not to heed the march of time signaled by her birthday and to go on seeing herself as an attractive young woman in lovely dresses. To what extent is she simply idealizing her youth? It's hard to say since none of her guests knew her then so that they are not in a position to confirm or deny her memories. But Lumbik is quite aware of her "romantic upbringing" (124), and her repeated outbreaks of tearful sentimentality certainly testify to her disposition to recall the good in the past and to forget the bad. This is corroborated above all by the hiatus in this story about anti-Semitism in Germany in the 1930s and the reasons for Sonia's and her guests' being in London now.

"A Birthday in London" offers a graphic portrait of a group of escapees, long resident in their new environment, holders of British citizenship, but in many respects still not naturalized. Middle-aged they look back to their previous lives with a medley of feelings. Lumbik, the realist, concedes the pleasures of his youthful existence in Vienna, but doesn't allow himself to grieve, savoring instead the security he has achieved through his newly acquired British citizenship. His present cheerfulness may be the outcome of the adventures and hardships he had surely undergone on his long journey before reaching this safe haven in London. The others, too, have all experienced some degree of adversity. Else is only just attaining financial ease with her compensation money and is therefore in high spirits, but she remains alone because all her family perished. Mrs. Gottlob's barbed tongue may stem from a certain dissatisfaction, for which she finds solace in overeating.

Of the four Sonia is the most labile, although her position is, objectively, better than that of her friends. Her husband, nineteen years her senior, would by then anyway have retired, aged, possibly be dead. Unlike her guests, none of whom speaks of family, she has a son, a daughter, and a grandchild. But she does not appear to be deeply attached to them, certainly not to Lilo, whom she merely pities. Nor, with the new photo in hand, does she dwell on her grandchild. Has she been to visit Israel? With her revulsion for the Kibbutz and its customs, it is unlikely. Sonia looks not forward to her family's future but always backward to its past glories. In London she has comfort again, money, and some friends, albeit not of the social level of those she had had in Berlin, whose invitations she would answer at her escritoire (the French word hints at a certain snobbishness). Despite her affluence Sonia has suffered a drop in prestige; she no longer commands the position of respect she once had as the wife of Otto Wolff, the Director of SIGBO. Because she had had the most, she also ironically had the most to lose. Her fixation on the parties and dresses of her youth suggests a streak of narcissism in her personality. However her childlike spontaneity is a source of her attractiveness. Jhabvala has performed a delicate balancing act in delineating the character of Sonia. Beneath the success story of her survival lurks a story of failure—failure to grow up and to adapt.

"A Birthday in London" captures a brief moment, the couple of hours of the party, but at the same time it gives insight into the quality of elderly escapees' lives. Although predominantly situational and apparently static, limited in place as well as in time, it has its own dynamism in its larger perspective on the characters' past in relation to their present. It is delicately balanced too in its evocation of their moods as they oscillate between nostalgia for the past and acceptance of the present as well as between a sometimes grudging gratitude toward the host country and a rebellious criticism. The bright jocular tone of the birthday celebration overlays the serious difficulties these characters have faced, and still cannot wholly shed or master.

British Provinces

4

"TRY TO FORGET"

Maureen Duffy, *Change* (1987)

" 'It's all behind you now. You must try to forget' " (45), Dr. Fentiman tells Tilde, his new German maid, the replacement for the English one who has been drafted to work in a munitions factory. The time is 1939, just before the outbreak of war. Tilde has come to Great Britain to do domestic work, the only kind of work she "was allowed to do" (47).

Tilde is one of the over 20,000 European women admitted to Great Britain on domestic permits in the 1930s, particularly in the latter years of that decade.[1] In 1936, 8,449 such visas were granted, nearly double the number in 1935; in 1937, the figure rose to 14,000, including some "domestic couples," although it then dropped to 7,000 in 1938 following a change in regulations. For most of the young women the domestic route was a last resort of escape; even those who held affidavits to enter the United States were afraid to wait in Europe much longer for their quota to come up. Some of the *Kindertransport* children were also directed into positions as domestics when they reached their later teens. Virtually none had any experience of such work; indeed many came from families that had themselves employed domestic help. Apart from dealing with separation from their families and anxiety about the fate of those left behind, learning a new language and different customs, they had to accommodate more than most escapees to a much lowered social status. And they were alone, without family support. " 'Tilde, Tilde, is the kettle on?' " (48) is the clarion call in *Change*.

These women were permitted to come to the United Kingdom in an attempt to alleviate the servant problem about which the employing class had been complaining since the end of World War I. At first the complaints were about the declining quality of domestic servants, but increasingly mere availability became an issue as other, more attractive forms of employment opened up for young women in factories or clerical positions, where conditions of work were better, pay higher, and personal freedom far greater. On the recruitment of the remaining British servants such as the Fentimans' maid into war service, the shortage of help became sufficiently acute to warrant the importation of foreign labor. A family such as Dr. Fentiman's absolutely needed help because, in accordance with British usage, the doctor's office was located in part of the house. One of the duties imposed on Tilde is the cleaning of the medical areas: " '[Y]ou will always remember to scrub the waiting-room floor with strong Lysol once a day won't you. Even if it looks clean, there are invisible germs' " (99). Her work isn't just a matter of making tea.

Attitudes toward this category of escapees were mixed. On the one hand the Trades Union Congress sponsored National Union of Domestic Workers protested against the presence of foreign labor; on the other such groups as the National Council of Women, which saw the old lifestyle threatened by the dearth of servants, were supportive. Government policy has been characterized as "clearly motivated by opportunism and blatant self-interest" (Kushner, 563). If its primary aim was to assure a supply of domestics, the policy failed, for most of the women moved into other occupations such as nursing or factory work within two–three years. In this respect Tilde in *Change* is atypical in staying on with the Fentimans.

As things went, Tilde was not badly treated.[2] For a minimum wage of fifteen shillings per week most British domestics worked for twelve hours a day six-and-a-half days a week with strict regulations concerning their limited free time. Some of the foreign maids were undoubtedly exploited, in part because of their ignorance of both housework and their rights. Tilde has "learned to bake" (47), does "all the cleaning and queueing and cooking" (136), and of course the washing up. When she takes the initiative by asking Dr. Fentiman for an afternoon off every week, he immediately accedes to her request: " 'Of course, of course you should. I ought to have thought of it or Evie should. And a whole day Saturday or Sunday, once a month' " (99). His generosity is somewhat blunted by the realization that she had till then apparently had no time off.

Tilde is one of the very large cast of characters in *Change*. By taking a wide cross-section of the British population from all levels of the class hierarchy Duffy shows how everyone was affected by the war between 1939 and 1945. The novel's five sections correspond to the phases of the war: "Innocence," "Iron," "Papers," "Overlords," and "Elegies." In each of them most of the various figures recur; all speak for themselves either in letters or diaries (in "Papers") or more commonly in conversations or through their musings in indirect discourse. Without direct narration Duffy cleverly conveys the progress of the war by the protagonists' participation in its major events: the evacuation from London, and the bombing of the city; the recruitment of women into factories, the Land Army, nursing, ambulance driving, wireless monitoring, decoding, and entertaining the troops; the landings in Norway, Dieppe, North Africa, Sicily, and D-Day; the desert campaign against Rommel, the fighting in Burma, the bombardment of Germany; the pilotless V-2s over the south of England toward the end of the war. Beneath these outer events the less tangible but decisive changes such as the loosening of the class structure and of morals occurred. The vast world events determining all the characters' fates are, as it were, personalized into particular but cohesive, at times intersecting, strands. Conversely as they are mounted onto the historical context, the individual vignettes assume a quasi-documentary significance. The wealth of precise detail about lifestyles such as the spectrum in speech and food creates cumulatively a strong sense of period and especially of class distinctions.

While the novel's time span is delimited to the six years of the war, its geographic expanse comprises the many landscapes where the fighting took place, although the focal point is London and the counties surrounding it. Where Tilde is located is not specified. However since the British government sought to prevent a concentration of the foreign domestics in north and northwest London, it is not unreasonable to assume that she is elsewhere. Manchester had a training hostel for the escapee domestics, and in Liverpool they formed their own association.

About "all" that is "behind" her, in Dr. Fentiman's words, that is, about her past, we know very little. Her name is perhaps an abbreviation of Mathilde, and her mention of Hamburg "where we were warmed a little also by the sea" (162) suggests that she may have come from there. We do hear obliquely that her mother had been deported; the last letter from Anna-Lise (her best friend?) had urged Tilde not to "worry. Mama was allowed to take an extra quilt with her in case it was cold where they were going" (45), hardly a reassuring piece of news. In this lack of information about her previous life and her escape *Change* departs from the majority of escapee fictions. But this absence of personal history is by no means unique to Tilde. All the characters in this novel appear, like actors on the stage, as if out of nowhere, and most have no last names. This mode of presentation turns them into representative types of people sucked into the war, which transforms their lives. It is left to readers to deduce their situations, family relationships, friendships, and the connections among them.

Tilde is the most isolated, desolate figure in *Change*. She is portrayed within the Fentiman household, but Dr. Fentiman's invitation to "feel like one of the family" sounds ironic—even though "they had given her a key which showed they trusted her" (45). To ask her to feel like one of the family is an absurdity, a hollow pretense; she is an employee hired to do the dirty work. She is more alone than the two other foreigners included in *Change*: Karol, the Polish aristocrat who is taken up by Gerald and his set and who later joins the navy, and the nameless Black American soldier who has an affair with Millie. Tilde has no friends at all. Not that she has time to socialize, yet on the rare occasions when she meets other refugees and they talk about things, " 'I feel I am very different from the rest of them too, as I am different from everyone else around me' " (163). Most of them look forward to the end of the war and possibly to going somewhere else, whereas Tilde doesn't " 'want to see the Promised Land in case it turns out to be just another country I can not belong to' " (163).

This sense of radical displacement, which dogs Tilde, is a direct consequence of her violent ejection from a place where she had felt a genuine belonging. Now she has "passed into limbo, into statelessness" (134) metaphorically rather than politically since the domestics were officially German citizens, and some were interned as "enemy aliens." Tilde describes herself to the book-seller from whom she buys a German dictionary as "a refugee" (134) by way of apology for requesting something German. Tilde's loneliness leads to depression. She goes so far as to envisage her death with a kind of black humor. Flooded with pain she would drop on the landing:

> The Fentimans would find her and all his doctoring skill would fail to raise her from the grave she fell into in slow motion every day. She laughed again at their long faces bent over her in concern. How would they explain it to the bobbies in their ridiculous hats. This young girl, this refugee, seems to have died of a broken heart (45).

In search of a cause for her dejection she wonders whether "it is the diet or the spirit's diet of loss" (163).

That "spirit's diet of loss" devolves more from her inability to forget those she had left behind than from grief at her own present lowly position. Apart from asking for some time off she never voices any complaint about the degradation to which she is subjected. Despite Dr. Fentiman's rational advice to " 'try to forget,' " Tilde's thoughts return insistently to Anna-Lise and to Fräulein Blumberg, her beloved English literature teacher. She has an intense longing to see them again, "come back from the dead" (163–4). Her phrase expresses her instinctive acknowledgment that they are dead, yet emotionally she cannot accept that they can never come back: it "was so unthinkable that the human mind couldn't encompass it; it was simply beyond possibility that they could go away and never come back, that somewhere out there were places where people died; were killed" (46). Tilde sees herself as a "keeper of history" (185), "a walking memorial" who had been "sent away" precisely "to survive and remember them" (100). This amounts to an acceptance on her part of a sort of mission. Not forgetting fulfills her need for self-justification, a means to deal with her survivor guilt.

That people are being deported to places where they are killed is the fundamental fact that Tilde is totally unable to understand. Like the feelings she herself experiences it is unprecedented in the history of humankind in the deliberateness of its planning and execution.

> Even the pogroms of Russia were spontaneous manifestations of the hatred the oppressed turn on each other when the oppressors are too high to reach. This is calculated with a basis in philosophy and politics, with its lists of those who are going away "to work," never coming back (135).

By 1942 reports had begun to percolate to Britain of the brutalities in the concentration camps. At a club for refugees Tilde meets Eva who had with her brother escaped from Poland and who has heard that "every day thousands are taken away from Poland in cattle trucks never to be seen again" (133). Dr. Fentiman tells Tilde that in Warsaw the Jews have been forced to build a wall and live inside it and not go out without permission. He insists that as she was born in Germany and grew up there, she must "understand" the Germans. But she responds: " 'I thought I did. I no longer understand anything' " (98).

Tilde is quite bewildered too at first by many aspects of life in England, but gradually she does come to understand better at least the population's capacity to endure wartime hardships stoically because "most of them did not have much before and therefore had less to lose. They are used to this life of enduring, of making do" (162). In the course of the six years that the action of *Change* covers Tilde does make some progress in coming to a deeper understanding of her new environment, but she cannot master her past or the realities of the Holocaust.

In trying to deal with these problems she is further alienated by Dr. Fentiman's persistent blindness to and detachment from what is happening to the Jews in Europe. For instance when he tells her about the wall in Warsaw, she immediately recognizes it as a " 'ghetto. We are used to them.' " He remains perplexed: " 'In the Middle Ages, yes. But not now. What would be the purpose?' " (98). Living in an offshore island had practical, protective advantages for Anglo-Jewry in sparing them some uncomfortable truths, but this physical isolation also generated a degree of cultural insularity, which further separated the new arrivals from the established community through the cultivation of avoidance. Their innocence elicits from Tilde "not anger but pity for them, the Fentimans" (98) because she realizes that "[T]hey were still deceiving themselves and she refused to be a part of it; she was tired of playing Cassandra" (99). Her role as Cassandra—or the realist—is certainly one factor in her isolation at a time when optimism was the dominant tone, certainly in public in Britain. So the Fentimans trust that their friends in Nice "will be all right" (99). Although Tilde is much younger than the Fentimans (her repeated references to her English literature teacher suggest that she may only recently have left school), she has an acute awareness, partly experiential, partly intuitive, of the implications of what is going on in the world at large. So when Dr. Fentiman discloses to her at a fairly early stage in the war that " '[T]he news isn't good, I'm afraid' " (97), Tilde is amazed at the fact that he evidently expects her to be surprised: "How could the news be good? . . . She would never see any of them again" (97). Unlike Dr. Fentiman Tilde has a strong and very personal stake in the progress of the war, symbolized by her recurrent plaint that she "would never see any of them again." Even at the end of the war when pictures appear of the liberation of concentration camp survivors, Dr. Fentiman remains naive: " '[H]ow shall we ever know who they were?' " he asks, to which Tilde replies laconically: " '[T]here will be lists,' she said. They always kept lists' " (212).[3] "Lists" are an obsessive theme in her mind; she recalls "the typed official list" (46) held by the man who came to remove her mother, and she imagines the list that would be drawn up if the Germans were to invade England.

On these imagined lists "Tilde and the Fentimans would both appear, she first and immediately because she was a traitor as well as a Jew but the Fentimans, who thought themselves so English, their turn would come too" (48). This insight on Tilde's part touches on a painful issue, which was long not openly discussed, namely, the tensions between British Jews and escapees. "They were English first, the Fentimans and Jews second" (46), Tilde observes; "the Fentimans ate English," "the taste of Protestant puritanism" that pervades their food extends metonymically and metaphorically to their entire lives. Hence their apparently puzzling dissociation from the fate of European Jews during the war. These dissonances between British and Central European Jews became most readily apparent in cases like Tilde's where a young woman serving as a domestic was in constant close proximity to her employers. Many domestics aimed for positions in Anglo-Jewish households, expecting to find a more familiar environment than in a gentile home. The Fentimans, in their limited way, show Tilde kindness; at Christmas (!) they give her "cards and little presents and make a celebration not for the God of the Christians but for hope, for a turning towards the light, for a new year" (163). But the no doubt well-meant advice to "try to forget" reveals a crass failure of empathy for Tilde's situation and her wholly justified fears for her family.

The veiled antagonism between British and Central European Jews rested largely on a cultural disparity. It surfaces too in "A Birthday in London" (1963) when Else ridicules her employer, Mrs. Davis, who, she maintains, would take the name Beethoven for a dirty term. As Anthony Greenville has recently summarized it:

> Wealthy Jews might be seen at the socially prestigious opera, but not at the theatre or at concerts, whereas for the refugees the Wigmore Hall became something of a cultural Mecca. . . . The ascent of British Jews up the social scale took place under a system of values quite different from that of the Continental Jews, accentuating the divide between the two groups.[4]

This cultural divide appears in *Change* when Tilde proposes to go to the free concerts on Sunday afternoons that she has read about, and particularly in her further study of English literature at the City Literary Institute, where she will go on her afternoons off. Already well read in Shakespeare, Dickens, and Galsworthy, authors widely known in Germany among the educated, she thinks less of improving her English than of looking "for the shade of Fräulein Blumberg among the English poets" (100). To attend the classes "would help me," she tells Dr. Fentiman without explaining that they would "remind her of beauty and timelessness and Fräulein Blumberg" (99). Even in a seemingly forward-looking activity such as studying English literature Tilde is actually harking back, that is, not forgetting in order to look beyond the present toward a timeless transcendence of evil.

She is, however, unable to achieve such transcendence. Unlike Hartmann and Fibich in *Latecomers* (1988), she cannot put the past behind her and move forward into a new life. Despite her youth she has no positive hopes for her future. She fears she will not belong anywhere, not in the Promised Land any better than in England. "What must it be like," she wonders, "to have

a country to love with every movement of your blood?" (162). The lack of
such attachment to a country and its ideology is one of the characteristics that
makes her see herself as "different from everyone else around me" (163).
She cannot participate in the patriotism that sustains the British through the
hardships of war. Cut off from her former home and unrooted in her new one
she has only memories that bring more bitterness than comfort.

These memories numb Tilde. She withdraws into a "shell," which she
creates for herself:

> Her shell must be kept intact while it grew inwards, calcifying the still soft inte-
> rior until the shell met the stone heart at its core and she became like the
> pumice people, left behind in the ruined city after a volcanic eruption with the
> tide gone out for ever from the ashen shore (99).

The image of the shell is a potent metaphor for her separation from the
mainstream, and it is greatly reinforced by its association with the ruined city
abandoned even by the tide. Her emigration to England has been "a volcanic
eruption," which has left her stranded "for ever" on an "ashen shore." The
violently destructive force of a volcano and the mass of lava debris it leaves in
its wake evoke the devastation that overshadows Tilde's current life. The shell
itself, though intended as a self-protective refuge, actually has the effect of
heightening her isolation. She is even hesitant to go to a concert or a literature class because "perhaps the words and music would make a crack in her
shell but that was a risk she had to take" (100). She believes that she will
finally become "stone" (100), "pumice" (99), inured against the grief of loss,
but this transformation is not a healing one since it is at the expense of her
openness to feeling and to living. So the shell is the cipher for her self-enclosure;
instead of putting her bad experiences "behind" her, she puts them within
herself, internalizing her pain. The result is utter desolation.

Aggravating her seclusion is her physical and psychological isolation: she
has very little opportunity for interaction with others partly because, as a
domestic, she is restricted to the house six-and-a-half days a week. Had she
been a factory worker or a nurse, she would have had more daily contact with
other people, more opportunity to make friends, or at the very least more distraction. Her only recorded conversations are with Dr. Fentiman, who has no
insight into her distress. Her confining environment is an important factor in
impelling her retreat into a shell, and beyond that in her failure to adjust
better.

The circumstances of her daily existence are conducive to fostering her
introverted reflections; housework, since it requires little thought, leaves
open space, which is flooded with her dark thoughts. The dullness and emptiness of her present also help to account for her attachment to a past that was
emotionally and intellectually more satisfying. To compare Tilde's path with
that of other young escapees in England brings out the drawbacks innate to
her situation. Joe Beech in *To the City* (1987) is taken in by a kind English
foster family, attends high school and Oxford. Hartmann in *Latecomers* serves

in the army, and even Fibich, who resembles Tilde in his inclination to hang back and to look back, is drawn into British life through his business and later his wife and son. The existence of a domestic, by the very nature of the work, enforces seclusion and indeed exclusion.

Tilde is excluded too from the camaraderie of the war effort, which lowers class barriers and encourages a sense of community. In contrast to the other characters in *Change*, Tilde makes no direct contribution to the concerted struggle to beat Hitler; as a servant her position is literally subservient. Whereas those around her are fighting to preserve ideals in which they believe, she is up against the blank wall of a man-made disaster, which defies either rational comprehension or emotional working through. In her visits now and then to the synagogue nothing moves her: "the singing is nice but I do not hear God speaking to me" (135). The silencing of God's voice is both a cause and a manifestation of her turning into stone.

Tilde's retreat into a shell implies too a resistance to the change that all the other characters undergo in the course of the war. She has undergone her radical change before the outbreak of the war. She has also lost her innocence long ahead of the other protagonists. From this angle her sense of her differentness from everyone else is justified. She does not have the British capacity for "muddling through" (135), which proves such a source of strength in the war. While the British "cannot visualize defeat" (135) Tilde has already experienced a defeat because "Germany is gone for me for ever" although she still identifies herself as essentially "a European" (135). Hemmed in by these internal conflicts she lacks the resilience to rebuild her life, remaining instead in the paralysis of depression.

The sense of Tilde's enclosure, of her introversion and separateness, is vividly captured in *Change* through the portrayal of this figure almost exclusively by means of indirect discourse. Readers are thus consistently placed within her mind, following her train of thought. Except for Dr. Fentiman's "try to forget," there is no corrective image of her. The disposition of the narrative does not permit any glimpse of how others perceive her. Tilde's containment (imprisonment?) within herself is objectified in the literary format in which she is presented. The eschewal of narrative comment results in a gap in our knowledge of what lies "behind" her, although it is not hard to make an adequate conjecture. Yet despite this area of shadowiness the intensity of the trauma Tilde has suffered emerges with great poignancy precisely because she is permitted to speak for herself and we are made to experience her hurt vicariously alongside her. From this, that is, her perspective, the injunction to "try to forget" is not just inappropriately glib but virtually impossible to carry out.

In several respects Tilde displays the symptoms of posttraumatic stress disorder: in her anxiety, her obsession with "lists," her flashback to her mother's deportation, her fixation on the past, and certainly in her absolute inability to project a future for herself. In this too she stands out from the other characters in *Change*. All of them, as the novel's title indicates, have to submit to changes during the war, many of them for the worse. The concluding section,

"Elegies," records a number of deaths as well as widespread loss not merely of property but also of "innocence" (the title of the opening section). Nevertheless the survivors manage to reconstruct and reshape their lives, often in positive new directions. Hilary, who has discovered that she is a lesbian, goes off to college; her schoolfriend, Sylvie, who was a nurse on the Egyptian front, marries a doctor; Wilf decides to enlist in the army instead of going back to his former dreary occupation; young Lennie is on the way to upward mobility in a career in the navy.

Tilde also has a good opportunity to start a new life and to gain an honorable foothold in British society when Evie Fentiman suddenly dies and her employer begs her to stay. When he encourages a greater familiarity with him, "[S]he knew what it meant of course. He was lonely and he needed a housekeeper. She could be Frau or Mrs. Fentiman if she wanted. It would make her a British citizen. But could she marry such an old man?" (211). Is it the age difference alone that deters her? Her enthrallment in her past and his lack of understanding for her feelings surely also play a significant role too. Now that he in turn has become acutely troubled she resents his dependence on her as he trails her through the empty rooms of the house, calling for her "like a lost child" (212). He is again described as "demanding like a child" (212) wanting reassurance whereas what Tilde needs is a supportive father figure, not a child. Perhaps she is afraid of taking on a commitment that could become a permanent servitude; perhaps after all her losses she is afraid to cast off her shell sufficiently to engage in any relationship, which could eventually lead to further pain. After all Dr. Fentiman is so much older than she is that he would likely die before her, and she would again be left alone. She is not sufficiently self-seeking to calculate the value of acquiring through marriage to him citizenship and a certain security. Her instinctive feelings override without a moment's hesitation the lure of the advantages that would accrue to her through marriage to him.

Tilde's future remains open and uncertain. She considers going back "to search among the ruins for her dead" (212), but the sight of the pictures of concentration camp survivors forces her to acknowledge the futility of such an attempt. Her final words concern the lists that she will scan. She is the saddest and most pathetic of the figures shown in escapee fictions, cast out from the place where she had loving ties and ill prepared to cope with the loneliness facing her. Duffy's epigraph to *Change* from Edmund Spenser concludes on these words:

> We daily see new creatures to arize,
> And of their Winter spring another Prime,
> Unlike in forme and chang'd by strange disguise:
> So turn they still about, and change in restless wise.

For Tilde there is as yet no sign of "another Prime"; she is trapped in "Winter," in her shell, her anxieties.

5

"To Serve under the Chimney"

W.G. Sebald, "Max Ferber,"
The Emigrants (1992)

"With every year I have spent since then in this birthplace of industrialization, amidst the black façades, I have realized more clearly than ever that I am here . . . to serve under the chimney" (192).[1] The words are those of Max Ferber, the titular subject of the last of W.G. Sebald's quartet of long short stories collected under the title *The Emigrants (Die Ausgewanderten*, 1992). Ferber's comment is reported by the anonymous first-person narrator who tells all four stories and is a strong presence throughout as he pieces together the fragments of Ferber's life and his family's earlier history. His cryptic statement about serving "under the chimney" can be invested with a double meaning: literally the "chimney" refers to those of Manchester in the North of England where Ferber has been a painter since the 1940s, but metaphorically chimney also evokes the crematoria of the Holocaust death camps, which Ferber escaped, although his parents didn't. The word "serve" suggests Ferber's subjection to both the city's physical gloom and to the haunting shadow of the past, which flickers in a protean mosaic of memories and amnesias.

The narrator had first chanced upon Ferber in a deserted area of Manchester in the Waidi Halfa transport café, "a curious hostelry . . . that resembled a field kitchen" (163). Run by immigrants from Africa, "it probably had no licence of any kind, and was located in the basement of an otherwise unoccupied building that looked as if it might fall down at any moment" (162). The dilapidation and marginality of this café (which is later noted to have disappeared altogether) signals a pervasive instability. Ferber invariably sits in front of a fresco "that showed a caravan moving forward from the remotest depths of the picture, across a wavy ridge of dunes, straight towards the beholder" (164). Because of the painter's lack of skill and the awkward perspective, "the human figures and the beasts of burden were slightly distorted, so that, if you half shut your eyes, the scene looked like a mirage" (164). This outlandish locale is an eerily appropriate setting for the narrator's conversations with Ferber. The apparently random details gradually coalesce into a pattern, though one studded with gaps and uncertainties.

The fresco, for instance, depicts the crossing of deserts of which Ferber speaks: "He himself once remarked . . . that in his dreams, both waking and by night, he had crossed all the earth's deserts of sand and stone" (164). The crossing of deserts of sand and stone (i.e., full of obstacles) can be construed as an analogy to his difficult life. The sand also refers to the dust that is the outcome of his idiosyncratic method of painting and that is as if incorporated into Ferber himself in "the gleam of graphite on the back of his hands" (164). His studio is

> layered with the dust of decades. Since he applied the paint thickly, and then repeatedly scratched it off the canvas as his work proceeded, the floor was covered with a largely hardened and encrusted deposit of droppings, mixed with coal dust, several centimetres thick at the centre and thinning out towards the outer edges, in places resembling the flow of lava (161).

Ferber insists "that nothing further should be added but the debris generated by painting and the dust that continuously fell and which, as he was coming to realize, he loved more than anything else in the world. He felt closer to dust, he said, than to light, air or water" (161). To the narrator it seems that Ferber's "prime concern was to increase the dust" (164) through an ironically progressive process of painting, erasure, and repainting, which thwarts a definitive conclusion. As a result of this "steady production of dust," the facial features on Ferber's portraits "remained ultimately unknowable" (162). The painter's methodology and indeed the whole scenario at the Waidi Halfa café, which initially seem merely bizarre, serve as an oblique introduction to the story's central implicit themes: movement, transience, a nomadic lack of permanence, dissolution, dislocation, uncertainty, evanescence, improvisation as a norm, mystery, unfathomability. And while most of the pieces in the puzzle that is "Max Ferber" can ultimately be placed in relation to each other and connected as in a jigsaw, the narrative always, as it were, remains enveloped in dust and debris, resisting finalizing interpretation, like Ferber's paintings. An aura of strangeness, of limited knowability permeates this story in a manner typical of Sebald's endlessly challenging writings.

The exploration of the unknown and the surprises which that effort entails is a dominant motif from the outset of "Max Ferber." It opens with the narrator's arrival in Manchester by plane in the autumn of 1966 at the age of twenty-two, a situation patently derived from Sebald's own experience (he was a lector in the German Department at the University of Manchester, 1966–1967). For the first time away from home further than a few hours' train journey, looking down on the orange sodium glare of the street lights, he realizes that from now on he would be "living in a different world" (149). He has become a voluntary expatriate, embarked on a journey of discovery, not across stretches of sand, but through "a blanket of fog" (150). Gloom and desolation are the keynotes of his perception of the once prosperous but now decayed city, "almost hollow to the core," with "dark ravines between the brick buildings," "soot-blackened" houses, in short "a necropolis or mausoleum" (151). The more he registers "the clearly chronic process of its [the city's] impoverishment and degradation" (156) on his Sunday walks, the more he is beset by a sense of alienation. In what had been "the immigrant city of Manchester" (181) he comes across traces of the large influx of European Jews who had played a key role in the development of the city's cultural life in its heyday starting in the later nineteenth century and extending into the twentieth century. Their absence is symbolized by "the barely decipherable brass plate of a one time lawyers' office, bearing names that had a legendary ring to my ear: Glickmann, Grunwald and Gottgetreu" (157).[2] Prosperity—and the Jews—had moved out to the suburbs and to satellite towns beyond the narrator's legs. This emphasis on the despoliation of the environment and the disappearance of the Jews serves above all the poetic purpose of evoking the backdrop against which Max Ferber paints to dust.

Mobile, ever wandering, almost compulsively, the narrator roams through industrial wastelands, past abandoned depots and warehouses, a long-disused gasworks, a bone mill, a slaughterhouse, and along the Manchester–Liverpool Ship Canal, which had formerly supported a lively export/import trade. These ciphers of dereliction form the frame to Ferber. The narrator happens upon a crude sign "TO THE STUDIOS" (160). In the remnants of what must have been a carriage business with stables and outbuildings he comes across a studio "in one of those seemingly deserted buildings" (160) where Ferber had been working ten hours a day seven days a week since the 1940s. A patch of grass and an almond tree in blossom are the only living things to mitigate the devastation of Ferber's surroundings. Sheer haphazardness has led to the meeting of the expatriate and the escapee that is at the heart of this story. The same kind of contingency marks both their lives.

The narrator and Ferber can be regarded as "twin souls," not directly as are Hartmann and Fibich in *Latecomers* (1988) but more subtly and figuratively in their reciprocal interdependence throughout the narrative. At first dogged by "a sense of malaise and futility" (156) in an unfamiliar place the narrator becomes more purposeful once he encounters Ferber because he wants to delve into his history in order to learn how he had become the eccentric he is. Ferber for his part exists from a literary angle solely through the intermediacy of the narrator. Not only is the perspective consistently that of the narrator, so also is the voice. Everything that Ferber says is *reported* speech. The narrative is repeatedly punctuated by the interpolated phrase, "said Ferber," sometimes in parentheses but mostly as an insert into the flow of the sentence. The narrator thus acts as a conduit for Ferber's words. This characteristic mode of indirection is clearly illustrated in Ferber's remark about serving under the chimney with which I chose to open this section. In stark contrast to the majority of escapee fictions, which abound in indirect discourse and dialogue, "Max Ferber" is a monologue by the narrator. We are therefore granted no immediate insight into Ferber's mind; he is always seen and heard from the outside through the narrator's eyes and ears. So the narrator's constant presence is also partly a device for distancing Ferber whose remoteness has the effect of heightening the mystery about him.

In the English translation Ferber is further distanced through the change of his name from the original German version where he is called Max Aurach. That name echoes all too obviously that of the actual painter, Frank Auerbach, whose life and work share many features with Aurach's/Ferber's. Born in Berlin in 1931 Auerbach was sent to England by his parents to avoid Nazi persecution. He studied art in London at the St. Martin's College of Art (1948–1952) and at the Royal College of Art (1952–1955). His work has been exhibited in major galleries in London, New York, the Yale Center for British Art, and throughout Europe. Since 1954 he has had a studio in the urban landscape of London's Camden Town. His mode of painting resembles that of Aurach/Ferber. He works and reworks his canvases to produce a powerful surface impact through the weight of the densely applied color and the expressive texture of the paint itself. Since Sebald habitually fuses reality with fiction it is likely that Auerbach was a model for Aurach/Ferber. In the fiction the painter is transposed to Manchester where Sebald himself lived for a time, and in the English translation his name is changed to Ferber, which resonates for German speakers with "Farbe," color.

Of far greater significance, however, is the change of the painter's first name to Max. For Maximilian was the third of Sebald's own names, and he preferred to be known as Max rather than by either of his other two names, Winfried or Georg. This coincidence of the protagonist's and the author's names hints at the subterranean affinity between them. In his consistent reporting of Ferber's words, the narrator is a fascinated, sympathetic listener who becomes increasingly drawn into Ferber's life and history. The closeness of the two figures is enhanced by the overlap between narrator and author revealed by the biographical data mentioned in the story: like the narrator, Sebald was in Manchester during 1966–1967 and later, after a year in Switzerland, returned to England "to take up the offer of a position I found attractive from several points of view, in Norfolk" (177). These interchangeable roles devolve from a certain Nabokovian strain. Nabokov, a recurrent figure in Sebald's work, makes two appearances in "Max Ferber," once as a butterfly catcher near Montreux during Ferber's visit to Switzerland with his father (174), and again in the memories of Ferber's mother of a Russian "leaping about the meadows with his butterfly net" (214). But this conflation of time periods and of persons is more than a playful element in a narrative game; it testifies rather to the fluidity intrinsic to the layering of memory and of personality. Despite the differences between them in age and religious background, the narrator and Ferber seem secretly conjoined by their status as creative artists, as outsiders, loners, and their negative attitudes toward their native Germany. This latent intermingling gives "Max Ferber" a special intensity.

*   *   *

Ferber's life story emerges slowly in discrete segments at various points in the narrative. Initially, at the Waidi Halfa café, it is an "extremely cursory version," and the narrator notices that Ferber is "loath to answer the questions I put to him about his story and his early years" (166). He divulges just as much as he is ready to tell. In 1943, at the age of eighteen, he had first come to Manchester as a student of art. Within months, in early 1944, he had been called up. During that first brief stay he had lodged in the very house where Ludwig Wittgenstein, then a twenty-year-old engineering student, had stayed in 1908. This seemingly irrelevant, interpolated detail sites Ferber in the tradition of Manchester as an immigrant city. The link to Wittgenstein gives Ferber "a sense of brotherhood that reached far back beyond his own lifetime or even the years immediately before it" (167). In this comment of Ferber's the theme of the continuities of history is introduced, a theme particularly important in a story concerned mainly with discontinuities. After completing basic training at Catterick Ferber had volunteered for a paratroop regiment, but when he contracted jaundice he was compelled to spend more than six months convalescing at the Palace Hotel in Buxton, a Derbyshire spa. In early May 1945, on his discharge from the army, he had returned to Manchester to resume his study of art. This is the first installment, as it were, of Ferber's account of himself. It is dense in topographical and historical detail, yet suspended in a blank about what had occurred previously.

The next, anterior part of the patchwork comes from an extraneous source, a magazine article that the narrator happens to read about Ferber in November 1989 at the time of his first major exhibition. The chanciness of the discovery is underscored by the narrator's statement that he had long avoided reading the Sunday papers, especially the color supplements. That he happens to do so on this occasion appears to be further evidence of a hidden connection between the expatriate and the escapee. It is indeed from "the rather meagre magazine account" (178) that the narrator comes to learn of Ferber's status as an escapee. He had arrived in England in May 1939, at age fifteen, from Munich where his father had been an art dealer. His parents, who had for a number of reasons delayed their departure from Germany, were deported in November 1941 to Riga, where they were murdered. With hindsight the narrator understands the "inhibitions or wariness . . . that had kept our conversations away from his origins" (178). In this reticence there is a hint of shame on both sides: on the narrator's part because he is a German and feels co-responsible; on Ferber's part possibly as a manifestation of survivor guilt.

When the narrator returns to Manchester after an interval of over twenty years he finds Ferber in the same studio. For three whole days and far into the night they speak of "our exile in England" (181) and of the narrator's moves in the meanwhile (they coincide exactly with the author's, thereby confirming the autobiographical strand). The first person plural, "our," again suggests an affinity between the narrator and the protagonist. By 1989, Ferber points out, the narrator is as far removed temporally from Germany as he himself had been at the time of their first meeting in 1966. Thus another recondite link is forged between the expatriate and the escapee. Ferber's memories are lapidary, going back no further than his eighth or ninth year; he recalls "little of the Munich years after 1933 other than processions, marches and parades," standing as a teenager "silently amidst the cheering or awe-struck crowds, ashamed that I did not belong" (182). "Not once," he tells the narrator, "was there any talk of leaving Germany, at least not in my presence, even after the Nazis had confiscated pictures, furniture and valuables from our home" (185), nor after Crystal Night when his father was interned in Dachau for six weeks. No explanations whatsoever are offered; Ferber does not speculate, and the narrator restricts himself to reporting.

The most striking feature of Ferber's recall is the engulfing silence, the "loss of language," which may be a consequence of Ferber's forfeiture of his mother tongue, German, a language he has not spoken once since his parting from his parents at Oberwiesenfeld airport in Munich in May 1939. That scene is a prime example of the inability to communicate, a muteness on both sides rooted in apprehension and a kind of embarrassment, which stems from repression and denial. When there is so very much to say, a lifetime of talk between parents and child, nothing at all is sayable.

> The drive seemed endless to me, said Ferber, probably because none of us said a word. When I asked if he remembered saying goodbye to his parents at the airport, Ferber replied, after a long hesitation, that when he thought back to that May morning at Oberwiesenfeld he could not see his parents. He no longer knew what the last thing his mother or father had said to him was, or he to them, or whether his parents had embraced or not. He could still see his parents sitting in the back of the hired car on the drive out to Oberwiesenfeld, but he could not see them at the airport itself (187).

All three seem as if anesthetized into a numbness, which blunts the pain of the parting. Perhaps because Ferber's visual abilities are predominant he can see but not hear his parents. In his last glimpse of them sitting in the back of the hired car they appear to be wax figures, as though they were already dead. In striking contrast to that gap in his memory Ferber "could picture Oberwiesenfeld down to the last detail, and all those years had been able to do so with that fearful precision time and again. . . . he could see it all with painful clarity" (187–8). Arguably Ferber is displacing a suffering too distressing to tolerate. He has veiled the ghastly moment of permanent separation from his parents in silence, frozen it into a stasis in order to defuse its emotional power to overwhelm. But unlike Fibich in *Latecomers*, who has also forgotten that dreadful moment but who desperately yearns for some recuperation, Ferber seems to have obliterated it from his consciousness. He even understands, at least intellectually, the psychological mechanism; recalling an incident of extreme pain from a slipped disc, he comments:

> I gradually understood that, beyond a certain point, pain blots out the one thing that is essential to its being experienced—consciousness—and so perhaps extinguishes itself; we know very little about this. What is certain, though, is that mental suffering is effectively without end. One may think one has reached the very limit, but there are always more torments to come. One plunges from one abyss into the next (171–2).

Like Joe Beech in Tindall's *To the City* (1987) Ferber here refers to the
mental suffering occasioned by memory as an "abyss."

The incident at the airport is a vivid illustration of the main theme of "Max
Ferber": the selectivity—and unreliability—of memory. This is a recurrent
motif in escapee fiction because all the escapees carry vestiges of a past life.
Some such as Hartmann in *Latecomers*, Joe Beech, and Max Ferber want to
put that past out of mind. Most, especially those who were older when they
left Europe and had established positions, such as Sonia Wolff in "A Birthday
in London" (1963) and Gottfried Rosenbaum in Jarrell's *Pictures from an
Institution* (1954), view their former existence with a certain nostalgia. The
issue of memory is particularly acute in "Max Ferber" because it deals with
several interrelated sets of memories, the narrator's, Ferber's, and his
mother's, all of whom harbor ambivalence about remembering, though to
different degrees.

The narrator's memories of Manchester are negative on account of the
city's desolation, but while this causes him temporary dejection, it does not
affect him deeply as he has no emotional ties to the place in either the past or
for the future. Its significance to him is primarily as the location of his meeting with Ferber. Ferber is, as it were, embedded in that desolation, although
the patch of grass and the blossoming tree outside his studio form an oasis of
a continuing, self-renewing life cycle. However the "impoverishment and
degradation" that have ravaged the city conjure up the similar fate during the
war of the European cities from which Ferber came. In the narrator's mind
Ferber is associated with that collapse of European civilization that necessi-
tated Ferber's emigration (and, mutatis mutandis, the narrator's/author's).
It may well be these subconscious associations of Ferber's fate with that of
Europe that motivate the patchiness of the narrator's memories: "I no longer
remember how Ferber came to tell me the extremely cursory version of his
life that he gave me at that time, though I do remember that he was loath to
answer the questions I put to him about his story and his early years" (166).
The narrator was impressed by, and therefore recalls, Ferber's reluctance to
speak about certain things or his total silence about them, whereas he has
eliminated the circumstances that led to the opening up of his story. Since
Ferber did not want to tell it, it may be that the narrator prompted him with
questions, and this is what he would prefer to forget.

The unreliability of the narrator's memory is borne out by his confusion
of time sequences. In the opening sentence he specifically fixes "the autumn
of 1966" (149) as the date of his arrival in Manchester. Later he writes of a
walk with Ferber: "[O]ne summer evening in 1966, nine or ten months after
my arrival in Manchester" (166). The discrepancy cannot simply be attributed to error; it confirms instead the fallibility of the narrator's memory.
It almost seems as if the fogginess of Manchester envelops the narrator too,
creating a penumbra, which fuzzes distinct outlines. This penumbra engulfs
Ferber too; between their meetings in 1966 and 1989 the narrator records
that "Ferber did come to my mind at various times over the long years, but
I never succeeded in picturing him properly. His face had become a mere

shadow" (177). In contrast to Ferber, the painter, whose memory is primarily visual, the narrator, a man of words, lacks the ability to "picture." The
nature of memory is individual and volatile.

Ferber's relationship to memory is at once more complex and more
transparent. He evacuates the most painful memories such as his parting from
his parents. Yet he does have the capacity to retrieve experiences anterior to
that point provided they are not laden with excessive anguish. For instance
his visit to Germany two years previously aroused "another old memory that
had long been buried and which I had never dared to disturb" (172)—a trip
to Switzerland with his father at age twelve. Memory is here conceptualized
as an archaeological process of retrieval. On his return thirty years later he
finds Switzerland "amazingly beautiful" but "also strangely threatening" (173).
On his last night his "incipient anxiety" worsens (173), and his final days in
Montreux together with his return journey to England "had disappeared
entirely from my memory" (174). "Why exactly this lagoon of oblivion had
spread in him, and how far it extended, had remained a mystery to him however hard he thought about it" (174). The "lagoon of oblivion"—a remarkably graphic image—does not remain a mystery to readers. Surely his last days
and nights in a European city whose name begins with an "M" and his travel
to England parallel the memory that he wants to banish of his last days in
Munich and his parting from his parents also to go to England.

By the time of the narrator's subsequent meeting with Ferber in
November 1989, when the narrator is nearly fifty and Ferber seventy, Ferber
has become more willing to speak and appears to have attained greater clarity in regard to his memories. He confesses that after leaving school he opted
to move to Manchester alone rather than join his uncle in New York because
" 'I did not want to be reminded of my origins by anything or anyone' " (191).
This, then, is an escapee who starts his new life in his teens and who consciously wants to put his past behind him. In Manchester in his studio he has
fashioned a world of his own, apparently in complete isolation. He feels
" 'nothing but a disquiet in the soul' " (181), a disquiet that he is able to
identify at this point as emanating from Germany: " '[T]he fragmentary
scenes that haunt my memories are obsessive in character. When I think of
Germany, it feels as if there were some kind of insanity lodged in my head.
Probably the reason why I have never been to Germany again is that I am
afraid to find that this insanity really exists' " (181).

These reflections on Ferber's part raise another question fundamental to
"Max Ferber": what "really exists," that is, the interplay of fact and fiction.
On the one hand memory consists of quicksands, essentially shifting, slip-
pery, and precarious; on the other hand, the story has a pronounced documentary air. This aspect is very much to the fore in the locations, especially
the names of the districts and streets of Manchester, which are so accurate as
to provoke nostalgia for that dark but cultured city in one like myself who
grew up there. The European places cited also do—or did—really exist: the
Hotel Terminus Bristol on the Place de la Gare in Colmar, the Palace Hotel
in Montreux, the Victoria Jungfrau Hotel in Interlaken, the Palace Hotel in

Buxton, and the Midland in Manchester. The known topography of these places and their openness to recognition by readers induces them to envisage the narrative as realistic. The foundation of ascertainable sites and venues grounds the action in a semblance of certainty, which counteracts the waywardness of memory.

As if to support such reality claims photographs are interspersed into the narrative. This is a distinguishing feature of all Sebald's writings; he himself was a keen photographer who habitually carried a Brownie camera and took snapshots. The vast majority (seventeen out of twenty nine) of the photographs in "Max Ferber" are of places, of which fourteen are exteriors and three interiors; seven are of objects, and five of people. The status of the intercalated photographs is quite ambiguous, indeed contradictory in effect. To begin with they are not captioned so that it is left to readers to discern the connection between the photograph and the narrative. Generally the photograph can be construed as an illustration of what is being told. The invocation of visible authority therefore appears at first sight to support the story's realism. Devised in the mid-nineteenth century in the heyday of realism, photographs have often been taken as a warranty of authenticity in the sense of being a truthful copy or replica. Sebald draws on this normative function of photographs to which readers' expectations have been conditioned.

However it then turns out that photographs are by no means always the direct, indisputable records of facts for which they tend to be taken. The possibility of manipulation, indeed of fraud is categorically raised within the narrative in regard to the photograph of the book burning on the Residenzplatz [main square] of Wurzburg in 1933. The specificity of place and time as well as the established fact that such book burnings did occur would lead readers to give credence to the newspaper clipping Ferber's Uncle Leo shows to Ferber's father. This photograph is one of the few in "Max Ferber" to be accompanied by an extended commentary:

> That photograph, said Uncle, was a forgery. The burning of books took place on the evening of the 10th of May, he said—he repeated it several times—the books were burnt on the evening of the 10th of May, but since it was already dark, and they couldn't take any decent photographs, they simply took a picture of some other gathering outside the palace, Uncle claimed, and added a swath of smoke and dark night sky. In other words, the photographic document published in the paper was a fake. And just as that document was a fake, said Uncle, as if his discovery were the one vital proof, so too everything else has been a fake (183–4).

The argument is powerful in its logic and the speaker, a grammar school teacher of Latin and Greek in Wurzburg, can be presumed to be a respectable, trustworthy citizen. On the other hand the report reaches readers at third-hand, as is indicated by the reiterated interpolations: "he said— he repeated it several times," "Uncle claimed," "Uncle said." Doubts arise: why does he repeat it several times? Does he fear he won't be believed? Or is his opinion after all a mere speculative hypothesis? Although his reasoning seems convincing his assertion is no more than a "claim," a "suspicion," and a shocking one at that. There is a further chain of repetition, and with it of distancing, as Ferber passes on what he has overheard his uncle say to the narrator who in turn transmits it to readers. The narrative strategy here is reminiscent of Denis Diderot's in *Jacques le fataliste et son maître* (1771; *Jacques the Fatalist and his Master*), which presents the doctrine of fatalism as one held by Jacques's master and merely reported by Jacques who turns out to be very skeptical of it. Suspicion of word-of-mouth transmission thus has a striking literary precedent.

What are readers to make of this episode? For sure it undermines the guarantee of authenticity, which might automatically have been invested in the photographs. If this one is a fake, what is the standing of the others, which are simply incorporated into the text without explanation? Are they too, or at least some of them, partially fabrications? The recent argument by Colin Jacobson in *Underexposed* (2002) is, to cite its subtitle, "Pictures Can Lie and Liars Use Pictures," that photographs are often used for purposes of political propaganda, as in this case. Readers can judge for themselves only those images with which they have a prior familiarity; so, for instance, the photograph of the Midland Hotel in Manchester is acceptable to me as unadulterated because it corresponds to what I knew (233). Like this photograph a number of others, including those of Withington Hospital and 104 Palatine Road, seem to me, for similar reasons of personal familiarity, to be accurate records of reality. But appeals to the personal memories of a very few readers are not a legitimate basis for interpretation. Doubts are inevitably aroused by the allegedly fake photograph, which challenges readers to scrutinize the others more closely. For instance in that of the Ship Canal the water looks brushstroked, while in that of the wasteland with clouds drifting in from the Irish Sea the artful design makes the impression of having been arranged.

The suggestion that one photograph is faked is a crucial point in "Max Ferber." Its context is as important as its mediated mode of narration. The incident comes back to Ferber during his three-day conversation with the narrator in 1989 when the painter is in his seventies, an age for reminiscing. Uncle Leo makes his startling claim after the funeral of Lily Lanzberg, Ferber's grandmother, who had taken her life. The family concludes that "towards the end she was no longer quite in her right mind" (183). This is a prime example of the family's consistent practice of silence: "of those things we could not speak of we simply said nothing" (183). So they remain "largely silent about the reasons" for her suicide (183). In resorting to their customary subterfuge of silence, they refuse even to contemplate the possibility that Lily may have correctly assessed the impending threat to the Jews. Suicide was an option not infrequently chosen especially by older people who felt unable to face the upheaval of emigration.

Only Leo breaks the silence. At the end of July 1936 Ferber recalls, he "was the only one I occasionally heard talking outspokenly about the situation" (183). That the word "situation" is a euphemism is underscored in the German text where it is designated "die sogennante Lage" (*Die Ausgewanderten*, 273; the so-called situation). Leo's outspokenness "was generally met with disapproval" (183). It is in consonance with this attitude maintained by the family that on hearing Leo's allegations about the faking of the picture, Ferber's father "shook his head without saying a word, either because he was appalled or because he could not assent to uncle Leo's sweeping verdict" (184). Probably both. For Leo's "sweeping verdict" concludes that not only this picture but "everything else has been a fake, from the very start" (184). "[E]verything else" refers to the entire Nazi regime. Leo alone is willing to face the danger, and, what is more, to act on it by arranging to emigrate. The rest of the family, immobilized in the silence of denial, shunned confronting the "situation" and pay with their lives. That the "situation" is not explored further can be explained by Ferber's youth at the time; the child would not be able to understand the implications of the happenings in the political sphere. His parents' denial ceases only at the last moment in May 1939 when they bundle their son off to England, also or still in silence. The unmasking of this photograph touches indirectly on the political tensions underlying "Max Ferber," and leads to the central theme of *The Emigrants*.

But the episode of the faked photograph illustrates too, the uncertainty that envelops the whole story. A plethora of contradictory information clusters around the claim that the document has been falsified. Each factor for or against this claim is balanced by another that potentially cancels it out. For instance although the uncle is an eminently respectable high-school teacher he has reason for wanting to discredit the regime on account of his dismissal from his position on December 31, 1935 (note the circumstantial detail). His certainty about the specificity of time and place ("on the evening of the 10th of May, he said—he repeated it several times" [183]) counters the recipients' doubts as to its veracity. The photograph comes from a newspaper, which should be a reliable source of information, but could be another vehicle for propaganda. The narrator also finds it hard to believe the accusation, but comes to accept what he at first sees as Leo's "suspicions" (184) after checking the photograph in a Wurzburg archive and becoming convinced that Leo's contention was actually justified. Far from establishing certainty the photographs ultimately open up apertures of uncertainty, which dovetail with the precariousness of memory.

* * *

The photographs that herald the final part of "Max Ferber" are especially equivocal in nature as products of the narrator's hesitant recall. They are color photographs of an exhibition he had seen the previous year in Frankfurt. On the other hand counteracting their almost hallucinatory quality is the named specificity of their timing and location. They are of "the Litzmannstadt ghetto that was established in 1940 in the Polish industrial center of Lodz, once known as *polski Manchester*" (235–6). The parallelism between Lodz and Manchester becomes apparent from a photograph, presumably of Lodz (235), showing a mass of buildings dominated by smoking chimneys much like the pictures of Manchester toward the beginning of "Max Ferber." The chimneys of industrialized production are thus associated with those of industrialized extermination even as the place of extinction for some of the victims of the Holocaust is linked to the place of survival for a number of escapees, Manchester having had the second largest community of escapees in Great Britain.

The confluence of Lodz and Manchester as counterparted industrial cities is an example of the essentially associative organization of "Max Ferber," similar in this respect to memory. Reminiscent of the expanse of the earth's deserts, which Ferber has crossed, the story is devoid of sharp boundaries either temporal or spatial. Within the basic linear movement from 1966 when the narrator meets Ferber to 1991 when he visits him in Withington Hospital, gaps intervene, the largest between 1966 and 1989 while the narrator loses sight of and contact with Ferber. The pattern of narrating and narrated time becomes most complex in the leaps backward such as that into Ferber's memories of his trip to Switzerland with his father in 1936, his parting from his parents in 1939, and his early years in England. The randomness of memory determines the narrative's meandering flow.

The most significant excursus from the present time and place of the central story occurs in the intercalation of the memoirs of Ferber's mother, a manuscript of almost 100 handwritten pages contained in "a brown paper package tied with string" (192) that Ferber hands to the narrator in Manchester in 1989. Again the physical details are overdetermined as if to emphasize the memoirs' actual existence. Penned in the Ferber home in Munich between 1939 and 1941 it deals with the difficulties of those years "(said Ferber)" (192), but mainly it offers a retrospective account of the youth of the writer, Luisa Lanzberg. Extending over some twenty-five printed pages in "Max Ferber," and like the Ferber narrative, illustrated with photographs, it reaches back into the history of the Jewish community in the small town of Steinach near Bad Kissingen, formerly under the jurisdiction of the prince–bishops of Wurzburg. The remarkably precise topographical information functions once more as a solid anchor to reality, and the historical account is presented with equal care. As far back as the late seventeenth century nearly a third of Steinach's inhabitants were Jews. The community was vigorous both in its preservation of Jewish traditions and its allegiance to Germany. The combination of separateness and integration was successfully accomplished. For example, in the school "exclusively for Jewish children," the teacher, Salomon Bein, saw himself "first and foremost as a loyal servant of the state" (202–203). Luisa's father is proud of the contract he had won "as supplier and provisioner to the army" (208). Luisa herself during World War I has two Gentile suitors, to one of whom she is formally engaged, although her father claims "that the proposed attachment was bound to cut [her] off from the Jewish faith" (214). The idyll of peaceful coexistence between Jews and Gentiles all too easily leads to intermarriage and assimilation.

In Luisa's case that danger is averted by chance through the two young men's death so that she eventually marries Fritz Ferber. Her German patriotism is rewarded by the bestowal of the Ludwig Cross "in recognition of what they called my self-sacrificing devotion to duty" (216). The implicit irony is that this Cross will not protect her from deportation and extermination in 1941.

That Luisa's memoirs are mediated reminiscences is underscored by the interspersed "(Luisa writes)," paralleling "(said Ferber)." Her perceptions may be tainted by the natural tendency to idealize the past, especially one's youth. But there are sufficient definite facts such as her father's contract with the army and her Ludwig Cross to support her picture of a happy relationship between the town's minority and its majority. The possibility of such harmonious cooperation in the past also emerges from Ferber's report of the German and Jewish immigrants to Manchester through the nineteenth and into the twentieth century when the local Sephardim "made little distinction between the Germans and other Jews" (192).

Luisa's memoirs prompt the narrator to visit Bad Kissingen and Steinach in June 1991. The narrative thus opens out geographically as well as temporally. The comparative remoteness of Luisa's home and, by implication, the extensiveness of Jewish communities in Germany is suggested by the length and complications of the narrator's journey: "I travelled via Amsterdam, Cologne and Frankfurt, had to change a number of times, and sit out lengthy waits in the Aschaffenburg and Gemünden station buffets, before I reached my destination" (218). Once more the circumstantiality of the topographical details in the actual and in part well-known place names buttresses the realism of the narrator's journey and extends metonymically to his experiences in Steinach. Because he has arrived there by a route readers accept as real, we are prepared to invest belief in his report of what he finds there.

Instead of the former thriving, active community he comes upon the remains of a synagogue "which was vandalized during the Kristallnacht and then completely demolished over the following weeks" (221). As for the Jewish cemetery neither of "the two keys with orderly labels" (221) handed to the narrator in the town hall fits so that he has to climb over the wall. The semblance of care ("orderly labels") is sheer hypocrisy. The official city ordinance, posted on the cemetery gates, shown in a photograph (fabricated or authentic?) is not translated into English: "Dieser Friedhof wird dem Schutz der Allgemeinheit empfohlen. Beschädigungen, Zerstörungen und jeglicher beschimpfende Unfug werden strafetlich verfolgt" (222; This cemetery is commended to protection by the community at large. Damage, destruction, and every kind of insulting misconduct will be judicially prosecuted). While there is no willful destruction there is total neglect:

What I saw had little to do with cemeteries as one thinks of them; instead, before me lay a wilderness of graves, neglected for years, crumbling and gradually sinking into the ground amidst tall grass and wild flowers under the shade of trees, which trembled in the slight movement of the air (223).

Shocked by this sight the narrator decides to leave Steinach sooner than he had intended because he feels "increasingly that the mental impoverishment and lack of memory that marked the Germans, and the efficiency with which they had cleaned everything up, were beginning to affect my head and my nerves" (225). The synagogue has become a labor exchange, the cemetery an abandoned jungle, the Jewish community exterminated.

The narrator's visit to Steinach completes the exploration he had begun when he first met Ferber and had conversations at the Waidi Halfa café. In piecing together the strands of Ferber's life and of his family's history the narrator has over and again encountered variants of the devastation he had seen in the cityscape of Manchester. The Jewish community of Steinach has disappeared leaving as its only trace a neglected cemetery. Ferber's parents were exterminated, Ferber himself lies in hospital dying of pulmonary emphysema. The Jewish community of Manchester has dispersed. It is in keeping with this overarching poetic theme of destruction that "Max Ferber" abuts in the Lodz ghetto, on "the strangely deserted pictures, scarcely one of which showed a living soul" (236). In Sebald's story too only a small proportion of the photographs depicts human beings, and all of them are from the past, long since gone into death.

Not even artistic creativity represents a bulwark against the ubiquitous break up of previously flourishing social systems. Ferber's peculiar method of painting produces more dust than anything else in his repeated erasures as if he were unable to approximate the ideal he has in mind. His endeavors result in frustration, not fulfillment. The narrator succumbs to the same malady of self-doubting dissatisfaction. During the winter of 1990–1991 he finds working on the account of Max Ferber

> an arduous task. Often I could not get on for hours or days at a time, and not infrequently I unravelled what I had done, constantly tormented by scruples that were taking tighter hold and steadily paralysing me. These scruples concerned not only the subject of my narrative, which I felt I could not do justice to, no matter what approach I tried, but also the entire questionable business of writing. I had covered hundreds of pages with my scribble, in pencil and ballpoint. By far the greater part had been crossed out, discarded, or obliterated by additions. Even what I ultimately salvaged as a "final" version seemed to me a thing of shreds and patches, utterly botched (230–1).

A similar discomfort is transferred to the reader. Putting together the "shreds and patches" is for us also "an arduous task." Like the narrator we not infrequently unravel what we have done, are constantly tormented by scruples of not being able to do justice to this brilliant, unconventional narrative. We construct, discard, obliterate, and are ill at ease with the "final" version. Yet we are, after all, accustomed to dealing with the fragmentariness of postmodern art. In "Max Ferber" the problem goes deeper because its roots are not merely technical but existential. What we confront in this story is the despoliation of an earlier civilization. Max Ferber escaped, and so, in a sense, did the narrator, but both live under the pall of profound traumas, which they are barely able to articulate. These losses are the smoke-belching chimneys under which they serve, and which overshadow their lives.

Although it certainly recounts the life of an escapee, "Max Ferber" does not fit comfortably among escapee fictions. Some of the common themes of such fictions do appear; for instance the pain of parting from home and parents, the vicissitudes of making one's way in the host country, and above all the irresolvable tension between forgetting and remembering. In not going to his uncle Leo in New York Ferber categorically declares his wish to cut loose from his past and to follow his own calling as an artist. Nevertheless his meeting with a German compatriot years later unleashes, albeit only gradually, a stream of memories. As his trust in his listener grows he is able to disclose more and more of his story until he even hands him the package of his mother's memoirs.

But other motifs prevalent in escapee fictions are noticeably absent. Perhaps because he is an artist, and an eccentric one at that, Ferber works and lives in total isolation. We have no glimpse of any existence outside his studio and the Waidi Halfa café, itself a kind of extraterritorial area. In contrast to the narrator who roams the streets and districts of Manchester, Ferber never seems to leave his little, self-created realm. He lives as on an island without any interaction with a surrounding community. That his studio is in the midst of a wasteland of ruined industrial plants is symbolical of his situation beyond the normal bounds. He also lacks identity other than as an artist. He is of Jewish extraction, has been forced to leave his homeland, and is bereft of his parents for that reason, but religion plays no role in his life. No mention is made either of his speech; having arrived at age fifteen and served in the army he probably mastered English with relative ease, although at the cost of largely losing his mother tongue.

What most potently distinguishes "Max Ferber" from most escapee fictions is the distance at which the reader is kept from him. Despite the welter of information, which slowly emerges in "shreds and patches," Ferber remains largely an enigma. It may well be that he remains an enigma to himself, a character who shuns introversion and who expresses his emotions in his painting. That alienating painting to dust definitely suggests an inner contradiction: self-destructiveness allied to an unremitting, obsessive commitment to an ideal. We can only hypothesize from what we are allowed to see/hear. For—and this is crucial to "Max Ferber"—the indirect discourse so prominent in many escapee fictions, a technique that permits immediate access to the protagonist's thoughts, is here replaced by reported speech. Admittedly reported speech is another kind of indirect discourse, although not entirely so in "Max Ferber" because it is punctuated by "said Ferber." This, then, is cited speech, which never allows us to forget the mediating presence of the narrator.

Yet, paradoxically, "Max Ferber" reproduces a most vivid sense of the escapee experience. To read the story is to mimic the escapee fate of taking a journey without a map or a known destination. We as readers suffer bewilderment and loss of assurance as we are exposed to chance and contingency. The narrative is at once realistic and heavily charged with symbolism; we cross deserts of sand and stone, and serve under chimneys. The specter of extinction—of the Jewish community in Steinach, of Ferber's family, of Manchester's prosperity, even of the Waidi Halfa café—hovers insistently over those who have succeeded in escaping it, and over us as readers too. The story's remarkably original elegiac power has its source in the reader's vicarious plunge into the disorientation and randomness of coping with being an escapee.

NEW YORK

6

"THE GREAT LOSS"

Bernard Malamud, "The German Refugee" (1963)

"To many of these people, articulate as they were, the great loss was the loss of language—that they could no longer say what was in them to say" (360). "These people" are the German refugees in New York in the summer of 1939, "accomplished men" (358), who had achieved high professional standing in their native land and who suddenly find themselves stranded because of their poor English. As one of them puts it, " 'I feel like a child, or worse, often like a moron. I am left with myself unexpressed. . . . My tongue hangs useless' " (358). "The German Refugee" is a powerful confrontation of one of the escapees' major obstacles to resettlement in the host country, the problem of acquiring the local language as quickly as possible.

Mastering the new language is crucial as an indicator of acculturation, for the formation of a revised identity, and not least for practical purposes. Knowledge of the language has wide implications; not being able properly to understand it bars one from fully appreciating the culture, and vice versa, thus contributing to a feeling of isolation and not belonging. Language therefore assumes a strong symbolical dimension. As the Grinbergs point out in *Psychoanalytic Perspectives on Migration* (1989), "[M]igration is such a long process that perhaps it never really ends, just as the emigrant may never lose the accent of his native country" (58). That accent is what Ruth Prawer Jhabvala in her autobiographical essay "Disinheritance" (1979) poetically and poignantly terms "the accent of the soul" (13) for which the escapee continues to long. Still more trenchantly Alice Kaplan emphasizes the "emotional consequences" of a language change, even if it is a voluntary change, as in her case:

> There is no language change without emotional consequences. Principally: loss. That language equals home, that language is a home, as surely as a roof over one's head is a home, and that to be without a language, or to be between languages, is as miserable in its way as to be without bread.[1]

Failure to achieve at least functional competence results in the "phenomenon of linguistic isolation"[2] and concomitantly of economic and social marginalization.

That this difficulty is one that besets an entire category of people is indicated by the generic formulation of the story's title, "The German Refugee." At the same time the issue assumes a personal specificity in the names of the four men being taught by the narrator, a student who makes a little money as an English tutor. Karl Otto Alp was formerly a film star, Wolfgang Novak a brilliant economist, Friedrich Wilhelm Wolff had taught medieval history in Heidelberg, and Oskar Gassner had been a critic and journalist in Berlin. Oskar is the story's central figure because his is the most pressing need. Within three months, by September, he has to give a lecture in the first week of the fall term at the Institute for Public Studies, where he has been offered a job teaching a course, in English translation, on "The Literature of the Weimar Republic." Journalists, together with lawyers, encountered the greatest trouble in transferring their skills; about half the journalists ended up teaching German language and literature, while the lawyers taught political science or international law.[3] The Institute for Public Studies almost certainly stands for the New School for Social Research in New York. Founded in 1919 as a bastion of intellectual and artistic freedom, it created in 1933 the University in Exile to rescue endangered scholars who had been dismissed from teaching and government positions by totalitarian regimes in Europe. It became a refuge for many eminent, subsequently original thinkers. By 1941 it had twenty escapee professors at various levels on its graduate faculty and a further thirty in other departments.[4]

Oskar's ongoing travail to write his crucial introductory lecture and to learn how to articulate it punctuate and structure the narrative. His English is execrable: "[H]e misplaced consonants, mixed up nouns and verbs and mangled idioms" (358). To compound his anxieties he has never taught before and is afraid to do so, doubting his competence, especially in a language he speaks so badly. This change of profession robs him of his self-assurance and erodes his identity. The time pressure and the magnitude of what is at stake for him aggravate his nervousness, which in turn further reduces his capacity to learn.

Oskar's desperate struggle with the language is told in a first-person narration by his tutor, Martin Goldberg. About to enter his senior year in college at age twenty, Martin is at once a contrast and a complement to Oskar. They are alike in their poverty, in their scant knowledge of each other's tongues, and in being Jewish. But Martin is young, at home in New York, with his future ahead of him; he describes himself as "a skinny, life-hungry kid . . . palpitating to get going" (357). Oskar on the other hand seems older than fifty with hair turning gray, heavy hands, sagging shoulders, and clouded eyes. His path is downward, while Martin's leads upward. At the beginning of "The German Refugee" when Martin walks into Oskar's room, he functions as a frame to the refugee's story and as an explanatory filter for readers' perceptions. As the narrative progresses, however, he becomes increasingly involved emotionally in the drama so that he moves from its periphery closer to its core.

It is Martin who summarizes how Oskar had reached the point where he is at the story's opening. He had come to the United States for a short visit in October 1938, a month before Crystal Night, to see if he could find a job, which "would permit him quickly to enter the country" (358); he has no relatives to act as guarantors. With the help of a foundation he was promised a position not in his own field, journalism, but as a lecturer. Back in Berlin he had a frightening delay of six months before being allowed to emigrate. Having sold whatever he could he managed to bring some pictures and boxes of books by bribing two Nazi border guards. He had parted amicably from his Gentile wife, who had gone to live with her anti-Semitic mother. This sketchy account is somewhat unsatisfactory. The U.S. government was stringently limiting the entry of Jewish refugees in order to reduce the dual threat of worsening unemployment and anti-Semitism. A restrictive quota system, initiated in 1924 by the Johnson Act, was still in force between 1938 and 1941 when a mere 124,000 German–Jewish immigrants were permitted to enter the United States.[5] The vagueness of Martin's rendition of Oskar's history can be attributed to a combination of Martin's own ignorance at the time with Oskar's inability as well as reluctance to communicate this painful segment of his life.

In contrast to Oskar's shadowy past the story's short action is precisely set in both place and time. Like many escapees Oskar lives first in temporary quarters in a dark hotel room on West Tenth Street in New York. After their hour-and-a-half lesson at 4:30 p.m. three times a week, Oskar and Martin sometimes ride the bus up Fifth Avenue and walk for a while around the Central Park lake. Later Oskar moves to a two-room apartment on West Eighty-Fifth Street near Riverside Drive, a favorite location for refugees; from there he and Martin often go to eat supper at the Seventy-Second Street automat. These walks, suppers, and the accompanying conversations lay the foundations for the personal relationship that develops alongside the professional one between teacher and pupil and that grows in importance as the story unfolds. The specificity of the locations in the city gives "The German Refugee" a firm grounding in a recognizable reality.

The exact timing of the action, which spans from June to late September 1939, reinforces this pronounced realism. The oppressiveness of those months has a dual source: the steamy heat of the New York summer, and the alarming deterioration of the political situation in the irreversible drift to war. The heat hits Oskar hard because he is totally unaccustomed to it and unprepared too. While he wears just a cotton-mesh undershirt and a light bathrobe indoors, he dresses to go out as if he were still in Germany. "He would put on full regalia—hat suit, coat, tie, no matter how hot or what I suggested," Martin observes (362). Oskar probably has no outdoor clothing appropriate to the New York climate (his suits are of wool), and no money to buy any. In addition, as the phrase "full regalia" implies, he feels an inner need to keep up the appearance he considers to be proper. His European style of dressing denotes his newness to American life and ways. "To a certain degree," Kent comments in *The Refugee Intellectual*, "the refugee is forced to adopt American culture, since his former culture has completely rejected him" (97). Oskar has not been in the United States long enough even to begin this process of adaptation.

If the physical tribulations of heat and humidity have a demoralizing effect, the news from Europe creates an extremely menacing atmosphere psychologically. In the story's second paragraph already Martin thinks of events across the ocean where "Adolf Hitler, in black boots and a square mustache, was tearing up all the flowers" (357). References to the gathering clouds of war go hand in hand with Oskar's endeavors: by mid-August the Poles are mobilizing; shortly after the Soviet–Nazi nonaggression pact is signed the secondhand fan that Martin had bought gives out; and the Nazis invade Poland as Oskar writes and rewrites his lecture. The happenings in the microcosm of Oskar's troubles are thus echoed and intensified by those in the macrocosm of the grave political crisis in the world at large.

This interpenetration of the inner and outer landscapes underscores the mounting tension in the story as Oskar's deadline draws nearer; his unproductive, frustrated summer is related to the impending outbreak of war. The date of his lecture virtually coincides with the start of active hostilities; Oskar's personal future and that of Europe both seem doomed. The blockage in the composition of his lecture appears emblematic of the world's powerlessness in the face of Hitler. Indeed Alan Berger has suggested a wider analogy: "The loss of speaking ability is Malamud's way of indicating that the terrors of National Socialism are, literally, unspeakable."[6] Such an extension into the metaphoric situates the escapees' difficulties in learning a new language in the context of their deeper dislocation in having to accept the betrayal of the homeland for which they had felt an affectionate loyalty. To Oskar Germany becomes "the damned country" (361) that has driven him into his current duress and penury.

Berger's metaphoric reading is supported by Malamud's repeated practice of charging physical denotations with psychological connotations. In the opening paragraph Oskar in his "stuffy, hot, dark hotel room" "fumbles" for the light switch (357). The details vividly and economically evoke his literal and figurative imprisonment and disorientation in a black hole. Malamud's imagery conflates the overt with a secondary, underlying meaning. Hitler, for instance, is "tearing up all the flowers" (357); Oskar's few utterances are "in handcuffed and tortured English" (361), and "his eyes looked as if they had been squirted with a dark dye" (362). Oskar's linguistic blunders and failures stand out even more painfully in contradistinction not only to Malamud's masterful language but also to Martin's fluent, colloquial idiolect.

Martin's own mode of expression modulates from his slangy breeziness at the outset when he is merely a student wanting to make a little money into a more sober, thoughtful manner in consonance with his evolution into an understanding friend to Oskar. Sucked into Oskar's predicament he tries to help him by going to the New York Public Library to find material for the lecture, even though he is unable to read German poetry. He puts forward parallels with Whitman's *Leaves of Grass*. When Oskar rejects this suggestion Martin himself feels "defeated . . . tasting a new kind of private misery too old for somebody my age" (366). He is "sometimes afraid I was myself becoming melancholy, a new talent call it, of taking less pleasure in my little pleasures" (365). He matures rapidly as he comes to participate vicariously in Oskar's despair. It is so frightening that he is on the verge of dissociating himself from this pupil: "It has gotten to be too much for me. I can't drown with him" (366). So Martin learns what it means to be a refugee: "displacement, alienation, financial insecurity, being in a strange land without friends or a speakable tongue" (364). Thus he articulates what Oskar experiences but is unable to put into words.

Because of his growing personal insight into Oskar's plight, Martin perseveres where two previous tutors had given up. Much of the first third of the story is devoted to Oskar's pitiful attempts to speak English. Although like most educated Germans he had at one time studied English, he is certain that he cannot say a word; he starts, then stops "as though it could not possibly be said" (358). Malamud resorts to phonetic notations to convey Oskar's thick German accent and his grotesque distortion of words: " 'How is it pozzible. I cannot say two words. I cannot pronunziate' " (359); " 'Do you sink I will succezz ?' " he asks Martin after doing exercises in front of a mirror for the correct positioning of his tongue (360). The insuperable hurdle of the English "th" led to the division of the escapees into the "sinkers" and the "tinkers" according to the way they chose to surmount this obstacle. While doing his best to cooperate with Martin, Oskar remains "melancholy . . . uneasy, fearful" (359). Sometimes he reverts to German: " '*Ich weiss nicht wie ich weiter machen soll*' " (359; I don't know how to go on). His loss of the means of expression entails beyond the loss of his self-confidence and his identity a certain infantilization. Intellectually and emotionally Oskar feels annihilated: " 'I have lozt faith. I do not—not longer possezz my former value of myself' " (364).

In counterpoint to the Polish army's mobilization Oskar stays immobilized, paralyzed by a writer's block, which stems from his profound estrangement not just from the language but also from the new form that his self must take. Martin summarizes the stasis by describing Oskar and himself like two figures in a Beckett play "once more enacting the changeless scene, curtain rising on two speechless characters in a furnished apartment" (363). Oskar's hatred of German and his anger at the memory of that culture is certainly an additional factor. The topic of his course, "The Literature of the Weimar Republic," may itself create an unconscious impediment since it takes Oskar back to happier days and to the fools' paradise in which German Jews lived. Conversely these same unconscious forces may come into play in Oskar's sudden ability in the first week of September at the outbreak of war quickly to write and rewrite the lecture, which is translated into English by the historian Friedrich Wilhelm Wolff. Oskar is undoubtedly energized by the autumnal cooling slowly setting in, and even more so by Martin's support and active assistance. Despite his initial dismissal of Martin's ideas he does eventually incorporate Whitman into his lecture. Above all he must realize at some deep level that he has found a real friend in this new environment.

The change that Martin observes in Oskar's appearance symbolizes once again the close interface between the psychological and the physical:

> He had awakened from defeat, battered, after a wearying battle. He had lost close to twenty pounds. His complexion was still gray; when I looked at his face I expected to see scars, but it had lost its flabby unfocused quality. His blue eyes had returned to life and he walked with quick steps, as though to pick up a few for all the steps he hadn't taken during those long, hot days he had lain torpid in his room (366).

Oskar's reclamation of his capacity for self-expression, albeit still in German, heralds an upturn in his appearance, his personality, and his prospects. With Martin as his coach he works very hard at the task of learning to pronounce the English version of his lecture. " 'All this can be a dreadfully boring business unless you think you have a future,' " Martin comments, adding: " '[L]ooking at him I realized what's meant when somebody is called "another man" ' " (367). After its gloomy start and protracted chronicling of both Oskar's and Martin's misery the story assumes a more hopeful note, especially when the lecture goes well. This turning point in Oskar's new existence is recorded by Martin who is a member of the audience. The auditorium is crowded, there are a number of prominent people, two reporters, and a photographer because Oskar is the first refugee to be employed by the Institute, and its directors are keen "to make the public cognizant of what was then a new ingredient in American life" (367). The novelty and rarity of a refugee in an educational role casts indirect light on the resistances escapees encountered in finding employment. Oskar looks the part in a blue suit and with his hair cut. His enunciation, to Martin's satisfaction, "wasn't at all bad . . . a few *s's* for *th's*, and he once said 'bag' for 'back,' but otherwise he did pretty well" (367). There is even a touch of humor when Martin thinks that Oskar's reading of Whitman sounds as though the poet "had come to the shores of Long Island as a German immigrant" (448). By the time of the lecture Warsaw had fallen, but this catastrophe in the macrocosm is now mentioned as an antithesis to Oskar's rising fortune.

"The German Refugee" could have ended there as a success story for this escapee thanks to an open-minded institution that gives him an opportunity to prove himself and thanks above all to his devoted, sympathetic tutor. But the story has a brief coda, startling though not wholly surprising. Coming to Oskar's apartment two days after the lecture, Martin finds him dead by gas poisoning.

The motif of death and specifically of suicide threads as a sinister undercurrent throughout the narrative. Oskar admits to Martin that he had made a suicide attempt at the end of May during his first week in America when he was living in a small hotel. He had filled himself with barbiturates, but the phone had fallen off the table, alerting the hotel operator that something was amiss. Revived in hospital he concludes that " 'it was a mistage' " (363). This early attempt can be ascribed to Oskar's feeling utterly overwhelmed by the task facing him. Significantly Martin urges him not to contemplate it ever again because " 'it's total defeat' " (443); in other words his rationale is underpinned by considerations of a moral nature in relation to pride and self-esteem, a central factor in the escapee's predicament. Oskar on the other hand is purely pragmatic: " 'I don't.' he said wearily, 'because it is so arduous to come bag to life' " (363). His answer already implies that if he were sure of being able to complete the act, he might try again.

The theme crops up repeatedly as if to foreshadow the story's ending. Once when Martin gets no answer to his knock on Oskar's door, he feels "chilled down the spine . . . thinking about the possibility of his attempted suicide again" (363). It seems a real possibility in the darkness of his severe depression. Martin comes to see Oskar every day, neglecting his other pupils and his livelihood, because he has "a panicky feeling that if things went on as they were going, they would end in Oskar's suicide" (365). Over and over Oskar is characterized as "defeated," looking "like a wounded animal" (365), emptied of faith in himself. His two previous tutors had not been able "to keep [him] from drowning in things unsaid . . . he wanted to swallow the ocean in a gulp" (360). Here the suicidal ideation is connected directly to the frustration induced by the language problem. The words defeated and "drown" are applied by Martin to himself too when he thinks of his own per-ceived failure to help Oskar and his consequent fear of likewise going under.

But why would Oskar commit suicide *after* he has successfully delivered his lecture when his future looks considerably brighter? It could be that he is still apprehensive about teaching in English without a prepared, translated script. Yet there is no indication of such a motive in the text. However there are hints that Oskar may have other problems besides that of learning English. This possibility certainly occurs to Martin who wonders whether there is "something below the surface, invisible . . . some unknown quantity in his depression that a psychiatrist might help him with" (364). For, Martin reasons, "not all [refugees] drown in this ocean, why does he?" (364). Confronted point-blank about the "unknown quantity," Oskar throws Martin off the scent: "He meditated on this, and after a few minutes haltingly said he had been psychoanalyzed in Vienna as a young man. 'Just the usual *drek* [dirt],' he said, 'fears and fantasies that afterwards no longer bothered me' " (364). His pause for meditation gives pause for thought on the reader's part, but can ultimately be attributed to his reflectiveness and his familiar linguistic hesitancy.

Only in the story's closing paragraph is the nature of that unknown quan-tity revealed, although in retrospect it turns out to have been at least partially foreshadowed. For instance on the day when Martin doesn't find Oskar at home and is anxious about another suicide attempt, he comes upon an air-mail letter from Germany. He can make out no more than one sentence: "*Ich bin dir siebenundzwanzig Jahre treu gewesen*" (363; I have been faithful to you for twenty-seven years). Since Oskar had told Martin that he and his wife had "parted amicably" (358), it is hardly surprising that she should write to him. Anyway this detail is easily overlooked because the locus of the story's suspense is in the composition of the lecture as the symbol of Oskar's ability to survive and make a fresh start. The wife crops up once more in Oskar's "fantastic frightening dreams of the Nazis inflicting tortures upon him" (365). In one such dream, when he had gone back to Germany to visit his wife, he had been directed to a cemetery and seen her blood seep out from a shallow grave, although her name is not on the tombstone. Anxiety dreams of this type were not uncommon among escapees as a manifestation of post-traumatic stress syndrome. In telling Martin of this dream Oskar confides that the marriage had not been happy; his wife had been sickly and unable to bear children. Nonetheless he had " 'offered her to come here with me' " but she refused because she " 'did not think I wished her to come.' " In response to Martin's question, " '[D]id you?' " Oskar utters one laconic word, " '[N]ot' " (364). Perhaps the parting had been a relief to both of them; but it is also possible that on her side it had not been quite as amicable as he makes out.

The latter scenario is presented in the story's final paragraph as Martin with a vast effort, which parallels Oskar's struggles to write, deciphers a letter from Oskar's mother-in-law giving news of what had happened to his wife. She asserts that Oskar had abandoned her daughter. This is an accusation that defies evaluation on the part of readers. Coming from this antagonistic, anti-Semitic relative, it may be no more than an exaggeration or indeed an invention. But how do we assess whether she is anti-Semitic except on the basis of Oskar's assertion? At this sensitive time in his life he may just feel rejected and persecuted by all German Gentiles. His perception is as subjective as his mother-in-law's so that the veracity of both is beyond Martin's and the reader's power of discernment. All Martin and we know for sure is that Oskar did not wish his wife to accompany him to America, and that she was aware of this. So maybe he did abandon her. What follows thereafter strains credibility. Martin learns from the letter that Frau Gassner had converted to Judaism, been seized by the Nazis, and transported to a small border town in Poland. "There, it is rumored, she is shot in the head and topples into an open ditch, with the naked Jewish men, their wives and children, some Polish soldiers and a handful of Gypsies" (368).

These are the closing words of "The German Refugee." Admittedly this astonishing twist makes the story end on a bang, but artistically this post-script detracts from the otherwise predominant focus on Oskar's wrestling with learning English. The report of his wife's fate, which is in part merely "rumored," introduces an ambiguity into the story: is Oskar's "great loss" as much, or even more, that of his wife rather than of his language? Is his guilt at having abandoned her the unknown quantity in his depression that Martin had sensed? Is that guilt then exacerbated into survivor guilt on her death, thereby precipitating his suicide? Somehow, though, such a reading doesn't quite hang together. Why would she convert after being abandoned when she had not done so in the course of the twenty-seven years of marriage? Is it she who is being vengeful (368) in a masochistic way rather than the rabbi to whom the adjective is applied. Why would he be vengeful? Conversion to

Judaism is, in any case, no easy process. The story's concluding paragraph doesn't make sense either rationally or aesthetically.

In light of the revelations about Oskar's wife and his own suicide, the references to Whitman seem an ironic commentary on the human condition as portrayed in "The German Refugee." When Martin offers Whitman as material for his lecture, Oskar maintains the "it wasn't the love of death" that the German poets had got from Whitman since that was already intrinsic to their tradition. Whitman's primary legacy, according to Oskar, was "his feeling for *Brudermensch* (human brother), his humanity" (366). As if to bear this out the passage that he cites in his lecture runs as follows:

> *And I know that the spirit of God is the brother of my own,*
> *And that all the men ever born are also my brothers, and the women*
>   *my sisters and lovers,*
> *And that a kelson of creation is love* (367).

The irony stems from the contradiction between this creed of human love as the heart of creation and the brutality of what happens to Oskar's wife and indeed the inhumanity of the treatment meted out to him by his homeland.

"The German Refugee" is a somber story, even setting aside its ending (if that were feasible). It shows the grim physical conditions under which formerly respected, professionally established escapees had to live in the early days after their arrival in the host country. Oskar has to submit to the discomfort and humiliation of "a round of diminishingly expensive hotel rooms" (359). His dark, stuffy room, "cluttered with clothing, boxes of books he had managed to get out of Germany and some paintings" (358), is an objective correlative to his unanchored, unsettled position. While these possessions must be impractical encumbrances on his multiple moves, they also represent a precious continuity with his previous existence and a reminder of his erstwhile standing and lifestyle. The sentimental value of objects brought along often outstrips by far their financial worth.[7] The substantive privations that Oskar undergoes are emblematic too of the underlying psychological tribulations. He voices his resentment at the destruction of his career and his uprootedness in a striking image when he describes himself as having been flung "like a piece of bleeding meat to the hawks" (362). And all this dislocation finds its most immediate incarnation in the inescapable necessity of acquiring a new language.

7

"An Abundance of Happiness"

Ruth Prawer Jhabvala, *In Search of Love and Beauty* (1983)

At her sixtieth birthday party, as her family and friends stand by the lit cake singing, Louise gives "thanks in her heart for such an abundance of happiness with all her dearest ones around her" (112). Those dearest ones are her daughter, Marietta, her grandson, Mark, her adopted granddaughter, Natasha, her friend since schooldays, Regi, and Leo Kellermann, who can perhaps best be described as a guru. Louise and Regi and their women friends are "German or Austrian refugees who had managed to get their money out but felt bored and stranded" (12). Only Leo had arrived "penniless" (11) and still lives off his circle of admirers, largely female. Otherwise these are prosperous escapees who try to continue to lead much the same life in New York as they had done in Europe. Do they in fact find "an abundance of happiness," or is this claim charged with irony?

When *In Search of Love and Beauty* opens Louise has been in New York for some thirty years. She is the novel's anchor figure, the matriarch who is a stabilizing presence for the three generations that the novel portrays. Through its lengthy time span of about seventy years, reaching back into Louise's schooldays in Germany and ending on her imminent death at age eighty-four, *In Search of Love and Beauty* can particularly well depict patterns of continuity and change in the process of adaptation, including resistances on the part of the older members of the family and a range of compromises among the younger ones. Its three sections focus, respectively, on Louise in her forties, in her sixties, and in her eighties, but within this overarching linear progression time also flows very fluidly back and forth between the present and the past through skillfully manipulated, associative transitions.

Curiously, however, nothing is divulged about the characters' actual escape from Europe. Maybe because they had ample means and left early their emigration from Europe and immigration to the United States was relatively easy, we have to assume. At most there is a passing reference to "those . . . strange times . . . when they were refugees who had lost their first hold on life and were trying to establish a new one" (45). The focus in *In Search of Love and Beauty* is on the new lives they build, especially on the

interplay between vestiges of their former habits and exploration of the possibilities in their host country. The experience is characterized as "exciting as
well as devastating," depending primarily on their age: "exciting for those of
them still young enough to start again" but "only devastating" for those who
were not (45).

Louise stands midway between the two categories. Still young and ener-
getic herself, she is married to a man eighteen years older than herself for
whom it proves nothing but "devastating" to have had to leave his homeland. Louise's story closely parallels that of Sonia Wolff in Jhabvala's short
story "A Birthday in London" (1963) except that Louise is a Protestant.
That she, like Sonia, had grown up in comfortable circumstances is denoted
by the "villa" her parents owned in the suburbs with a garden full of fruit
trees (42). An attractive, well-developed teenager, already inseparable from
Regi, Louise becomes a "devotee" (43) of the town's excellent theater and
opera. It is there that Bruno Sonnenblick sees her and falls in love with her.
He is the stereotype to the verge of caricature of the well-to-do, cosseted,
upper-middle-class European Jew:

> Bruno was thirty-six years old . . . He was the director of his family firm of
> thread manufacturers and lived with his widowed mother in the family mansion
> in the Kaiserallee. Every day he was driven home from the factory in a
> Mercedes-Benz to lunch with his mother, and then she saw to it that his nap
> was not disturbed. Only she herself came tiptoeing in, to replace his freshly
> laundered shirts or arrange gloves and spats on their appointed shelves (44).

His name, Sonnenblick (Sunnyview), holds out the promise of abundant
happiness for Louise as he runs "the entire gamut of breathless courtship" (44)
with flowers, chocolates, and the Mercedes coming for her every day. When
away on business trips he sends letters "on pale stationery with the family
watermark" in writing "as neat as his English suit, his spats, and Homburg
hat" (44). The theatrical, overblown "passion" displayed in the sample letter
reproduced in the novel is fertile soil for the narrator's ironic mockery,
devolving from the contrast between Bruno's middle-class conventionality
and his adoption of a quasi-Wagnerian mythology and terminology of
goddesses and extravagant gestures.

Bruno's deep immersion in German culture as well as his age (like Otto
Wolff's in "A Birthday in London") are major obstacles to his adaptation to
new ways. Many years after his arrival in New York, when his daughter is old
enough to become engaged, he is still reading Goethe's idyll *Hermann und
Dorothea* in German. As in her short stories Jhabvala uses such small telling
details to make a point obliquely. Thus while Marietta addresses Louise as
"Mother," Bruno remains "Vati" (15). He is not only "born to money"
(120) but just as much into German cultural and behavioral traditions. For
instance when Marietta is a schoolgirl, "Bruno put his arm around her and
told her to curtsy—he always told her to curtsy when there were visitors,
automatically using the exact same German phrase and intonation he had

heard his mother use with his sisters" (89). He is so committed to the conduct considered suitable in his youth that he cannot see how times and customs have changed. His white handkerchiefs are monogrammed and "beautifully laundered by himself" (16) since there are no more servants to perform such tasks—this seems to be the extent of Bruno's concession to the United States. On his long walks in Central Park he is immediately recognizable, even in those less informal days, as the European gentleman:

> In the winter he wore spats and an overcoat with a fur collar; in the summer lightweight suits of dove-gray and a dove-gray Homburg. When Marietta was small, she sometimes accompanied him; she walked sedately, her white-gloved hand in his. When they met acquaintances—which was rarely—he raised his hat and inclined in a small bow; he encouraged her to curtsy (121).

This passage illustrates how Bruno is invariably envisaged from an external perspective through notation of his appearance and behavior. Readers have no access to his mind so that we know nothing of his thoughts, specifically his reactions to his existence in New York. The only indirect glimpse of his feelings comes in the observation that the apartment was the "one place that felt familiar to him, for not only was it filled with his family furniture but it also had the same high ceilings, vestibule and corridor, and sliding doors between the living and the dining rooms as the house in the Kaiserallee" (45). Even the needlepoint cushions his sisters had embroidered are still there. This is a salient example of the way in which furnishings function throughout *In Search of Love and Beauty* as objective correlatives of their owners' emotional state. Bruno does not pursue any business or occupation; apparently the Sonnenblicks have sufficient assets to live on. They are thus exempt from one of the main worries of most escapees, namely, how to eke out a living. Without the economic pressure to work, Bruno lapses into an inactivity, which must weigh heavily on him, with only reading, walks (and a little personal laundry!) to fill his days, compared to his rigorous, purposeful routine in Germany. His removal from the business world also leads indirectly to his isolation, his confinement within the small family circle. Yet unlike Otto Wolff in "A Birthday in London" he does not let himself go; on the contrary he maintains his appearance with utmost meticulousness. However it is no surprise when he dies quite rapidly after surgery. He represents that group of older, formerly highly respected, successful escapees who proved unable to rebuild meaningful lives or come to terms with their altered position.

Virtually a generation younger than Bruno, Louise has more flexibility to accommodate to new surroundings and circumstances, but she doggedly preserves, even guards the status quo in the apartment where she goes on living after her husband's death:

> It was a large, lofty, old West Side apartment, which she had had for over thirty years. All the furniture—the cabinets, the velvet sofa the size of a Roman bath, the Steinway grand, which no one ever played—came from Bruno's family

house in Germany. She never changed anything and didn't have the place cleaned often enough, so that the carpets, the velvet upholstery, and the convoluted carvings of screens and furniture had an accumulation of dust that seemed to add to their ponderous weight. Every now and then she declared that she would change everything, including the apartment, which was of course much too big for her alone. But she never even changed the photographs (14).

By staying so tenaciously attached to the past, Louise seems almost to be living in a kind of mausoleum. Time is arrested here; the photographs show Bruno in his "dapper forties" (14), Marietta as a sixteen-year-old, and Mark as a cute little boy. The heavy pall of dust is the visible sign of the unseemly, demoralized neglect that has befallen those icons of the past. Even as she preserves these relics, Louise seems no longer emotionally invested in them.

Unlike the idled Bruno Louise as a woman maintains her basic function of caring for her family, no matter where they live. Among escapees women often fared better psychologically precisely because of their obligations to their families. While Leo dwells critically "on her limitations, such as her bourgeois housewife mentality" (86), this trait is an asset to her in keeping her busy and making her feel useful to her family. Nevertheless in some respects she resembles Bruno, notably in her adherence to the conventions of outer decorum by never going down the street without hat and gloves; even at age eighty-four, when she is summoned to an emergency at Regi's, she dons her hat, albeit askew, before hurrying out. She faithfully and enthusiastically observes the various rituals customary in German families such as the celebration of birthdays with cake and candles and Christmas with a goose and a splendidly set table. It is Louise in her mid-eighties who takes the initiative in organizing a birthday party for the already demented Regi. She is thus very instrumental in maintaining continuity between the old and the new life by upholding some of the important institutions of German family ceremonial.

But at the same time Louise acclimatizes to some extent, even though she had always been the conservative one in comparison to the far more adventurous Regi, the "chaste bride, the 'Ceres' of her household, for she adored Bruno and no other man ever counted for her" (56). Still, in her widowhood Louise does not abide rigidly by the moral principles of her youth, yielding instead to the freer atmosphere of the 1960s and 1970s. She is as enthralled by Leo as the other women he seduces. Natasha comes upon her gamboling naked with him in the family apartment, playing games that are far from innocent. Louise also shows her ability to move with the times in her relationship to her gauche granddaughter, that is so much more progressive than the stern, old-fashioned expectations that Bruno tries to impose on Marietta. Louise takes Natasha on an annual vacation in the Hamptons, treats her without the condescension that other family members show toward her, understands her need for her own emotional space, and even confides in her. Because Louise is able to bridge European and American ways, she can experience "an abundance of happiness" through her dual affirmation of continuity and change, past and present.

The third member of the original generation of escapees is Regi, whose life story is the accompanying parallel and foil to Louise's from their schooldays into old age. From the outset she is utterly different to Louise: "Regi was tall, thin, nervous, with short skirt, short hair, a cigarette in a holder. She was sharper and more daring—altogether more modern—than Louise" (43). The disparity between them is graphically displayed in the crass contrast between their respective styles of dress: the thrice married and twice divorced Regi tends to flamboyance "in a long-skirted crepe de Chine dress with masses of jewelry hung like booty all over her," while Louise favors "sober, well-cut suits of very expensive material with a fox-fur piece round her neck" (51). Regi, too, has brought furniture from Germany, though it also is the antithesis to Bruno's and Louise's traditional pieces; her "smart Park Avenue apartment [is] done up in the Bauhaus style" which she had seen as "the latest thing" (12): "all glass and tubular metal legs . . . white wolf rugs on the floor" and "an expressionist painting" of Regi herself in the nude (62). For all her zest for life in its latest, ultramodern forms Regi has no "abundance of happiness"; eternally critical and restless, she leads a life of pleasure, which brings no pleasure so that she feels "cheated, shortchanged" (63). For her life in the new world is at once "exciting" and "devastating."

Far more than Louise, Regi is the target of narratorial irony. For instance while she prides herself on having kept her figure, she has in fact become skeletal. Her insistence on clinging to a dated European concept of what is proper (like Bruno), even on vacation beyond New York, makes her "a complete misfit in her elegant black" (136). In middle and even more in old age, her appearance verges on the grotesque: "Regi looked at her with her shaved and penciled eyebrows raised high; one pointed crimson fingernail, hard as a bird's beak, tapped the table" (138). By adamantly remaining as she had been in her youth and refusing to accommodate to her changed surroundings, Regi becomes a parody of herself. She is as if frozen in a past to which she has fallen captive; what was once so "modern" is now distinctly passé. Eventually she declines into a senility, which is at once pathetic, revolting, and comic as she huddles on her bed naked except for her mink coat in paranoic fear that her helper is out to steal her valuables. Again Jhabvala makes striking use of details to give a vivid picture of Regi's dementia. Her helper is a young man who brought her home one day from a dancing club patronized by lonely, elderly women. Eric is one of the very few Americans shown in this novel interacting with escapees. Regi withdraws more and more into her own world, fashioned out of remnants of her first life until she loses contact with reality.

The fourth and most puzzling member of the older generation is Leo whose past is as enigmatic and eccentric as his present. Handsome and charming in his youth, he thrills the affluent "bored and stranded" (12) escapee ladies with vague hints about his early associations with Reinhardt, his meeting with Freud, his publication of a poem in a famous magazine, and so forth. His evasiveness arouses readers' suspicions about the authenticity of these claims. While his admirers feel "in the presence of a yet undefined

genius" (12), Jhabvala's irony, at its most intense at Leo's expense, suggests
the exploitative essence of that "genius":

> Fortunately, he was by no means an aloof genius. He didn't just sit there and let
> himself be admired. It was a two-way traffic, and while he allowed them to
> glimpse into his soul, he also looked into theirs. Yes, he had that wonderful gift
> of making each one feel—even those who were no longer so very young or
> good-looking—that he was in intimate contact with her, on the deepest and
> most thrilling level; and moreover, that he had absolutely no difficulty in under-
> standing as well as condoning whatever secret, or secret longing, she might be
> harboring (12–13).

It is a long time before this charismatic sponger is "given up as a charlatan" (13).
   Meanwhile, with funding from Mark and probably others, Leo has established in the Hudson valley his Academy of Potential Development where he
expostulates his "doctrine" and prescribes devotional exercises, which aim at
"becoming a truly more integrated person (or, as they put it at the Academy,
a more *become* person)" (140). It is surely another irony that the person *least*
integrated in any way should preach the centrality of precisely that quality.
Leo's commune attracts a variety of young and not so young bewildered
Americans who accept his "odd behavior" (140) as an additional incentive to
have faith in him. The pseudo-religious nature of his power is made apparent
in his famous Saturday night lectures, which Natasha shrewdly recognizes as
comparable to "the Sunday morning sermons the original owners of the
house had gone to hear in the white clapboard church" (153). The lectures
are followed by parties, which give ample opportunity for Leo's sexual preda-
toriness. The climactic "Point" (175) that Leo's disciples are supposed to
reach is more likely an orgasm than a profound psychological insight. In a
novel that systematically uses homes as a tool for characterization, the fact
that Leo's house is "heavy and dark," its grounds "tangled and wild" strongly
implies that he does not spread much enlightenment. With passing years he
becomes at once more solemn and more ludicrous. To hide his middle-age
spread he takes to wearing a kind of child's bib-pinafore, and later his obese
body is shrouded in a loose flowing throw like a monk's habit, which sends
mixed signals of venerability, religiosity, and the necessity for concealment.

*   *   *

Among the successive generations, efforts at assimilation become increasingly pronounced. Louise's daughter, Marietta, is very much a transitional
figure. It is not clear whether she was born in Germany or in New York (*In
Search of Love and Beauty* is scant on precise dates). There is no doubt, however, that for her life in the United States is "exciting." She symbolically
makes herself over by shedding the European name she had been given and
that her father persists in using, Marianne, renaming herself instead Marietta.
This rather glamorous, artsy version is more congruent with the self-image

she is cultivating; before her marriage she trains briefly as a dancer. Renaming is a form of self-reinvention, of shaping an amended identity removed from that into which she was born. But later when she starts a fashion business in sportswear she becomes very successful "for, in spite of her erratic, high-flown nature, she turned out to be a first-class businesswoman—a talent perhaps inbred in her through her father's line of German–Jewish entrepreneurs" (33). The fashion business suits Marietta perfectly by enabling her to fuse her own creative, somewhat Bohemian inclinations with her solid financial heritage from her ancestors.

To be transitional means for Marietta in effect to be torn in opposite directions throughout her life. She makes an early, probably rather impulsive, marriage to an American, Tim, with whom she becomes "disillusioned" (24) after less than a year, admittedly with good reason since he is an alcoholic. This brief alliance gives her the opportunity to experience a milieu totally different from that in which she had grown up. Tim's mother and two sisters reside in the Hudson Valley in a venerable old house, which had belonged to them for generations; they lead "spare but active lives in a converted farmhouse standing on a few acres of land which were all that was left of the original family holdings" (68). There is an almost Faulknerian aura of decline about the family. One of the sisters, who has periodically to be checked into a mental hospital, eventually dies of an overdose of her tranquilizer. When Tim's mother succumbs to a carefully concealed cancer and the remaining sister sets up an antique store on Martha's Vineyard, the house is sold and the family disappears. Self-destructiveness is characteristic of its male members: Tim's father had driven his car over a cliff; his grandfather had died by drowning in the ocean at Southampton; and Tim himself had combined both these violent deaths by falling with his car, one perfectly still summer night, into Lake Kennebago after a party in a cabin there. No "abundance of happiness" in this family, whose suicides contrast sharply with the escapees' strong will to survive.

Marietta's misdirected experiment in assimilation into American rural life ends quickly and unhappily: she "could find no place for herself in this family group. Nothing was more boring to her than the conversation around that dining table—except perhaps the food" (92). As so often in *In Search of Love and Beauty* rooms and their furniture are the outer manifestation of feelings:

She felt trapped with him in their bedroom—narrow and sloping like all the upstairs rooms and too small for the furniture in it: the high mahogany four-poster, the carved chest-on-chest, a walnut armoire that had a strange smell in it as of dead people's clothes. She sat by the window and looked out over the landscape: the fine tall trees, the handsome houses separated from one another by respectful acres, in the distance the Episcopal church with Tim's ancestors in its graveyard. It was all as alien to her as this room with Tim slumped on the bed; so that suddenly she jumped up and, not even bothering to pack her clothes, she went downstairs and let herself out the front door. She got in her car and drove straight to New York (93).

The narrow, grave-like room is as smothering and menacing to Marietta as the Episcopal Church with the graves of her husband's ancestors. By the "strange smell" they seem to be invading the bedroom and driving her, the intruder, out as a foreign, disruptive element.

Apart from her son all that remain to Marietta of this marriage are rather unpleasant memories of a Thanksgiving, the major American family festival, she had endured there. Irrationally she extends her disillusionment with Tim and his family on to "their entire race and nation" (24). Still she retains a certain nostalgic longing, or more likely an abstract notion that she would like to belong to an American family, for she visits the house when she is in the area and peers in through the windows as though trying to recapture some dreamlike mirage. She never realizes the futility and irony of her attempt to integrate into a family that is essentially dysfunctional and self-destructive. This is not the milieu in which she can find the new identity for which she is searching.

The New York apartment in which she lives from then on is as different as possible from the housing of both her parents and of Tim's family. It is as if she were defining herself by opposition:

> Marietta's apartment was as light as Louise's was dark. She had low, deep furniture upholstered in raw silk, a shining gold Buddha, and on the walls some exquisite gold-framed Indian miniatures. Her Oriental rugs bloomed with delicate floral motifs. One wall was entirely taken up by windows, framing her view of Central Park (39).

When she, too, makes love to Leo, she fears that her "delicate little chaise longue" might break beneath his weight (111). The incident pokes fun at Marietta's hardly serviceable furnishings, whose modernistic delicacy is the antithesis of the antique sturdiness of the chest and armoire in Tim's bedroom and the heavy solidity of her parents' furniture. The fragility of Marietta's decor is emblematic of her life, beset by frequent "moments of crisis" (33).

Marietta's Oriental rugs, gold Buddha, and Indian miniatures indicate her attraction to the East. In another form of her quest for her appropriate place, she goes through an "Indian phase" (33). After meeting Ahmed, an Indian musician visiting the United States, with whom she shares an interest in dance, she pays several extended visits to India. At first enthusiastic about everything and in close touch with Ahmed's family, she comes increasingly over the six years of her visits there to withdraw from the local environment (partly out of fear of infections), staying instead in luxury hotels with showers and air conditioning. She thus removes herself to an impersonal, international sphere rather than attaining a connection to a distinctive local culture. Her inability to settle definitively on any one thing becomes manifest in her increasing tendency to flightiness and flirtatiousness as she grows older; she flirts with handsome young Indians and with a string of American men younger than herself, as well as with the exotic. Her only lasting commitment is to her business, which is, interestingly, a vestigial reminder of her

German–Jewish origins. As the child of escapees, one of the second generation, Marietta never resolves the question of the place and position truly congenial to her. While she mostly separates herself from her past, she cannot
forge a viable, stable self in the New World.

By the third generation assimilation if not integration is well underway.
Marietta's son, Mark, flourishes in business and also has the self-confidence
to assert his own personality. Mark's remarkable acumen in real estate, like his
mother's in fashion sportswear, is clearly a legacy from his paternal grandfather's side but in other ways he follows his own path. He is to some extent
reminiscent of Werner, Sonia Wolff's son in "A Birthday in London." Both
are handsome, travel frequently and impulsively, and show a strong streak of
willfulness, which surfaces in a tense, distanced relationship to their mothers.
But they differ fundamentally too; whereas Werner is rather a playboy and at
age twenty-six still lives with his mother, Mark is serious in his devotion to his
business and far more independent. He has a splendid loft in New York in a
late-nineteenth-century building, once a warehouse, now converted into
huge apartments, one to each floor:

> Mark had the topmost story—an enormous space into which his architect had
> been able to fit as many rooms as into a complete town house, though at the
> same time leaving it open to a surge of cityscape. The warehouse windows, tall
> as a cathedral's, gave out onto a different scene on every side. There were
> round water towers and a round Greek Orthodox church, a Romanesque
> tower, an unconverted warehouse and another converted one, a neon-lighted
> airline, a building with a silver spire, another like a black glass pencil with an
> adjacent Gothic old hotel mirrored in its side—all crowding and jostling
> together as they rolled away toward the horizon where the river flowed into
> the sea (65).

The spaciousness of Mark's place and especially the global view from the
uppermost story convey a sense of Mark's physical and metaphorical command of the city. But the extraordinary variety of the edifices visible from his
windows robs the scene of specificity; it is so anonymous as to be potentially
anywhere, and so paradoxically nowhere in particular.

Later Mark buys two houses in the country, one for Leo's Academy, and
the other "not as an investment but for himself and his friends on weekends
and summer vacations" (75). The acquisition of a half-ruined country man-
sion and the land on which it stands is obviously an attempt on Mark's part
to strike roots by inhabiting something more permanent than a rented apartment. This is borne out by his choice of location and building: not just in "his
father's part of the country" to which he had "developed an attachment" (69)
but the actual house, partially burned, that had been owned by his father's
family. So his attachment becomes "in due course proprietary" (69), much to
the indignation of his mother who had fled that house and area: " '[A]nd
why *there* of all places?' " she protests (94). Leo is equally disapproving
although he shows greater insight into Mark's motivation when he condemns
"people trying to buy back their own or someone else's ancestors" (96).

Mark is determined to reconnect with his father's family and thereby to legitimize himself as a settled American. His act is an expression of the third generation's wish to become fully integrated. In reaction perhaps against the older generation's depressive tendency to cling tenaciously to their established customs, Mark engages in what the Grinbergs in *Psychoanalytic Perspectives on Migration* (1989) have deemed "manic overadjustment" (89).

> Mark's efforts to restore and furnish the house definitely smack of the obsessive: His paternal grandmother would have been pleased to see the care he had lavished on the pieces he had inherited from her; and to supplement them, he had selected only those—drink table, gentleman's secretary, lyreback armchair—that exactly matched them in period and style. But although everything was at least 150 years old, it had all been so polished and refurbished—gleaming mahogany and rosewood with gilt bronze mountings—that it might as well have been entirely new. The floors too had been stripped and restored to their pristine pinewood planks; the walls and ceilings with their cornices and moldings were painted stark white; the carvings on the wooden mantels had also been carefully restored and repainted in white (224–5).

Ironically his endeavor to recreate the house as it had been backfires; what emerges instead is the pronounced impression of the *newness* of it all, reflecting his own standing as an American with as yet shallow roots. He "had reverted in style to his father's family," we are told (224), but it is in "style," not in spirit.

Mark's house and its furniture offer another prime example in *In Search of Love and Beauty* of the use of the environment fashioned by the persona as a means of characterization. This house and its furniture indirectly yet eloquently bespeak Mark's whole story. It is part of his need to emphasize the continuity with his father's, that is, the American side of his family, which makes Mark reject outright Marietta's offer of Louise's furniture when her apartment is dissolved in her old age. " 'It's the wrong period!' Mark exclaimed, truly shocked" (226). It carries, too, quite the wrong origins and associations, coming from the European side of his family, from which he wants to distance himself. Does Mark succeed where his mother had failed? There is more than a shadow of doubt: "the house, shining with new paint whiter than the new snow, stood like an ice palace on the hill" (235). The repetition of "new" in that brief description underscores that the house is too brash, too contrived to meld well into the landscape any more than Mark himself, the grandson of escapees.

Whether Mark can find "an abundance of happiness" there is another open question. He breaks away from family tradition in his homosexuality, an issue he is unwilling to discuss openly with his mother, who urges him to get married. His taste in boys is as emblematic as his house and furnishings of his urge to belong; he chooses

> fair, wholesome, Anglo-Saxon [boys], from simple families from somewhere within the heart of the country; so that, in being with them, he also felt that he

was acquiring a greater share of something—a landscape, a country, a way of being—that he longed for but only half possessed (69–70).

Here is the same longing and the same at best half-possession as with the house. Mark's young lover, Kent, causes him considerable grief by his mulishness, and eventually leads him into real danger when Anthony, a much older man also in love with Kent, comes to the country house and physically attacks Mark with a knife. Like his grandparents, mutatis mutandis, Mark has a fortunate escape, for only his expensive cashmere sweater is pierced. It is another irony of this novel that Mark, through his homosexuality, reiterates his grandparents' position in belonging to a group set somewhat apart from the mainstream.

The youngest member of the Sonnenblick clan is Natasha whom Marietta adopts on the rebound from her marriage. In her revulsion against the American way of life, including the Episcopalianism represented by the church visible from her ex-husband's bedroom window, she sets "about finding a one-hundred-percent guaranteed Jewish child" (24). This is the only mention of Judaism in the entire novel, and it reveals Marietta's remoteness from religion in the fact that she "had tended to mix up Jewish and Russian, and when she thought of a Jewish girl, it might have been more of a Russian she had in mind: a Turgenev or Chekov heroine, an embodiment of music, moonlight, and poetic feeling" (24). Natasha falls so far short of this extravagant ideal that she is a parody of Marietta's expectations and a caricature of the Jewish stereotype: short and thin, with thin dark hair, hair on her upper lip, a curved nose, and bad posture. With "her back bowed like a seamstress, her pale ghetto complexion, her dark inward-looking eyes" (75) she appears as a throwback to a more primitive East European stage in the family's history. Her clothes, too, which she buys from men selling them out of cardboard boxes on the street, are like a conspicuous rebellion against her grandmother's formality and her mother's fashion consciousness. She wears "long dragging cotton skirts and cheesecloth blouses made in underdeveloped countries" (128). She favors this garb as loose, unconstricting, very cheap, and above all, as helping to feed a starving family in some famine-stricken part of the world. Louise is the only one who understands, and defends her against Regi's criticism, explaining that "the child is an idealist. She has very high principles" (128).

However though overtly complimentary, that phrase also shows that Natasha is dismissed as a "child," clumsy, dreamy, absent-minded, though by no means unintelligent. She never has a boyfriend, nor a home of her own, nor a job except as an assistant at Leo's Academy, where a wage for her is secretly provided by Mark. Natasha feels herself to be "inadequate" (182) in every way, yet she has an endearing honesty, tact, and sincerity. At the Academy she remains the detached, observing outsider, housed in the attic, whereas others are allowed to move to the more desirable lower floors in time. While she possesses nothing she appreciates the significance of solid furniture as a symbol of stability:

> She longed for things to stay as they were, and above all for people to stay
> where they were: for a permanence that she imagined to have been there in the
> past. One only had to look at the furniture of the past—those heavy beds and
> sideboards—to know that it belonged to people who expected not to have to
> move. Only permanence wasn't the right word: she had no word for what she
> meant (189).

Herself of unknown origins Natasha experiences the escapee's yearning for
the settled conditions she attributes to some more certain past. Her attachment to Mark is partly admiration for the handsome, successful older
brother, partly also the desire for connection to someone who appears to be,
not least through his ownership of real estate, more rooted than she is. Yet,
like Mark, Natasha is an outsider to mainstream American life through her
allegiance to the counterculture in her choice of clothing and in her beliefs.

Despite the varying degree of their assimilation the status of these figures
in *In Search of Love and Beauty* as escapees is confirmed by the extent to
which they share the customs that bind the members of the subcommunity
to each other. Continuities as well as changes are conveyed by the repetition
of recurrent motifs in the telling details favored by Jhabvala. For instance the
protagonists go on using the same German eau de cologne, "the original
from Cologne with the blue and gold label, which even Louise's mother had
used" (133; readily recognizable as the 4711 brand). They go to the same
German doctors, Dr. Hirschfeld in New York, and when Natasha falls sick on
vacation in the Hamptons a very old, retired physician, who discovers that
Louise and he used to go to the same place in the mountains for their vacations. The bond of common past experience holds the escapees together, and
extends into the present, into their second lives. So cakes for birthdays and
pastries for coffee Klatsches are always obtained from Blauberg's; when
Louise at age eighty-four orders the cake for Regi's birthday, "she had been
going to the same place—Blauberg's—for over fifty years, and one of the
assistants, a Mrs. Weintraub, had been there for the last thirty of those" (233).
In Search of Love and Beauty projects the sense of a flourishing German–Jewish
subculture sustained by the escapees in order to replicate, at least partly, the
rituals of their former lives.

Of utmost importance among those rituals are visits to the Old Vienna
café, which serves as a register of change within continuity. The Old Vienna
in this novel may well be modeled on the famous Blue Danube in northwest
London, a social center for escapees, which reproduced Viennese coffeehouses.
In their early days in New York Louise and Regi regularly meet there for coffee at their habitual table (*Stammtisch*) in the center aisle. They know the
waiters and many of the customers so that the place functions, as European
coffeehouses used to do, as a sort of home from home. It is to the Old
Vienna that Bruno takes Marietta after their walks in the park: "she drank hot
chocolate with whipped cream and had the cake trolley come around several

times" (122). Years later Marietta chooses the Old Vienna as the locale for her meeting with Kent, her son's lover: "the Old Vienna with its mixture of coziness and glamor seemed the right place for it. And Marietta was amused to find herself there, in that family place where as a child she had eaten such quantities of Sacher Torte, with this youth who was Mark's friend" (206). Although she has doubts about choosing such "a very public place for so secret an assignation" (206), Marietta opts for it nonetheless perhaps because it gives her the advantage of being on home ground, as it were, for this charged rendezvous whereas Kent is at a disadvantage in being on foreign territory. It is also suffused in her mind with literally sweet memories that may counteract the bitterness of the situation she now has to confront.

Similarly it is under the chandeliers of the Old Vienna that Mark catches his first glimpse of Kent meeting with Anthony. Unlike the two previous generations Mark is not an enthusiastic patron; on the contrary "for his own social pleasure, Mark wouldn't have gone anywhere near the Old Vienna" (145). In his desire to be fully American the Old Vienna is precisely the spot he would eschew as the gathering place for the escapees; it thus becomes obliquely a barometer for his endeavor to separate himself from his European origins. Much frequented by the original escapees it is still patronized by the second generation, but shunned by the third. Mark goes there only because it suits his business interests. He takes along businessmen from Oregon and Oklahoma, with whom he has property dealings and who are eager to see "exciting aspects of New York" (145). The Old Vienna is always a great success with them despite its changed character:

> The management had, over all these years, not only maintained the standard of its performance but brought it up to a higher pitch. Chandeliers, mirrors, and blue velvet were there in such profusion that they were almost a parody; the dishes on the menu had retained their exaggeratedly Viennese quality; and while the cooking was nothing to write about—. . .—there were some wonderful drinks (145).

The Old Vienna has become a tourist attraction, "almost a parody" as its former clientele ages and disappears to be replaced by out-of-towners, gawkers, to whom it is the epitome of the exotic, not an extension of home in the dual sense of habitat and former environment, as it had been for the escapees.

The repetition of the motif of the Old Vienna is an effective way to denote the passage of time through the modulation of its nature and clientele. *In Search of Love and Beauty* is divided into three sections, the longest of which centers on Louise at age sixty at the point of her birthday party when she feels "an abundance of happiness." The opening section shows her at age forty, while in the final one she is in her eighties. By covering such a considerable span in her life and the lives of her family and her circle of friends, the novel can depict the changes that overtake the escapees through the years. However instead of a simple, linear progression the narrative moves constantly between various time phases, often reverting to the past as, for example, in the episodes of Louise's and Regi's youth and of Bruno's courtship. The flow is associative, the transitions smooth. So in Part I, after the description of the two friends' "tête-à-tête sessions at the Old Vienna" (56), we leap to "forty years later, Louise and Regi still met at the Old Vienna, though not very regularly" (58). Similar time-shifts occur in: "[Y]ears and years later—two generations later—Regi told Mark about that night" (61), and "it had been different in Louise and Regi's time" (81). Memory is handled indirectly and obliquely here. The characters do not generally engage in reminiscences, as in many escapee fictions. Jhabvala is an omniscient narrator who prefers scenic dialogue interspersed with description, though description is often infused with irony. The fluid shifts in time are a crucial means to convey the interpenetration of the past and present, the lingering presence of the past as a factor, at once explanatory and motivating, in the characters' responses and conduct.

The tensions between the three successive generations reveal the clashes between the old and the new behavioral patterns. Such tensions are, of course, not unique to escapee families, but they assume an added charge when they are complicated by the differences in standards and customs between countries as well as over the years. Reminders of the march of time come in the progressive aging of all the protagonists. As is her wont throughout the novel, Jhabvala resorts to the condition of interiors to denote their owners' state. When Regi lapses into senile dementia, Louise becomes fully aware of her disintegration through the nastiness of her apartment:

> The place was dusty, and the floors had lost their shine. In the past, Regi had been fanatical, firing maid after maid for not looking after her floors properly; . . . As for the smell in her bedroom, the cloud of stale perfumes—it was the ambience of her latter years, as of a shuttered, shut-down beauty salon; and yet, piercing through it, there *was* something else—what was it? A strange smell, acrid, sweetish, foul (192).

The same sort of disarray is found a little later by Marietta in her mother's apartment:

> now the room had an air of utter neglect, with dust ingrained and settled into each crevice of the carved and convoluted furniture and on the clustered grapes of the chandelier. Inside Louise's bedroom, Marietta found the bed unmade and Louise's old-fashioned flannel nightgown abandoned on the floor. When she stooped to pick it up, she saw some more clothes lying on the carpet—old woman underclothes that Louise must have stepped out of and left there. A pair of stockings had rolled under the bed too far for Louise to retrieve. Marietta had to stretch out to reach it, and when she did, she found it covered with fluff like something lost long ago and overgrown (219).

The two old ladies' aging, at once pathetic and grotesque, has its incarnation in the squalor of their homes, which demonstrate the extent to which they have lost control. The stealthy inroads of aging are ubiquitously apparent: Marietta's hand is not only "veined and thin" but also "twitch-ing" (211), a sign either of nervousness or possibly of disease; in Anthony's face, "strained and old," Mark recognizes ominously that "he might have been looking at his own face, twenty years later" (245); Leo confesses to feeling "old and tired" (229), and Mrs. Weinberg at Blauberg's tells Louise "about her latest complaint" (234). Having escaped the Holocaust the Sonnenblicks and the members and associates of their subcommunity are subject to the normal physical and mental processes of human decay.

*   *   *

So do the escapees and their offspring in *In Search of Love and Beauty* find the "abundance of happiness" Louise purports to have, or is this claim an overarching irony immanent to the entire novel? Its title is a phrase coined by one of the students at Leo's Academy; it raises the novel's central motif, the "search for love and beauty" (184) in which each of the characters is engaged in his or her own way. That search is particularly pressing for escapees as they start anew in an unfamiliar culture and have to find the most apposite path for their second lives. What is more the Constitution of the host country in this instance categorically spells out the individual's right, indeed the imperative to pursue happiness. The spectrum of escapees in *In Search of Love and Beauty* go about their quest in very diverse manner. Bruno and Regi remain fixed in their European lifestyles, as their furnishings and clothes indicate. By contrast the subsequent generations, Marietta and Mark, attempt to go native to different degrees and with varying success. After her short experi-ment with local mores Marietta recoils so decisively as to cultivate instead the exotic in her adoption of Natasha and her fascination with India. Louise's position is an uneasy compromise as she stays outwardly in conformity with her German past while privately breaking away from it. Leo and Natasha per-sist in standing apart from the norm, each tending his or her own garden as they see fit by creating an eccentric environment: Leo's clearly to his personal advantage, Natasha's an expression of her innocence and sometimes misplaced idealism.

Yet despite Louise's affirmation of "an abundance of happiness," it is doubtful whether any of the escapees achieve this in their second lives. Even Louise only lays claim to that blessed state in the fleeting moments of her birthday celebration. At other times she has to face an abundance of prob-lems in her relationships to the melancholy Bruno, the temperamental Regi, her impetuous daughter, her headstrong grandson, the demanding Leo, and the wayward Natasha. Said to have resembled a Wagnerian singer in her youth, in her seventies Louise is "more like a French tragic actress: tall, stately, draped in dark silk, her white hair disheveled, she appeared always to have heard some terrible tidings" (95). This image hardly corresponds to a life abundant in happiness. For the search for love and beauty, as Leo's disci-ple woefully remarks, results paradoxically in entanglement "in one harmful relationship after another" (184). This certainly holds true for Marietta in her

marriage and her successive flirtations, for Mark in his disappointments with
his lovers, for Regi in her serial marriages and later in life her paid friendships
with young men. Whether Leo attains love and beauty, or happiness, is highly
questionable; even in his commune he has to have an "escape hatch" (54, 76).
What is certain is that he creates disturbances in the lives of all those with
whom he comes into contact. Even Natasha, the self-contained introvert, is
not wholly exempt from harmful relationships in her attachment to Mark,
who makes financial provision for her but is unconcerned, as are nearly all the
others around her except Louise, about her emotional needs.

The difficulties encountered by the characters in this novel in their search
for love and beauty—and happiness—are, arguably, intrinsic to the human
condition. But escapees are more vulnerable than others on account of their
dislocation from their native environment (and language), and the necessity
of dealing with a culture where they are strangers. Bruno's life would unques-
tionably have been far happier if he had remained director of his firm in
Germany. Marietta, as Marianne, would likely have made a more suitable
marriage in the milieu in which her family was rooted instead of venturing
onto utterly alien ground. Regi, in her thrust for the ultramodern, might
have been able to keep up with the latest trends if she had stayed in her
homeland rather than being stranded in the past as a transplant to the United
States. Admittedly these are all speculative "ifs"; however they devolve from
the incontestable fact that the Nazis' advent to power and their persecution
of the Jews caused radical deviations in the lives of their quarry.

In Search of Love and Beauty is one of the rather few fictions that follow
escapees into the later years of their second lives. Many works concentrate on
the more immediate and dramatic problems after arrival in the host country
such as language acquisition, the establishment of a home, the quest for a
livelihood and a modus vivendi in the new environment. Because of their
affluence the Sonnenblicks and their friends are initially spared some of these
difficulties. What is more they take up residence in New York, the most
thoroughly cosmopolitan destination, where they can shape their lives among
the likes of themselves. The prominence of the Old Vienna testifies to the
cohesiveness of the subcommunity, certainly through the lifetime of the first
generation. The lack of a comparably congenial meeting place greatly intensifies the isolation experienced by the Hoffmans in Topeka, Kansas, in *The
Flood* (1987), and the Rosenbaums at Benton in *Pictures from an Institution*
(1954).

So despite the rather favorable circumstances under which they live the
Sonnenblicks do not find "an abundance of happiness" in their second lives.
Curiously they take no satisfaction, as does Lumbik in "A Birthday in London,"
in the mere fact of their survival, perhaps because their relocation was made
without the long struggle he had undergone. Also unlike the middle-aged
protagonists in "A Birthday in London" many of the younger characters in
In Search of Love and Beauty have a strong commitment to the present. This
certainly holds for Marietta and Mark who are intent on making a success out
of their respective businesses, though understandably less so for Bruno and

Louise, who are surrounded by objects from their past. Bruno surely must look back with a good deal of nostalgia; however because of the absence of indirect discourse to give insight into his mind, we cannot know. The recall of the past is carried out by the narrator, who interweaves retrospective accounts and scenes like collages grafted onto the present time of the action. But that past is always implicit in the present through the otherness that marks the characters and leaves them essentially outsiders to their new environment.

At the end of the novel the Sonnenblicks are close to extinction. Louise falls at Regi's birthday party, sustaining a serious injury, probably a hip fracture, which may at her advanced age lead to her demise. Mark will have no progeny, nor, it seems, will Natasha. Indeed her very existence is threatened as she hurtles into the dark in a very old, small car without lights, driven by Leo, "a mad, erratic driver," acting "crazy" (249) in pursuit of two members of his commune who have taken flight. A disastrous crash is imminent. It is in keeping with the pervasive undercurrent of irony in *In Search of Love and Beauty* that the Sonnenblicks survived the Holocaust only to die out within the two succeeding generations.

8

"A Bizarre Double Game"

Isaac Bashevis Singer, *Shadows on the Hudson* (1998)

The phrase "a bizarre double game" occurs some two-thirds of the way through Singer's posthumously published *Shadows on the Hudson*, which takes place primarily in New York City between November 1947 and November 1949. The verdict that he is playing "a bizarre double game" is made by Dr. Solomon Margolin, who had attended a yeshiva in Poland before becoming a physician in Berlin. A tall, erect man with a severe face and "the cold grey eyes of a Prussian Junker" (10), always fashionably dressed and beautifully manicured, a devotee of the athletic pastimes of the upper classes, able to speak Russian like a Muscovite, German like a Berliner, and English with an Oxford accent, Dr. Margolin stands astride the orthodox Jewish circles of his old friend, Boris Makaver, the novel's central patriarchal figure, and the secular world to which he had been assimilated through his aristocratic clientele in Berlin. In New York too, "he belonged to all sorts of Gentile clubs" (10). The duality of his life is epitomized in his continuing intimacy with Boris on the one hand, and on the other the secret resumption of his marriage to Lise, the German woman who had been his wife in Berlin.

When Margolin had emigrated to the United States in the 1930s, Lise had not only deserted him to remain in Germany but had taken to living with Hans, an active Nazi. Her father had been a Nazi too, and her brother a storm trooper, and Mitzi, the Margolins' daughter "had attended a school where they taught her that Jews were lower than lice" (406). Nonetheless Dr. Margolin had brought his errant wife and daughter to New York after the war, and set them up in an apartment on First Avenue next to the East River. Lise, who speaks perfect English and knows French well and who had run an exclusive fashion boutique in Berlin, finds a job immediately, while Mitzi enters Vassar. Their transition is easy, without any of the economic or adjustmental difficulties experienced by most escapees. It is Margolin who struggles with his conflicted existence: "[H]e would eat the Sabbath meal with Boris, would recite the blessings over the wine and the bread, would sing Sabbath hymns, say the Grace after Meals, and then go back to sleep with a woman who had left him for a Nazi" (408–409). Because of Boris, "his

Jewish conscience" (407), Margolin maintains two separate apartments, but his "hideous secret" (408) creates in him "an irreconcilable conflict" (409). Once in Berlin when he had had the opportunity to marry an exceptionally beautiful woman of the highest social class, he had gone so far as to consider conversion, but however little he believed in either Moses or Jesus, he had refused to change his religion. So he finds himself to be "neither a Jew nor a Gentile, neither an American nor a European" (336). With Lise, who proves ironically to be the perfect wife, Margolin "had the urge simultaneously to lie with her and to strangle her" (412).

Although Dr. Margolin's split is extreme it is to some degree characteristic of many of the characters in *Shadows on the Hudson*. In various ways they engage in a bizarre double game in their attempts to steer between the traditional values and lifestyles they have brought along from Eastern Europe and those of the culture of their adopted country. A parallel tension between old established orthodoxy and modern urban secularism is the dominant theme of Singer's multigenerational saga, *The Family Moskat* (1950), for which he was awarded the Nobel Prize for literature in 1978. Singer himself knew some of these schisms personally as the scion of a family that represented two opposing strains within Judaism, the Hasidic and the Rabbinic, as well as a product of big city, antitraditional tendencies within Judaism. Having left Poland in 1935 and lived the rest of his life in New York City, he can himself be deemed an escapee. He certainly has the capacity to portray from within the paradoxes and conflicts, in short, the bizarre double games of his tortured, complex fictional characters.

Like *The Family Moskat, Shadows on the Hudson* is a vast panoramic novel with a large cast of characters. It resembles the earlier work too in its handling of place, with Warsaw and New York City, respectively, as the unifying location and episodic excursions from there by various protagonists. However the time frame of a mere two years is much shorter in the later work, although retrospective vistas are opened up onto the characters' past histories, which give the novel temporal depth.

Boris Makaver, for instance, had escaped from Warsaw by a devious route via Paris, Casablanca, and Havana before finally settling in New York. No specifics are offered about that journey; he is seen in the novel's opening sections hosting a dinner party at his apartment on the Upper West Side between Broadway and West End Avenue. His guests, who include Dr. Margolin, are all from Eastern Europe so that there is an immediate sense of a rather close-knit subcommunity. The apartment's furnishings are, like those of the Sonnenblicks in *In Search of Love and Beauty* (1983), a replica of those Boris had had in Warsaw: "heavy mahogany furniture, ornate chandeliers with dangling crystal prisms, and plush and velvet upholstered sofas and chairs draped with lace antimacassars and fringed covers" (4). This is an obvious attempt on his part to recreate in the New World his familiar old surroundings. Indeed in his study Boris can imagine himself back in Warsaw as he looks out over the building's quiet courtyard with its small garden enclosed by a picket fence[1]: "the bustle of America evaporated and he thought

European thoughts—leisurely, meandering" (3). But in other areas of the apartment "the din" of Broadway reverberates up to the fourteenth floor with the noise of automobiles, trucks, and the roar of the subway from under the iron gratings. So Boris's physical situation, even within his own home, is a figuration of his dyadic psychological position.

Boris's heritage from his past is one of ultraorthodoxy. Although he had changed his name from Borukh (blessed) to Boris "out of business expediency" (4), he had never abandoned his Jewishness, and after the Holocaust he had heightened his strict religious observance. He is therefore among those escapees whose faith is strengthened rather than undermined by their experiences. He observes the regular daily prayer rituals, even maintaining a small sanctuary in his apartment. The celebration of the Passover Seder at his table is described in expansive detail (273–83), but with an undercurrent of irony because several of the guests have scant acquaintance with the ceremony. Despite the festive atmosphere on the streets and the availability of Passover provisions in that part of the city, Boris, it is implied, is among the few concerned with the spirit of Judaism. A widower for many years when he remarries his choice falls on Frieda Tamar, herself a learned woman, a descendant of an illustrious rabbinical family, whose first husband, also a rabbi, had perished at Auschwitz. Her entire appearance and demeanor, "unpowdered, unrouged," without lipstick, wearing her black hair combed into an old-fashioned bun, and in a black dress with sleeves to her wrists and a high collar that hides her throat proclaims her "a lost fragment of nineteenth-century Europe" (230). She and Boris spend the High Holy Days with a rabbi at a Hasidic inn in upstate New York.

Nevertheless despite his piety Boris is engaged in a kind of "bizarre double game" through his compulsive involvement in business. He had "regretted more than once that he had not become a rabbi, a scholar, or simply a hack writer" (71) since he loved both Torah and knowledge, but he is seduced by business. He has such rapid success that he becomes enthralled, almost obsessed by it: "after only four weeks of wandering about the city, he knew exactly where to make money" (8). The din from Broadway reminds him of all his business affairs, of the need to telephone his broker and to arrange a meeting with his accountant. He has a bad conscience about his acquisitiveness; as he scribbles his sundry appointments in his notebook, he recalls that Elijah had heard the voice of the Lord not in the strong wind or the earthquake but in a still small voice.[2] He has survivor guilt too as he acknowledges that "he was a materialist, a maker of money, a glutton, and a drunkard—for that he had been given an American visa and been sent to the United States to get rich" (50). He feels unclean to utter his prayers, and thinks that he should be mourning those exterminated in the Holocaust:

How odd it was: by day he was absorbed in commercial dealings like any businessman, but at night he was overcome by self-condemnation, an enormous remorse, a grief that harrowed his heart like a physical pain. What am I doing? What am I doing? To what end are we all so feverishly buying and selling?

I should sit on a low stool and mourn, not for seven days but forever. I should
rend my garments and keen until my death, taking a piece of bread with water
once a day and sleeping fitfully on a hard bench (51).

But such self-reproaches do not stall his escalating greed any more than do
his religious scruples. He becomes involved in a potentially highly profitable
shipping salvage venture, which turns into an utter disaster so that he sees
himself facing the prospect of becoming destitute. When his blood pressure
rises dangerously and he shows symptoms of heart failure Dr. Margolin
orders him to " '[D]rop your stinking business' " (330). Boris's religious
fervor is not a true spirituality; it is undercut by his passion for business so
that he experiences "an inner darkness . . . an emptiness" (53) as a result of
being so fundamentally torn between the two poles that dominate his life.

Boris's adult daughter by his first marriage, Anna, also plays bizarre
double games, in her case on the marital and sexual plane. Her early marriage
in Poland to Yasha Kotik, an actor, whom Boris regards as "a lunatic, a rogue,
a jack-of-all-trades" (27) had quickly collapsed. During their flight Anna had
precipitously married Stanislaw Luria, who is "both violent and sickly," "bel-
licose, and, moreover, a chronic failure and a liar" (12). Of a wealthy family
in Warsaw and well educated (he knows Shakespeare thoroughly) Luria had
been a lawyer, but in New York he does nothing; Boris realizes that he
"would leech off him all his life" (27). Physically and psychologically he is "a
broken man" (80), embittered by the extermination of his first wife and children. Like his father-in-law he feels survivor guilt, but unlike Boris he has had
his religious faith shattered. The couple's apartment on fashionable
Lexington Avenue reflects the hollowness of their marriage, looking "as if the
dwelling were a stage, and husband and wife the actors" (34). The habit of
pretense, intrinsic to her first marriage to a "comedian" (27), is carried over
by Anna into her subsequent relationships so that her life becomes devoid of
authenticity.

Anna's apartment is, like Marietta's in *In Search of Love and Beauty*, a
complete contrast to her father's:

> How different this living room was from Boris Makaver's salon. Here every-
> thing was bright and modern. The beige carpet spread from wall to wall. The
> walls themselves were brightly papered. Built-in bookshelves held volumes with
> colorful covers. The chairs, the sofa, the coffee-table—everything had been
> chosen for the comfort of the guests who smoked, drank, and did not remain
> long in the chairs assigned to them. On the walls hung various paintings and
> drawings that Luria had bought in Havana and New York—a jumble of sym-
> bolism, expressionism, and every other modern trend—the most striking of
> which was a representation of an androgyne. Even the lamps here were
> designed not solely to light the room but also for the sake of effect (34).

The emphasis on modernity and brightness is a foil to Boris's cultivation of
continuity and traditionalism. Anna's decor suggests that, like Marietta in *In
Search of Love and Beauty*, she wants to break away from what her father's

furnishings represent in order to partake of a more up-to-date lifestyle. Yet a certain brittleness and lack of direction is apparent here, as in Marietta's fragile pieces. Although "everything had been chosen for the comfort of the guests," they do not "remain long in the chairs assigned to them." This restlessness is the antithesis of the long discussions of philosophical issues in her father's cozier apartment. The showiness of Anna's place, the "jumble" of artistic styles, subsumes the superficial glitter of the new world, whereas the solidity of Boris's apartment is the incarnation of an outdated old world.

Still Anna resembles her father in her business acumen: "she became a carbon copy of Boris Makaver. She smoked cigarettes, went back and forth [from Florida] to board meetings, continually fiddled with numbers" (187). Anna follows in her father's footsteps by going into real estate, perhaps because it offers the optimal possibility for turning a profit. However this preference for the ownership of property, shown too by Mark in *In Search of Love and Beauty*, denotes also the escapee's desire to strike roots in the adopted country through tangible possessions in the form of land and houses. Boris is the first to recognize in Anna "a shrewd New York survivor, a cat that always landed on her feet" (369), who is driven by "an atavistic desire to make money" (341). As her modern decor indicates Anna wants to adapt to her environment, telling herself: "[T]his is America, not Europe! Here one has to shake a leg and do things" (542). She appreciates the fact that a woman too has the opportunity "to make money in America" (124). Again like Marietta, Anna reshapes her image by cutting her hair, losing weight, and acquiring a glowing tan. But Anna's transformation into a new woman is motivated primarily by the need for emancipation from her father in order to attain the financial freedom to indulge in her sexual adventures. Long before Luria's suicide, she embarks on an adulterous affair with Grein, whom she had known in Poland. The turbulent relationship with Grein signals her simultaneous desire to reconnect with her past and to enjoy the free-and-easy mores of her new country. Instead of her former "aimless flirtations which involve no obligations" (33), her affair with him is from the outset more serious: "[O]ur plan is to go first to a hotel and then to Tasmania" (44). But when they do in fact run away to Florida, they only become aware of the differences in their personalities so that they drift apart. Coming full circle Anna eventually joins up again with her first husband, Kotik, proclaiming: " 'I'm one of those who cling to the old days. You were part of my past, and after all I can't bury the past' " (424). So Anna's double game takes the form of appropriating those aspects of the American scene that she sees as to her advantage while at the same time wanting to retain certain facets of the past also to her own good. Her return to Kotik, who is undoubtedly a tricky operator, parallels Dr. Margolin's resumption of his marriage to Lise. Both continue to cherish an instinctive attachment to their former lives, although Anna is less apologetic and certainly less beset by qualms of conscience. She selfishly embraces what/whoever is to her immediate benefit.

Grein's double game differs from Anna's in stemming above all from his vacillations and indecision. He stands apart from the more recent escapees in having been in the United States for twenty years. The reasons for his earlier emigration are not stated; they may have been economic since he is something of a rolling stone who has not achieved prosperity in any of the various jobs he has held. Perhaps his lack of success is connected with his failure to acclimatize to, let alone understand, America as Anna does: "he retained a greenhorn's wonder and a tourist's curiosity. Everything amazed him" (30). During his stay in Florida, for instance, his dark city clothes look quite out of place. "No, Grein really did not understand America . . . Nonetheless, Americanness had entered his bones" (73–4). This ambiguity may underlie his paradoxical pattern of behavior. His repeated tendency "to lose all sense of direction" (45) is symptomatic and symbolical of the confused uncertainty of his intent.

Grein's double game consists of violent swings between lustfulness and religiosity. He oscillates between these two extremes "with the abstractedness of someone doing something against his will, against all logic, propelled by an alien hand, driven by a hidden force" (70). For years he has been unfaithful to his hardworking wife, Leah, in a long-drawn-out affair with Esther, a forty-year-old woman of good family who still has beauty as well as an air of refinement lacking in Leah. The sordidness of Grein's apartment on Central Park West with its smells of overheating and stale cooking and its clutter of food debris, old newspapers, and neglected mail projects the disorganization and absence of cohesion in this fragmented family, whose members go their separate ways without heed to the sensibilities of the others. Moving in and out of Grein's thoughts Singer exposes the "double standard that had been pointed out to him [Grein] countless times" (75). He would never, he asserts, divorce Leah whom he regards as the ideal of the virtuousness and chasteness he values in a woman. Yet he not only returns again and again to Esther but also promises to marry Anna who breaks up with her husband and, more seriously, probably with her father for Grein's sake.

The hypocrisy of Grein's conduct is aggravated by his own awareness of it: " '[O]ne thing is certain—I know what is right, and I do what is wrong. How does the Gemara put it, "Though he knows his Master, yet he desires to rebel against Him" ' " (75–6). Grein even tries to quieten his conscience by invoking biblical precedents: " '[H]ad not Abraham, Isaac, Moses, David, and Solomon all kept concubines?' " (75). But although he attempts to justify his course in this way, Grein acknowledges in his heart of hearts (and not by coincidence surely his first name is Hertz, heart) his wrongdoing:

> Like a criminal, he was preparing to commit a wrong in full awareness of the law and knowing in advance the consequences of his action both in this world and perhaps in the next. Nothing here has happened by chance; it was all premeditated, he said to himself. What does the Gemara call it? Sin out of lust for forbidden pleasure . . . and only today I was mouthing words about religion and religious discipline. Absurdly, he was overcome by something resembling piety. He felt a strong urge to appeal to the higher powers, to pray. But he dared not turn to God at the very moment he was breaking one of God's holiest laws (48–9).

Grein's deeply ingrained religious background leads him not only to judge his own conduct by those traditional standards but also to try sporadically to reconnect with his roots. After reaching a nadir when he sleeps on a park bench and is dislodged by a police officer, he enters a nearby synagogue to participate in the weekday morning service for the first time since his arrival in America. He has grown so distanced from Judaism that he "already only half recollected how phylacteries were worn—the leather straps, the rolled back sleeves" (371). In a surge of self-incrimination he censures himself as "an adulterer, a murderer, a liar. . . . I have broken the eternal bridle which God's immutable law places on human conduct. I belong with the Bolsheviks, the Nazis, the criminals of all nations. I embody the limbo of the underworld" (372). In the short service Grein realizes that "he had to play by the rules of the game" (376), that he cannot turn away from these tenets because "[T]his picture of God was in his blood" (375). "I must play this game to the end. Without it," he concludes, "I cannot breathe. Without it I have no identity" (376) . Significantly he envisages his religion over and again as a "game" he has to play, not as a set of moral principles to guide his life. Little wonder that he abandons this game to run away to the country in New England with Esther, another of Grein's experiments doomed to failure.

Little wonder either that Grein's two children break away from Judaism. His son, Jack, marries a young woman from Oregon, that is, as far away from New York as possible. Yet it is Patricia who develops an interest in Judaism, learning Jewish cooking and laws from her mother-in-law, acquiring books of instruction until she grows quite orthodox. Grein's daughter, Anita, on the other hand, who had always been at loggerheads with her father, marries a German with a thick accent and a contempt for everything American. An unattractive personality he arouses immediate suspicion in Jack as well as Grein of having been a Nazi. Through his default in giving his children a sustaining heritage Grein precipitates intermarriage in the second generation, although in an ironic twist the trend away from Judaism is reversed by his Protestant daughter-in-law of Scottish–Irish–German descent. Greins's double game with lustfulness and religiosity contrasts with Patricia's marital faithfulness and her sincere observance of Judaism.

Another bizarre double game, though essentially comical, is enacted by Morris Gombiner whom Grein and Anna encounter in Florida. Morris is actually not an escapee but a concentration camp survivor who has been in the United States barely a year. A "tiny person," "a miniature man," thin with glistening black eyes and two shocks of white hair on either side of a broad bald patch above his wide forehead (158), Morris is far from the image of the typical American. He wears a loud shirt with flowers all over it, prescribed for him by his wife who, he explains to Grein, " 'wants to turn me into an American' " (160). She is an oversized, overbearing woman with "huge earrings resembling bedsprings" bouncing from the lobes of her ears (166). Florence is a realtor who tries to inveigle Anna into investing in a defective house. She bullies Morris incessantly, directing his every step and constantly plying him with food and orange juice. Intimidated he mostly complies, but in private is highly critical of America and retains Central European manners; for instance he kisses Anna's hand when introduced to her. Morris's double game is a grotesque masquerade.

Equally grotesque, albeit in a tragic vein, is the practice of spiritualism by Mrs. Clark, the landlady of old David Shrage, once a professor of mathematics at Warsaw university. She purports to be able to conjure up his wife, Edzhe, who had perished in the Holocaust. She arranges a séance, hiring a Polish actress to impersonate Edzhe. While professor Shrage goes along with the charade, he knows at some level that "[T]his was all lies, falsehood, and deception, he thought, but it did not necessarily follow that Edzhe was not here" (61). His rationalism as a mathematician does not preclude his acceptance of an irrational practice. He accedes to a wishful double game even as he doubts its validity.

* * *

The repeated bizarre double games apparent in so many of the characters of *Shadows on the Hudson* are partly a product of the improvisational nature of their lives. Once deprived of their firm grounding in their original lands, they all too easily tend to lose their bearings—and their self-assurance—in new surroundings, which are strange, often puzzling, or indeed, incomprehensible to them. The decor of their homes reveals the dichotomy between the older escapees' wish to reproduce, that is, to restore their former environment, as does Boris, and the younger ones' thrust to venture into the new arena, as Anna does. The instability of their housing and their forfeiture of direction are expressions of the profound uncertainties to which they are prey. In counterpoint to the policy of the more affluent toward investing in real estate, the escapees mostly live in apartments (as was customary in New York City). Several are in even more transitional places such as furnished rooms or, in Kotik's case in a seamy hotel. When Anna and Grein begin to cohabit they move out of their respective marital apartments into a luxurious sublet one belonging to a couple away on an extended trip.

To lose one's way physically, like Grein, is a transparent metaphor for the escapees' bewilderment in the hurly-burly of New York City. The motif recurs in *Shadows on the Hudson* in the figure of Shrage who also keeps losing his way in the city:

> [H]e believed that his blundering about New York could be explained only in Freudian terms: it was rooted in his subconscious and must have a symbolic meaning. Moreover, Professor Shrage's eyes took in less and less. There was nothing physically wrong with his sight, yet his ability to see was continually diminished. Even by day he saw as if through a mist. At night his vision virtually vanished altogether (57).

The narrator here accedes to Shrage's interpretation of his blundering through the reference to Freud, as an analogy to his inner perplexity; his inability to steer his way home mirrors his psychological confusion, his sense of no longer possessing a real home, just a rented room. Notwithstanding the categoric statement that "there was nothing physically wrong with his sight," another explanation is possible, namely, the presence of cataracts, given Shrage's age and his symptomatology. However the psychosomatic reading is favored here as elsewhere throughout *Shadows on the Hudson.*

As their double games show the characters fluctuate and flounder between alternatives, which frequently run to extremes. These polar swings can and should, as with Shrage, be read on the two discrete but conjoined levels on which the novel operates: the literal and the figurative. The protagonists of *Shadows on the Hudson* are explicitly portrayed in a realistic manner rich in circumstantial detail. The variations in the characters' personal histories are skillfully displayed immediately in the novel's opening sections through the introduction of the guests at Boris's dinner party, which affords the omniscient narrator the opportunity to give an overview of the background, beliefs, and stance of each of those present. They comprise a wide range of professions and occupations as well as a spectrum of religious positions from ultraorthodoxy to agnosticism and Marxism. At the same time, collectively and figuratively, the long narrative uncovers the pervasive disorientation these escapees suffer as a result not just of their physical relocation but also of their existential dislocation. Although some manage to prosper financially at their new destinations, emotionally most of them remain suspended in a state of uncertainty. Their deficient sense of direction connotes their unsteady identities and their wavering loyalties.

They are all beset by tensions of various kinds. The novel's title hints at one major source of inner conflict: while they live in the here-and-now in the shadow of the Hudson River, they also live in the larger shadow of the Holocaust. It is constantly present in their subconscious, and often it surfaces in overt references. Frieda has lost her husband, Shrage his wife, Luria his wife and two children, Esther one half of her family. "All these shadows accompanied them, each played its own role, demanded its own share of immortality" (144). Looking at his fellow passengers in the subway Luria sees in his mind's eye those he had lost, and in contemplating suicide he asks defiantly:

> For what purpose did God—if there is a God—need six million Jews to be wiped out in agonizing pain? And why was it necessary to burn children? Perhaps the adults had sinned, or God wanted to put them to the test. But what about those infants whose heads German officers smashed in? (135)

Boris and Grein, in their phases of self-castigation, invoke the Holocaust as a yardstick to condemn their own behaviors.

Implicitly the novel raises the question of the appropriate balance between remembering and forgetting. Boris advocates the necessity of remembering with typical vehemence:

> Why did they forget? Boris believed that the whole Jewish people should go into mourning. A *Bet Din* or a Sanhedrin should institute a mourning period of

a hundred years: the Jews should be forbidden to wear bright clothing, to play music at weddings, to drink wine; instead, they should be compelled to sit on the ground for an hour each day and recite the Book of Lamentations to memorialize the destruction of Jewry (407).

The extremism of Boris's reaction is juxtaposed paradoxically with the equal fervor with which he pursues his current business concerns, apparently unmindful of the very losses that he believes should be memorialized by exaggerated, wholly unrealistic measures. Grein responds to the Holocaust rather differently by querying whether the Lord is indeed "gracious and full of compassion . . . slow to anger, abundant in goodness" (373). But he, too, casts these reflections aside as he becomes embroiled in his love interests.

A more complicated tension occurs in the relative attitudes to Europe and America. Europe is, on the one hand, home, the place where these characters had grown up, where they were socially and professionally established, and whose cultural values they understood and endorsed. On the other hand, however, Europe is now also the locus of the Holocaust, the place of death and annihilation. America is equally two-faced as the land of freedom and opportunity, the haven to which they have escaped with their lives, but it is still the land where they feel marginalized outsiders unable to find an enduring sense of direction. Memories of the past and longing for its (impossible) restoration clash with the realities of the present. These divided loyalties are implicated in most of the bizarre double games: Boris's allegiance to orthodoxy and his obsession with profit; Margolin's career as a Jewish physician and his reconciliation with his guilty wife; Grein's repeated adulteries and returns to Judaism. The ambivalence of the relationship to the past is revealed in Grein's dream that he is back in a small East European village in late spring under an enormous moon, very likely a wish projection. He is in the courtyard of a synagogue where he wants to join the congregation, but suddenly realizes that he is naked. His nakedness can be read as a cipher for his adulteries, the Americanness that has got into his bones. While he does not understand America he is not fit either any more to enter his original setting into which he no longer belongs.

On the whole in *Shadows on the Hudson* vestiges of Europe are idealized, while American mores are vilified. For instance Luria condemns American women as "whores" (245) motivated by "only one love . . . love of the dollar" (252). By contrast Esther strikes Grein as "magnificent, pale, European, almost as if her trip abroad had stripped her of the Americanness she had acquired over the years" (476). Ironically he ignores the fact that Esther is as much of a whore and as much impelled by love of the dollar as the other women except his wife, Leah. Other aspects of America are also exposed to criticism: discrimination against Jews in the South, in universities, and in posh hotels. But since these are voiced by the fanatical Marxist, Herman, Boris's cousin, who disappears in the Soviet Union, they spring from an obvious political bias. However Dr. Halperin, too, complains of the way his scholarly book is being handled by an American press; it is being cut and, in addition, published in two volumes. Whereas scholarship, he asserts, is respected in Germany, "[H]ere they regard a book as a shapeless mass from which you can lop off slices. Yes, yes, this is America" (310).

A weightier objection to America concerns the tendency to accelerate the erosion of Jewish values and faith: " '[U]ncle Sam's a hopeless rationalist,' " Grein asserts (31), while Boris maintains that " 'in America all Jewish laws have been abrogated' " (306). Boris himself, so vociferous in his defense of Judaism and so ardent in his observance of its rituals, is far from really educated in his religion: "[W]hile he could make out a page of Gemara, when he had occasion to write in Hebrew, it was riddled with errors. Boris had one aptitude—for trade" (8). Grein's situation is more serious still since he does have the necessary knowledge, having been a tutor in his youth in Poland and a teacher in the United States. When he considers why he has become " 'a liar, a seducer, a murderer—every evil there is,' " although his " 'saintly parents are only a generation removed from me,' " Dr. Margolin responds bluntly: " 'they had faith and you do not' " (444). Yet Grein himself recognizes that "when one removed the Jew's faith, precious little that was Jewish remained, and even less that bound all these modern Jews together" (150). At a minyan during the seven Days of Mourning following a death Grein hears the young "whispering all the time about baseball because the World Series was being played" (185). Hardly better is Kotik who is described as "in his own depraved way . . . superstitiously observant" (144), but who doesn't hesitate to throw a bacchanalian party on Yom Kippur when he is riding high. The abandonment of the genuine observance of the Jewish religion leads the characters into the moral "limbo" (368), which is fertile ground for their bizarre double games.

Indictments of and laments about America resonate throughout *Shadows on the Hudson* as the escapees repeatedly express their unhappiness with the country that has given them refuge, even as they grudgingly affirm the opportunities it affords, notably for making money. As they egg each other on, nurturing reciprocally their discontents and prejudices, the members of this escapee subcommunity seem singularly demanding and unlikable, in contrast to their counterparts in Jhabvala's "A Birthday in London" (1963) who are mostly content enough with the modest success of survival, security, and a modicum of financial ease. The protagonists in Singer's novel hover between continents in a no man's land of their own creation. Their sense of their own superiority alienates indigenous Jews, who in turn harbor their own conceits such as preferring "not to socialize with *Ostjuden*" (176; Eastern Jews). The absurdity of the standoff between successive waves of immigrants is epitomized in the criticism by the recent arrivals that the earlier ones no longer looked Jewish and that "they all spoke English" (276).

English is not spoken widely in *Shadows on the Hudson*, and for that reason the question of language is a central one. A veritable Babel of languages is used by the characters: Polish, German, English, Russian, Hebrew, and of course Yiddish with varying accents. The retention of fragments of Yiddish connotes the preservation of both cultural and personal identity in the reversion to the mother tongue. Yiddish is in fact called in Yiddish the "Mame lushen," literally mother tongue. The vestiges of Yiddish emphasize the characters' unassimilated status and their differentness from those around them in their new country. It is almost as if the secular new languages were a form of disguise or of alienation, while Yiddish as the original language is a measure of authenticity.

Languages are readily mixed or switched; Mrs. Clark speaks to professor Shrage "sometimes in English, sometimes in German, and occasionally in broken Yiddish" (60). Similarly Grein makes his notes "sometimes in Polish, sometimes in English, sometimes in biblical Hebrew, and sometimes in all three languages at once" (150). Lise repeats Hebrew words "with the same perfection as she spoke English or French" (411). Yasha Kotik speaks "only his own argot, half Yiddish, half English, with bits of Russian, Polish, and German, and words that he had made up himself" (495). Or a character may speak English, as Dr. Alswanger does, but with an accent incomprehensible in New York because he learned it in Palestine. This linguistic cacophony is a cogent means to represent the international diversity of the escapee subcommunity. The medley of languages both unites the members of the group internally and separates them from monolinguistic Americans externally. Juggling so many tongues the escapees have a foot in many lands and roots in none. But their linguistic versatility is also symptomatic of their mutability, their lack of a well-defined, integrated identity. Their shared multilingualism and multiculturalism sustain their networking, which stems ultimately from their common origins in Poland.

The languages spoken are frequently named because *Shadows on the Hudson* abounds in dialogue. This not only enhances the novel's liveliness but also gives readers direct access to the characters and their mannerisms in their speech patterns. Throughout, however, Singer is an omniscient narrator who provides very explicit information about the protagonists, such as their past histories, their professions, and their proclivities. This predominantly direct narration yields at crucial junctures to indirect discourse, especially when a quandary in a double game needs to be explored from the viewpoint of the character experiencing the dilemma. An intimacy with the protagonists, is thereby fostered, allowing readers insight into the contradictory directions in which they are being pulled and the pressures, inner as well as outer, to which they are subject.

The range of tone is equally great. Overall Singer tends to draw figures who are larger than life and whose predicaments and actions border on the extreme. For instance Dr. Margolin takes back a wife who had not merely deserted him but who had actually had Nazi connections. Likewise Anita is involved not just with a German but with a particularly objectionable young man who revels in ranting against all things American (why he has come to the United States is unclear). Fritz Grenzl's diatribes are so hyperbolical as to be grotesque. The same kind of exaggeration marks the portrayal of the Gombiners, notably Mrs. Gombiner, and also Yasha Kotik. Singer goes beyond the more discrete tropes of irony and satire into parodistic caricature.

Esther's superrich, eccentric husband (for a short time), Morris Plotkin, with his factotum is ludicrous. " 'He should be in a novel' " (207) is Grein's skeptical comment on him. Yet even in a novel he stretches the bounds of credibility. While it is mainly the subsidiary characters who are overblown in this way, a certain inflation occurs with the more central figures too, for example, in the extravagant alternations of Boris's, Grein's, and Dr. Margolin's double games.

Shadows on the Hudson paints a jaded, pessimistic picture of escapees. A few of them, such as Boris and Anna, prosper materially; but even this financial success is precarious. Boris loses much of his wealth in the disastrous shipping salvage scheme, and Anna, remarried at the end to Kotik, is likely to have to disburse a good deal to satisfy his whims. Grein never manages to do more than eke out a living; Dr. Alswanger and the painter Jacob Anfang are hardly able to do that. Emotionally, as their double games suggest, they are fundamentally insecure and chronically unsettled. The language of their adopted country remains alien to most of them as they persist in their preference for their native idioms. This subcommunity is so self-enclosed that no Americans are central to the action; Florence Gombiner and Morris Plotkin, two figures of fun, appear on its outer margins as inappropriate spouses.

Instead of tracing the upsurge that would be expected as the escapees settle into their new environment, *Shadows on the Hudson*, on the contrary, portrays a decline over the two years that the novel spans. The three dinner parties at Boris's apartment, which punctuate the narrative, serve as milestones in the decline. The first one at the novel's opening is an occasion of considerable splendor with sumptuous hospitality and a large number of guests, Boris's relatives and friends. The second occasion is the Passover Seder toward the middle of the novel. Since Boris had recently married Frieda, "he was determined to hold a Seder people would remember" (273). However he immediately runs into "the problem of whom to invite" (273). Anna, who as the youngest had always asked the Four Questions, has run off with Grein, another formerly regular participant, and Anna's husband, Luria, also makes it known that he will not attend. This leaves only four possible guests: Dr. Halperin, now Boris's brother-in-law, professor Shrage, Dr. Margolin, and Boris's nephew, Herman, to whom Boris doesn't want to entrust the Four Questions because he is "a disciple of Stalin" (273). In order to have a few more people at his table Boris invites the controversial scholar, Dr. Alswanger, who proves to be ill at ease because of his unfamiliarity with the ceremony. The core group, clustered around Boris, has begun both to disperse and to be undermined by internal tensions and strife among its members.

The third gathering, at the close, is to celebrate the first birthday of Boris's and Frieda's son. By then "[T]here was no one to invite" (531). Shrage has died, Anna is drifting round Hollywood with Kotik, Herman has vanished in the Soviet Union, Grein, too, has disappeared (rumor has it that he had become "a penitent" [531] in the Me'ah Shearim, the orthodox district of Jerusalem), while Jacob Anfang, on the other hand, is found by Frieda huddled into a room on Seventh Avenue reading the New Testament. Dr. Halperin is still there, having survived his book's mortifying reception, and so is Dr. Margolin. After the presence in New York of his German wife had become common knowledge, an angry rift had existed for a while between Boris and him. But when Frieda needs medical attention Boris insists on calling his old friend in, and so a reconciliation takes place. It is Dr. Margolin who makes the devastating diagnosis of the baby's condition:

> This child looked perfectly healthy, but over the little face lay a dullness and a foolishness difficult to identify or to define. The infant's lips were too thick, and Margolin didn't like the smile that hovered over them. The child seemed to be sunk in the abnormal complacency of those whose mental development is arrested. Its eyelids were heavy and slanted. A mongoloid baby! something inside Margolin screamed out (540).

This shattering news, which signifies the end of the Makaver line and probably of Boris's happiness, brings *Shadows on the Hudson* to a dark closure. The baby's retardation represents a further shadow on the Hudson. The final gathering, "not a party like those of earlier days" (532), completes the dissolution of the group present at the beginning. The novel is structured symmetrically through the three parties that mark the stages of the decline. And the epilogue, a letter from Grein in Jerusalem to Gombiner, confirms the apocalyptic strain as Grein expresses his conviction that modern culture is the product not of God but of "the underworld" (545).

The pessimism of *Shadows on the Hudson* is undoubtedly connected to the age of the majority of the escapees. Except for Anna all the main characters are in midlife. Their previously already established careers in Europe had been violently disrupted, and they find it difficult to make a fresh start. The older the escapee, the harder this naturally proved to be. Hartmann and Fibich in *Latecomers* and Joe Beech in *To the City*, who arrived at their destination in childhood, come closest to achieving good second existences, even if they turn out not to be as fully integrated into their host country as they would wish or would like to believe. At the opposite pole Otto Woolf in "A Birthday in London" and Bruno Sonnenblick in *In Search of Love and Beauty* are simply too old to make the effort. The protagonists in *Shadows on the Hudson*, on the cusp of middle age, are still able to try and succeed to some limited extent, although they remain within the bounds of their subcommunity with little contact with American institutions beyond. The mongoloid baby symbolizes the shortfall in their success. Boris and Frieda have both remarried and want to found a second family. But, as Dr. Margolin reflects, "Frieda was an older woman when she had conceived" (540), a known risk factor for the baby's Down syndrome. So these escapees' advancing age is expressed biologically; it results in another—the saddest—form of duality: a viable but damaged future.

U.S. PROVINCES

9

"CAN YOU HARMONIZE?"

Carol Ascher, *The Flood* (1987)

" 'Can you harmonize?' " nine-year-old Eva Hoffman's father asks her
as he hums a tune that he wants her to accompany on her violin (4). The
Hoffman family—father, David, mother, Leah, Eva, and her six-year-old sister, Sarah—are enjoying the cool of an early summer evening in 1951 in a
green pasture outside Topeka, Kansas, where they now live because the father
is a psychiatrist at the Menninger Clinic. Eva is somewhat hesitant about her
ability to harmonize, but she manages quite well. Whether the Hoffmans are
able to harmonize metaphorically with Topeka is a much thornier question.

David and Leah had "almost waited too long before we ran from Vienna,"
frightened by an incident when David was nearly arrested on the street as
they were returning from a psychoanalytic training session (31). Psychoanalysis,
with its origins in Freud and its predominantly Jewish adherents, was spurned
as a Jewish invention. However David's and Leah's expertise proved crucial
to their escape for it enabled them to "get out as counselors for the children's
transport train" (32), as David explains to Eva, the first-person narrator of
The Flood. How they came to the United States or what they did in the years
between 1939 and 1951 is not filled in, although Leah recalls some of the
hardships of emigration:

> We had to start all over . . . I left with a small cardboard suitcase. David had the
> leather one that's still in the attic. "How lucky!" I laughed with him, "that we
> only recently married. That way we don't have so much to lose." But David
> was more upset. He had so many books. He tried to sell them to a dealer in
> a second-hand bookstore, but the dealer wasn't supposed to buy anything from
> Jews (124).

Although considerably older than Hartmann and Fibich in *Latecomers*
(1990) or Joe Beech in *To the City* (1987), the fact that David and Leah are
still relatively young and not yet professionally established meant that it was
much easier for them to resettle in a totally new environment than it was for
older people already in mid- or late-career in the 1930s and probably less
flexible such as Otto Wolff in "A Birthday in London" (1963) or Bruno
Sonnenblick in *In Search of Love and Beauty* (1983). Both the Hoffman

children are born in the United States but brought up in a home with decidedly European values and standards of behavior so that they are liable to some of the second generation's adjustmental difficulties.

The shadow of the Holocaust hangs over *The Flood*. In response to her question how her grandfather had died Eva remembers her grandmother speaking in "a thorny tangle of German and English" of "thirty of our people taken away, many more even 'to the east,' " in the years after she had come to America ahead of her husband. " 'And they had all been killed, nearly all . . . the ones who hadn't got out' " including Eva's grandfather (158). Before David's mother left, Leah recounts, " 'the Nazis just marched in and scooped all her silver and china into a sheet and took it away' " (168). When Dr. Hoffman and his colleague and friend Mordecai, an orthodox Jew also from Europe, argue about the role of therapy in a particular case, Eva's father grasps the deeper roots of their disagreement: " 'We've both been bruised by the Nazis, only in different ways. So now we fight' " (33). It may also be such bruising in Vienna that has made Leah "so nervous and awkward when she was with people" (33), a trait that Eva repeatedly notices without being able to understand its cause. Despite their personal more-or-less unharmed escape the Hoffmans have nonetheless in some not quite definable way been traumatized by the psychological baggage they carry from their past.

Eva's reply to her father's question, " 'can you harmonize?,' " " 'I don't know' " sums up her entire situation in *The Flood*. There is much that she doesn't know or understand not only about her parents' history but also about their present position. All the happenings in the novel are focalized and filtered through the perceptions of a nine-year-old. Ascher, an anthropologist and educator, who grew up in Topeka and is herself the child of escapees has recorded her memories of a train journey to Texas when she was a few months older than Eva, which raise many of the issues that the fictitious narrator of *The Flood* faces.[1] Eva is presented as inquisitive, intelligent, and precocious, but still essentially innocent as she endeavors to understand what is going on round her. An unusually articulate and self-aware girl as well as an astute observer she soon discovers that even her parents are unable to give her satisfying explanations of the many puzzling behaviors that disturb her. Sometimes overheard conversations, such as those between her father and Mordecai, allow Eva a glimpse of difficulties with which she wrestles. This frame of the enquiring child is a fine narrative device for the exposure of the problems inherent in that society at that time, and especially of the aggravated form in which the Hoffmans as outsiders encounter them.

The Hoffmans' first dilemma occurs when a neighbor invites them to a picnic at the church. Mrs. Hoffman firmly refuses but Eva and Sarah want to go, and their father thinks " 'it would probably be a good experience for them' " (36). Their mother wishes they would go to a synagogue sometimes: " 'It's confusing for them if they keep visiting churches' " (36). Like many Viennese Jews the Hoffmans are completely secularized and nonobservant, yet Leah's unease about her daughters' church visits suggests that her consciousness of being Jewish had perhaps been raised as a consequence of the persecution she and her husband had undergone. Nazi persecution affected escapees in different ways. Some sought to jettison the ethnicity that had caused them so much trouble, while others had intensified faith because they had escaped. Leah "half-heartedly" considers lighting candles on Friday night—an idea that merely provokes "a sarcastic look" from David (36).

The actual supper at the church is uneventful. However when the purple-gowned choir files in and the organ becomes "brooding and somber" (40), Sarah takes fright. " 'It's just church music,' " Eva reassures her, although she herself feels "anxious and unsure about what was to happen" (40). Young as they are the girls sense that they are in an alien environment. This is under-scored by the snippets from the hymns about Jesus, Christ, and "my Savior" (41). Eva begins to join in the singing, feeling both "fearful and daring" (41) as if she knew that this is a transgressive act. She also recognizes that her father would call the music "emotional or even trashy" (42). The cultural disparity between the standards in her home and those of the milieu beyond the home is already mooted here. The episode reaches its dual climax in the coincidence of an apocalyptic thunderstorm with lightning and drenching rain with the preacher's sermon. In a terrifying performance he warns of the possibility of a flood, which he ascribes to the prevalence of atheism, alco-holism, and, worst of all, communism. When Sarah falls asleep Eva is glad of the comfort of her sister's body against hers, and wishes "it were all over and we could go home again" (46). Eva's disquiet at not belonging does not need to be expressed in so many words. The image of the church is decidedly negative, dominated by the tactics of fear that the preacher uses. So the invitation to the picnic backfires making Eva draw away from her environment; the visit confirms her view of herself and her sister as "two Jewish girls" (38) who cannot "harmonize" despite her attempts to sing along. They are outsiders, in but not of the community.

The second source of the Hoffmans' detachment from their surroundings emerges more slowly in the course of the narrative but comes to assume increasing importance. They do not share their community's attitude toward blacks. Hanging in their living room is a large portrait of a Negro at which their neighbor darts uneasy glances when she comes to invite the girls to the church picnic. The Hoffmans are considerate, indeed even friendly to their black cleaner, Mrs. Johnson, who arrives late because the bus wouldn't stop for her. After years of working for the Hoffmans she has finally been persuaded to stop bringing her own lunch since "Mother had slowly con-vinced her to eat whatever we were eating along with us" (8). Eva gives Mrs. Johnson a small brooch to hold her dress together when a button comes off, but Mrs. Johnson refuses to keep the little violin pin, obviously afraid of being accused of theft. Eva also chatters to her about the books she is read-ing and asks whether the youngest Johnson girl, Mayella, is reading the same ones, and whether Mayella couldn't come with her mother one day. " 'Uh huh' " is Mrs. Johnson's laconic response, avoiding any sort of commitment, either negative or positive (13). She is patently very reluctant to get into conversation with Eva, maintaining the distance she considers proper. Yet she does disclose that her niece, Lureen, a teacher, had recently got notice from the Board of Education.

This information inserted into the narrative provides the opportunity to touch on the sociohistorical context of *The Flood*. In the opening chapter already Dr. Hoffman speaks to his wife about "a suit that a Negro man was bringing against the Board of Education" (2), but as he communicates in German, Eva does not catch it. Hearing about the dismissal of Mrs. Johnson's niece she suddenly realizes that there are neither Negro teachers nor indeed Negro children in her school. So the highly charged topic of school desegregation is introduced. In the early 1950s Topeka was at the very heart of the storm about school desegregation.[2] The Brown v. Board of Education suit followed a series of Supreme Court decisions on specific educational challenges. The first was that universities must admit blacks to graduate facilities if a desired course of study was not offered in a black institution. Then in Sipuel v. Board of Regents of the University of Oklahoma in 1948 the Court ruled that blacks must be admitted to state universities because they offered many opportunities not available in black institutions. In 1950 in Sweatt v. Painter the Court ruled that a separate black law school, established for Sweatt after he sued for admission to the University of Texas Law School, was unequal not only in facilities and curriculum but also in reputation and opportunity for stimulating professional contact. In Laurin v. Oklahoma State Regents, also in 1950, the Court ruled that the state violated the "separate but equal" doctrine when it required isolated cafeteria and classroom seating for black students because this resulted in unequal educational opportunity.[3]

The Brown suit contested the separate but equal doctrine on the grounds that separate schools were ipso facto unequal, and extended the challenge too to black children of elementary school age. The plaintiffs in this action, brought in the United States Court for the District of Kansas, aimed to enjoin the enforcement of a Kansas statute, which permitted but did not require cities of more than 15,000 population to maintain separate school facilities for black and white students. Based on that authority the Board of Education of Topeka had elected to establish segregated elementary schools. The three judge District Court found that segregated public schools had a detrimental effect on black children, but denied relief because they found that the schools were essentially equal with respect to buildings, curriculum, transportation, and the educational qualifications of teachers. The ultimate decision in Brown's favor in May 1954 was a major landmark in the fight for desegregation, although opposition to it continued, notably in the "Southern Manifesto" issued by a group of Southern politicians.[4]

The shadow of the Brown v. Board of Education suit is a vital factor in the action of *The Flood*. In a sense it hangs over the population of Topeka in 1951 in a manner somewhat parallel to that of the Holocaust over the escapees. Whichever way the decision were to go it threatened to bring radical, perhaps violent, change to the lives of both blacks and whites just as the advent of the Nazis had done to European Jews. That Lureen had been given notice by the Board of Education is a precursor of the turmoil about to break out. And the Hoffmans, as a result of their own bad experiences in Vienna, are acutely sensitized to prejudice and discrimination rooted in racial bigotry.

Clearly Topeka is a difficult place for them to settle. What had brought the Hoffmans to Topeka is the Menninger Clinic, a private hospital dedicated to mental illness. Established in the late 1920s by Karl Menninger and his father, Charles, who were soon joined by Karl's younger brother, Will, it emphasized the so-called family spirit in the running of the institution as well as in relationships between patients, doctors, and staff. At a time when most psychiatric care was still primarily custodial, Karl Menninger believed strongly in the possibility of cure, or at least of melioration. He also endorsed the therapeutic potential of psychoanalysis, and himself underwent a training analysis with Franz Alexander, one of Freud's most brilliant pupils, who had moved to Chicago, where he founded the Chicago Psychoanalytic Institute. In 1934 Menninger visited Freud in Vienna with Alexander, but the visit was a disappointment. Nevertheless the Menninger Clinic, more than any other hospital in the United States, integrated Freud's view of emotional life into its treatment plan. One of its main models was Schloss [Castle] Tegel, an exclusive, experimental psychiatric hospital outside Berlin run by Ernst Simmel, another pupil of Freud's. The Topeka Institute for Psychoanalysis, under the directorship of Karl Menninger, organized seminars for the study of Freud's writings.

The opportunity to recruit emigré psychiatrists versed in psychoanalysis seemed a godsend to Menninger for the development of his clinic, which was short of expert training analysts for the American staff. What Menninger sought to import to Topeka was not just a methodology but the broad culture that underlies psychoanalysis. Several emigrés who had already arrived in the United States were employed in the 1930s, while others were actually brought from Europe. Of all medical specialists psychiatrists enjoyed "the most favorable reception among the public. The American stereotype of a psychiatrist as a foreign-looking gentleman with a thick beard and an accent of like thickness helped the refugee neurologist and analyst."[5] But from early on the enterprise was beset by tensions and frictions. The newcomers' English left much to be desired; when Simmel visited in early 1936 his lecture was barely comprehensible. More serious most of the physicians were accustomed to private, independent practice and were uncomfortable with the "family spirit" mentality so central to the clinic. Salaries became another significant bone of contention. Culture shock was inevitable:

> Though Karl sentimentally regarded Topeka as his hometown, the contrast between the Kansas capital and the great European cities can hardly be exaggerated. The newcomers characterized Topeka as a cow town. Deprived of classical music, art, and theater, they were bored. Even the routine social services of European cities were missing.[6]

The wives, without even the benefit of association with the hospital work, were still more affected by the provincialism, "the cultural poverty," and "the icy stares of neighbors suspicious of foreigners."[7] Under these circumstances it is not surprising that few of the escapee psychiatrists stayed in Topeka for any extended period.

Young and inexperienced Dr. Hoffman was unlikely to have been among the first wave of foreign psychiatrists recruited to the Menninger, but might well have participated in the postwar training program. In 1945 Karl Menninger initiated a psychiatric residency program at the nearby Winter Hospital. The Menninger School of Psychiatry (MSP) was immediately flooded with over 700 applicants, of whom 92 began their training in 1946. The school rapidly became the major training agency for the nation's psychiatrists, constituting one-third of all psychiatric residencies and one-half of all those in the Veterans' Administration system. But the social problems, which had troubled the earlier influx, still persisted. Most of the MSP fellows came from urban centers, over 40 percent were of European origin, and about 30 percent were Jewish. "Some referred to Topeka as 'the sinkhole of the United States,' a hick town that lacked foreign films, classical music, even a delicatessen."[8] Topeka, for its part, "tended to be suspicious of the newcomers. Rumor spread among them that Karl Menninger had imported lots of foreigners, Jews, and Reds."[9] These conflicts were compounded by the civil rights actions, which came to a head in Topeka in the Brown v. Board of Education suit.

Topeka is thus certainly not a place where the Hoffmans can readily harmonize. Even as Mrs. Hoffman teaches her daughters, " 'You know, when you live in a country, you have to try to fit in' " (103) she herself is not good at doing so. She is quite torn; on the one hand she disapproves of the escapee doctors at the Menninger who "still want to be in Europe," whereas she wants to "become a real American" (77). On the other hand she still keeps a certain judgmental distance from American mores, for instance, from "the fashion" of letting each child have its own room because she "couldn't allow one to be a little princess while whole families live crowded together in basements. That's just not right" (123). She would like to bestow the customary American privileges on her children, however not at the cost of social justice. Such opinions alienate her from her neighbors with whom she does not mingle easily. The gulf separating her from them is denoted by the forms of address they habitually use; the others who immediately call each other by their first names, "Betty," "Mary Ellen," etc., note that " 'Mrs. Hoffman here always stays real formal.' " To which Mrs Hoffman replies, though "stiffly": " 'You should call me Leah. That is my first name.' She wanted to be like the other women but didn't know how" (131). It is ultimately not just her European habits of formality, much less such little things as mending clothes rather than throwing them out that sets her apart from the women in her neighborhood; it is her fundamentally liberal views on equality. She does not realize, for example, the shocking transgressiveness of her insistence that Mrs. Johnson should eat along with the family.

The escapees infringe local customs in many facets of their conduct. "We were the only people who walked in town, and even the animals seemed to think it odd," Eva remarks (28). Their food is of course different; Mother makes *Butterkuchen, Pflaumenkuchen*, a Viennese *Torte*, all of which contrast with the green and red jello molds, the succotash, and the sliced ham at the church picnic. As in many other fictions about escapees food serves as the concrete symbol of their differentness. And even more so language. Having come to the United States at a fairly early age, probably in their mid- to late twenties, the Hoffmans could be expected to have acquired fluency in English. *The Flood* contains none of the mimicry of mispronunciations or foreign accents commonly found in connection with older escapees; however David and Leah frequently interweave German words or expressions into their speech, especially Leah at moments of emotion. In discussing the Brown v. Board of Education suit, for instance, they converse in German. In this case the use of German is a means to protect their children from a disturbing matter. Nevertheless Eva knows that "we were looked upon as strange" in the neighborhood and at school (143). They are definitely not integrated even though they are white.

To compensate for their otherness and loneliness in Topeka the Hoffmans cultivate friendships with several Europeans who live there. Apart from Mordecai who is a professional colleague—and something of an adversary—to David, a group gathers at the Hoffman house to play chamber music. Beyond their names little information is given about them, presumably because Eva, the child-narrator, is not familiar with their personal histories. Hans, the violinist, and Anna Mandelbaum are German, while the cellist, Micha, a psychiatrist, is Hungarian as is her husband, Janos, a painter. The melodious classical music moves David to tears: "the three sounded like thoughtful birds who had reflected on the pain of the world" (73). The communal music making is thus more than merely a social coming together; it is also a means to express and above all to share feelings with a few like-minded companions. This offers a striking example of the formation of a subculture of escapees building a new life in an environment that is alien to the point of hostility. Whereas in the major cities such as London and New York entire areas were colonized by escapees (Washington Heights, New York was nicknamed "the Fourth *Reich*"), in remote provincial places, such as Topeka, the subcommunity is shaped by personal contacts and mutual interests. The conversation over coffee and cake between the music making shows how this gathering functions as a support group too; at least within the group they can harmonize both literally and metaphorically. Anxieties are voiced about the imminence of flooding from the deluge of rain, the number of polio cases, the possible threat of typhoid. Much of the discussion centers on the Brown v. Board of Education suit. The group is unanimous in its support of desegregation and in its praise of Helene, an escapee social worker who has testified on behalf of Brown. On this occasion we hear that Brown has lost the case, "but in a useful way" because "they have the structure of their argument, and the case will go up to a higher court" (78–9). While favoring integration, not least on account of the negative psychological effects on black children of having to attend a segregated school, some members of this very discerning group are concerned lest blacks " 'lose the dignity of their autonomous culture' " (79). " 'And who wants a white Protestant culture?' " David asks sarcastically (79). The discussion uncovers the extent of the conflicts with which the escapees have to contend. Yet they accept their lot with stoicism: " 'We are the Jews of the diaspora. We have to learn to live in America,' " Hans concludes, adding " 'We have to be grateful for America' " (80). *The Flood* depicts just how complex that learning process may be. As if to emphasize the continuity of European culture the chapter ends with David calling on his daughter to get out her violin and begin tuning it.

The escapees' situation in Topeka is sketched in the first part of the novel, "The Rising Waters." Its second part, "The Refugees," depicts the crisis caused by the displacement of families in certain sections of the town by the flooding. The parallelism between the dislocation suffered by the European Jews and the ousting of the flood victims by the water is quite obvious, although one disaster is man-made and the other natural. The very title of the second half of *The Flood*, "The Refugees," evokes the Europeans who lost their homes and possessions and had to start life anew. The Topeka refugees are in considerably less dire straits insofar as they can stay in their native place, do not have to learn a new language, and will within a reasonable length of time be able to clean up their houses, return to them, and resume their former occupations and lives. The crisis they face is acute and finite in contrast to the protracted and fundamental process of resettlement confronting the escapees.

Mrs. Hoffman sets to work at once to help the flood victims. " 'Leah identifies with all refugees,' " her husband notes "gruffly" (78). She recalls how twelve years ago she too had had nothing. She takes bedding and towels to the collection center in the church basement to lend to the refugees. " 'Ma, the people are called evacuees,' I corrected her, wanting to keep her from thinking she and they were the same" (96). Leah does not care for such verbal distinctions: " 'It's not fair. Imagine, here we are, dry and safe, with good food and beautiful music, while so many people have their homes and crops destroyed' " (78). Yet it is important to her to draw a line between the church's religious and philanthropic functions. " 'I believe more in what they're doing downstairs,' " (101) she determinedly tells Eva who prefers the clean, pure, fragrant choir room to the crowded, smelly basement. This second visit to the church to donate to the flood emergency counterbalances the earlier picnic and sermon. This time Eva is attracted to the beautiful interior. " 'Wouldn't you like to go to a church like this?' " (101), she asks her mother, who responds with tears. She realizes the danger of her children becoming assimilated in the bad sense of losing their Jewish identity. The innate contradictoriness of the Hoffmans' position is very apparent in this episode when Leah implores her daughter not to forget that she is Jewish, and almost in the same breath urges her " 'to try to fit in' " (103). Eva assures her mother, " 'I really don't get confused about who I am' " (104), but the pull of the church leaves some doubt about the direction of her future development.[10] Leah's worry that her daughters may lose their Jewish heritage echoes the qualm expressed by some of the Hoffmans' friends that the blacks may forfeit their culture as a by-product of desegregation. Integration has its price.

The clash between mid-Western Protestant and European liberal-Jewish attitudes surfaces most sharply when the Hoffmans extend hospitality to an "evacuee" family, the Willigers, who have a daughter midway in age between Eva and Sarah. Since the Hoffman house is not large this entails some sacrifice, especially for Eva who is turned out of her room and relegated to an attic where her pet goldfish expires from the heat. From the outset Eva is resentful of the intruders whose radio blares out all day, who drip toothpaste onto the bathmat, and who boast of owning a TV. The peace and quiet of the house is disrupted, as are their habitual cultural activities: father's piano playing in the evening, Eva's practicing the violin and her reading. She feels isolated and bereft even within her own family because Sarah plays with Jolie Williger, and she no longer has her father and mother (nor do they have each other) since they are so preoccupied with dealing with their guests. The disparity between the Hoffmans and the Willigers comes into the open at the dinner table in a succession of telling details. The Willigers are accustomed to saying grace, "giving the good Lord His due" (121), a practice that elicits an amused smile from David. When Mrs. Williger in turn smiles Eva notices that she is missing a front tooth. Eva is too young to grasp the class implications of such a gap, which would hardly be tolerated among European professionals of her parents' standing. Mr. Williger and Dr. Hoffman talk about the unionization of labor, which the former opposes and the latter endorses, probably arousing thereby the suspicion that he is a "red." What the Willigers think of the Hoffmans is also left to readers' conjecture when Mrs. Williger says to her friend, Mrs. Rogers, " 'The Hoffmans have real interesting art, don't you think?' " as her eyes roam over the small pictures and come "to rest on the Negro man above the couch" (133). " 'Interesting' " sounds like a euphemism for something more forceful and disparaging.

It is in regard to blacks that the most searing rupture between the Willigers and the Hoffmans comes into the open. As outsiders the Hoffmans simply do not grasp the vehemence of the ingrained prejudice against blacks. To some extent they come across as " 'rather naive' " in this respect; that is the phrase that Mordecai applies to David: " 'if you're taking the side of the Negroes, or someone who's fighting for the rights of Negroes' " (138). We don't know how long the Hoffmans have lived in Topeka, but they must certainly have become aware of the prevailing prejudices. When Mrs. Johnson comes late because the bus wouldn't stop for a black person Leah exclaims: " 'Ach! I don't understand this country,' " to which Mrs. Johnson responds, " 'It ain't a country fixed for colored folks, that's for sure' " (9). Leah also comments on the fact that there are no black families at the emergency shelter for flood evacuees in the church. Eva seems dimly more aware of the great divide of segregation than her parents appear to be:

> A disturbing thought was crossing my mind. Except on those days when Mrs. Johnson came to clean, we never had Negroes in the house. . . . The other people on the street, who didn't hire anyone to clean, never had Negroes in their homes. And, of course, Mrs. Rogers hadn't wanted a little Negro girl [for adoption]. For all Mother's wishes for a better world, she must have hung back from inviting Mrs. Johnson's family (115–16).

By confining themselves to a little circle of their European friends the Hoffmans are avoiding, perhaps even denying, the immense problems in their community. They discuss them, that is to say, take cognizance of them on an intellectual level, but otherwise seem to bypass them as best they can. Maybe they would like to idealize America, the country in which they found refuge, as the traditional land of freedom. However Leah identifies not only with the flood refugees but also with blacks when she proclaims that in Germany " 'we were the Negroes' " (80).

The sheer virulence of the Willigers' contempt for blacks is brought out in the incident when Jolie, looking for the plastic gift, shakes out a whole box of Cracker Jacks over a Persian rug Mrs. Johnson had just vacuumed. Naturally Mrs. Johnson is upset: " 'Young lady, I just cleaned that rug,' " she chides Jolie. When she asks: " 'Miss, did you hear what I said?' " Jolie bursts out with: " 'I ain't taking no orders from a nigger!' " (144). The contempt contained in that word "nigger" summarizes Jolie's defiant sense of her absolute prerogative to act at will without the slightest consideration for Mrs. Johnson *because* she is black. Jolie "calmly and methodically" eats her Cracker Jack while Mrs. Johnson has to vacuum the dining room again. Sickened by Jolie's ruthlessness Eva wants to throw herself "at Mrs. Johnson to ask her forgiveness, and to tear Jolie's eyes out" (145). She goes outside to ponder on this gratuitous cruelty; like the church picnic it is a chastening experience of her milieu for her, another, far more traumatic milestone in her knowledge of the world.

The prejudice against blacks encompasses Jews too. " 'You know, for the longest time, we didn't even realize you folks was Jewish,' " Mrs. Williger confesses, adding that she was "surprised" when her friend Mrs. Rogers had told her (163). Her concession " 'you don't act any different' " (163) hints at the possibly bizarre expectations she has of Jews. Though taken aback the Hoffmans react with as much dignity and restraint as they can muster, pointing out that they thought they had said something at dinner on the first night. Again it is Jolie who acts out and voices the prejudice against Jews. " 'Jews smell bad,' " she bluntly tells Eva (170), and when the three girls are playing in an improvised backyard swimming pool, she complains that it isn't like the public swimming pool " 'because here we got to swim with Jew-Niggers' " (186). Is this an environment with which the Hoffmans are able to harmonize, or that even permits them to do so?

Eva is deeply hurt by this—her first direct encounter with anti-Semitism. However much she tries literally and metaphorically to wash off Jolie's insults she has persistent "dirty feelings" (187). Unable to tolerate any longer the Willigers' invasion of her home she makes an attempt to run away. She has no plan, and takes only a shopping bag. This instinctive flight from anti-Semitism reiterates on an almost parodistic level her parents' escape from Vienna with minimal baggage. Eva is soon totally at a loss where to turn. Near the river she sees a pickup truck "like Rosie Williger's, but older and more rickety" (190). Its open back is piled with stray objects left by the flood: a baby carriage, wooden planks, pieces of steel, and tires. Eva sees "a thin old Negro man with dazzling white hair" (190) bent over, struggling to extract a spring stuck in the mud. Although so far in her adventure Eva has heeded her mother's injunctions not to speak to strangers, not to accept rides, and so forth, she addresses this man to find out what he is doing. It turns out that he lives in his truck, and is hoping to sell what he can of the things he has retrieved, keeping just a few finds useful to himself such as the tires. " 'I could help you first, and then you could take me home,' I said" (191). Those are the closing words of *The Flood*.

The symbolism of this episode is pretty transparent. That the black man has a truck like the Williger's suggests resemblance rather than difference between the races. His dazzling white hair denotes a further parallelism between blacks and whites, physical and also figurative in the white element in the black man. Eva dignifies him by perceiving him as "a thin old Negro man," an individual, not just a generic Negro, let alone a "nigger," like Jolie. His thinness, reminiscent of Mrs. Johnson's, hints at his poverty, especially as he is homeless. His work of salvaging debris from the flood is another pointer to his marginality, yet it can be seen too as an act of rescue, even of environmentalism insofar as he is cleaning up the mess. Eva's harmonizing with the black man consolidates the alliance of the outsiders to the community (Jews were to take an active part in the civil rights movement). Their mutual help forms a positive conclusion to *The Flood*.

Whether it is convincing is another matter. As the action of an idealistic, curious (and lost and bewildered) nine-year-old it is quite credible. Eva doesn't know—doesn't *want* to know—the prohibitions that govern behaviors in Topeka. She has witnessed her mother's friendliness to Mrs. Johnson, and therefore has no hesitation on principle in speaking to a black man. He, on the other hand, is less plausible, largely on account of his speech patterns. Standard white English is attributed to him: " 'I don't know if I can get anything for it or not' " (190) instead of the black dialect ascribed to Mrs. Johnson. Eva's pact with him seems a device to provide the novel with a conciliatory, though wishful resolution.

This episode is the most extreme instance of the rather heavy-handed symbolism throughout *The Flood*. The picture of the Negro hanging above the couch in the Hoffmans' living room is a prime example; it signifies the Hoffmans' open-mindedness and interest in art as well as the distance between them and the Willigers and Mrs. Rogers who are all shocked by what they see as a flaunting of convention because they focus solely on the subject matter, ignoring any aesthetic dimension. Similarly the hymns at church contrast with the secular, classical music favored by the escapees, the *Lieder* by Mahler and the chamber quartets by Brahms and Bartok. The pack of derelict horses being driven helplessly to slaughter, seen by Eva on a trip to town, evokes the memory of Jews hustled to the gas chambers. The flood itself is at once reminiscent of the biblical story and of the Nazis' overrunning of Europe. The Hoffmans' house is "an ark" (119) for the Willigers just as America is for the Hoffmans themselves. " 'Did Noah take both Jews and Christians into the ark?' " Eva asks Mordecai (173).

Despite—or perhaps because of—its overarticulation of problems, *The Flood* gives a striking glimpse of escapees in a particular environment at a particular point in their host country's history. The Hoffmans must on the whole be deemed fortunate. Young professionals they have established a home and a family and a modicum of security through David's honorable position in his own line of work. The fact that the action of the novel takes place in 1951 must be taken into account; they have had twelve years in which to get settled, but of their struggles in those intervening years we hear nothing. This gap in their history is motivated by the narrative focalization through the child's eyes. The Hoffmans have retained their original identity as liberal, secular Jews; the only very minor change is the dropping of the final "n" in their name, which would almost certainly have been "Hoffmann" in Vienna.

It is precisely their adherence to their original identity and values that prevents them from integrating into the community in which they now live. Their humanistic tolerance is utterly at odds with the bigotry dominant among their neighbors. What is more as Jews they are themselves objects of that bigotry. Apart from the small band of their escapee friends, who are in a similar situation, the Hoffmans remain isolated in Topeka. That disconnection is felt by Eva too. Thinking of her forthcoming birthday she imagines a party for which her mother would set a table on the lawn with a pink tablecloth and pink napkins: "The trouble was I didn't have any friends my own age to invite" (96). This exclusion from their ambience cannot but affect the Hoffmans adversely. Leah is chronically tense, irritable, she "frets" and "fidgets" (6) when among people, is "strained with worry, or with holding back an unbearable worry" (26). David, too, usually buoyant, after the Willigers move in,

> never troubled to disguise his gloom or worry, he was not the one to volunteer information about his more private thoughts. And now, as in the cold winter when Grandmother had died, he drifted further into his books and music, and his drawn face showed he was in another world (143).

Mordecai, by contrast, speaks openly of "avoiding my own depression . . . and also doubts" (141). Yet even when the latter's professional disagreements with her father make Eva "itchy and upset" (141), there is a measure of civil, if at times heated, interchange such as is wholly out of the question with the Willigers or Mrs. Rogers. The educational discrepancy between them and the Hoffmans is merely one factor in this failure of communication; the underlying problem is the narrow-mindedness to which they have been programmed, as the preacher's sermon shows.

The restriction of the viewpoint, while giving coherent unity to *The Flood*, also has the effect of raising some questions, which must inevitably remain unanswered since they are beyond Eva's horizon. How, for instance, does David relate to his colleagues at Menninger's? Do they provide collegiality, a forum for an exchange of ideas, or are they, too, enmeshed in the web of local prejudices? In his postwar residency program "Karl [Menninger] balked at making a firm commitment to racial equality."[11] What about the synagogue that Leah mentions twice and where she thinks she should take her daughters? Why doesn't she do so? Does her own nonreligious background make her hesitant, or is the congregation as unwelcoming to outsiders as the community at large? On these matters readers can only speculate. But a clear picture emerges from *The Flood* of the heightened obstacles faced by escapees who land at a destination torn by internal tensions. The interaction between the indigenous and the newcomers is foredoomed by conflicts intrinsic to the community onto which the escapees are grafted.

10

"An Inconsequential Appendix and Coda"

Randall Jarrell, "Constance and the Rosenbaums" in *Pictures from an Institution* (1954)

"An inconsequential appendix or coda . . . in some real sense, the Rosenbaums' lives were over" (163–4). Is this an appropriate assessment of the lives of Gottfried Rosenbaum, an escapee from Austria, and Irene, his Russian singer wife?

Rosenbaum is a composer in residence at Benton, a small exclusive women's college. Neither its location nor the time of the action is specified. The time seems to be the early 1950s, contemporaneous with the writing of *Pictures from an Institution*. The location is uncertain; no place names are mentioned except New York on the distant horizon in contrast to the provincial Benton, which is vaguely in the South, perhaps in the mid-Atlantic region. On the other hand the immediate microscopic scene is vividly evoked as all the action is sited on the college campus or in faculty homes. This tightly knit community has both advantages and disadvantages: its genteel atmosphere derives from its Southern tradition of hospitality and sociability, but the constant proximity also inevitably spawns tensions, gossip, a sense of enclosure, and remoteness from the world at large. The Institution in the title refers to an educational academy; however the word also comprises a certain ambiguity, for to be institutionalized normally means to be shut away against one's will in a medical establishment usually dedicated to mental illness. How good an environment then is this for the Rosenbaums?

While the information about the Rosenbaums' present lives is rich, that about their past is patchy. Gottfried had left Austria after the Germans entered, "at the eleventh hour, by the skin of his teeth, without a garment," as he puts it (135). This brief, dramatic account sounds quite thrilling, but as it were generic, because it is lacking in specifics. However it is categorically stated that he is a Jew, although his mother was "a braided Austrian type, all *himmelblau* and *zuckerlrosa*" (69; sky blue and candy pink). Does this mean that she was not Jewish? Under the then prevailing Judaic law of matrilineal descent, her son would not be a Jew; although in the Nazis' eyes he would be since his father evidently was, judging by his name. The composer's own first and middle names, Gottfried Knosperl, were given to him by his mother. They translate into God-Pacified Bud of the Rose-Tree (70) with the fanciful "Knosperl" (literally Little Bud) curiously sandwiched between the two quite common names, Gottfried and Rosenbaum. Does this strange combination already signal the ambivalences surrounding him?

What Gottfried did in the twelve–fifteen-year interval between leaving Austria and coming to Benton is not explained. This hiatus, which reiterates that about his escape, is more troubling because the Rosenbaums are now pretty affluent: "She [Irene] and Dr. Rosenbaum had money of their own, too, and not just his salary; they had a cook, a summer cottage on Cape Cod, and a new Simca convertible" (139). Mrs. Rosenbaum "had brought with her, from the Old Country . . . jewels, a couple of fur coats . . . dresses of some of the finest vintages, and her new dresses were almost as astonishing as the old" (139). Had she escaped separately from her husband who had arrived "without a garment"? Had she been able to emigrate more easily, tak-ing her possessions with her because she is not Jewish? What is the source of their money? They certainly seem comfortably settled and secure at Benton, at least from the material point of view. Yet we do not know how long they have been there nor, more important, whether his is a renewable or a securely tenured position. These lacunae in our knowledge of them intensify their enigmatic quality.

The presentation of the Rosenbaums is typical of the narrative strategy of *Pictures from an Institution* in which the characters appear as they are in the present at Benton with relatively little exploration of their background or previous doings. In the case of the Rosenbaums this leads to a complete gap about their early years in the United States. It could be that Jarrell, a Southerner born in Nashville and educated at Vanderbilt, was not suffi-ciently familiar with escapees to envision a convincing history for them. However, since he treats all the protagonists in much the same way it is more reasonable to conclude that he simply had a greater interest in their present interactions than in filling out their past. But the absence of more than a min-imum of history results in a certain flatness of the figures and also often renders them more puzzling through the gaps in our knowledge of what previous experiences might be affecting their current reactions. This is more disturbing in relation to the Rosenbaums than to other fairly stock figures (such as the college president) since we sense the likelihood of an adventurous path before they landed at Benton.

This silence about the characters' past paradoxically at once detracts from and heightens the realism of *Pictures from an Institution*. On the one hand it detracts from it in the manner I have just suggested by diminishing readers' capacity to understand the protagonists' motivations or responses. On the other hand it heightens the credibility of the narrative situation. *Pictures from an Institution* has a first-person narrator who remains anonymous and largely veiled. His profile is shadowy: he is a married poet, who had lived in

New York and is now teaching at Benton. How long he has been there is not divulged although he evidently knows the college, its faculty, and students well. He is thus simultaneously an outsider and an insider to this community, functioning as the perceiving eye, the recording voice, and the critical filter. Rarely an actual participant he is nevertheless often present at various college events, although the first-person convention is not upheld with absolute consistency for the text also comprises conversations that he would not have heard himself. Yet he is a frequent visitor to faculty homes and college social doings so that he has personal familiarity with the people and the tone. His dominant stance is detached, often quite scathing in his ironic insights. For instance he questions the self-image on which Benton prides itself as "progressive":

> Benton was a progressive college, so you would have supposed that this state would be a steady progression. So it had been, for a couple of decades; but later it had become a steady retrogression. Benton was much less progressive than it had been ten years before (234).

The tone of the narrator's irony is in keeping with the genre of *Pictures from an Institution*, which is designated in its subtitle as "A Comedy." Within this framework the Rosenbaums, like all the characters, are portrayed as having a distinctly comic dimension. This image contrasts with the much more customary emphasis on escapees' struggles and difficulties in their host environment. The "comedy" of the Rosenbaums' lives in *Pictures from an Institution* may be in the eye of the beholder whose impishly irreverent gaze mediates the Benton community to readers. We are not allowed to see it other than through his vision, including his irony, so that we are unable to assess the degree of its accuracy. The phrase "an inconsequential appendix and coda" certainly projects a much darker picture of the Rosenbaums' situation than the brightness of comedy. Perhaps the hiatus about their early years after their escape is a means of passing over any of their struggles in order to emphasize the more amusing aspects of their lives.

The Rosenbaums are pivotal figures in *Pictures from an Institution*. The structure of the work is episodic, consisting of seven sections loosely connected through the recurrence of the faculty at Benton and members of their families. The opening piece is devoted to Benton's president and his wife and son, while the concluding one, "They All Go," is about the faculty's dispersal for the summer. Of the five intermediary sections one, "Art Night," deals with a college event; the other four present various segments of the faculty. The Rosenbaums are the focus of the fourth, that is, the middle piece titled "Constance and the Rosenbaums," but they also crop up elsewhere in their interactions with others at Benton. Their centrality is indirectly underscored by the prominence of their primary critic, Gertrude Johnson, the novelist from New York, who comes for the year to replace a creative writing teacher who has proved to be unexpectedly unsatisfactory. The months between her arrival and her departure, a little less than a school year, mark the temporal span of *Pictures from an Institution*.

Gertrude's equivocal attitude toward the Rosenbaums is paradigmatic not only of the opposing opinions about them at Benton but at a deeper level also of the ambivalences intrinsic to them. The section "Constance and the Rosenbaums" begins on Gertrude in an exchange between her and the narrator who recounts her views on writing and on humankind. Thus she frames the Rosenbaums in the same way as the narrator frames Benton. " 'I can't *stand* that Gottfried Rosenbaum,' " she explodes (134). Her dislike of him is clearly rooted in her jealousy of a rival, another creative artist in residence. Threatened whenever "she met someone who was either good or clever, she looked at him in uneasy antagonism" (134). Gertrude's dream that Gottfried had come to America in a submarine is obviously comical, yet it reveals too how she envisages him as a rather sinister person. She is sorry that he is a Jew "since that made it impossible for her to say what she felt was really somehow true: that he was a Nazi, *the* Nazi" (69). Again a comic absurdity covers an instinctive rejection. Many escapees in fact encountered suspicion (and were interned) because of the populace's (and indeed the authorities') inability in the panic of an acute wartime crisis to distinguish between Nazi Germans and those Germans in flight from the Nazis. Gertrude has to content herself with condemning Gottfried's "decadent, sensual (once she said by mistake, *sexual*) Viennese chromatics" (70).

The slip of the tongue perhaps hints that Gertrude's anger at Gottfried stems from a covert attraction to him as well as from jealousy, especially as her husband is a dreary, weak vassal. This hypothesis is corroborated by Gertrude's modification of her initial negativity: "After a while Benton seemed to Gertrude a little different from other places because Dr. Rosenbaum lived there" (67). "Different" is an open word, which could mean better or worse. Gertrude's phrase suggests a certain degree of approval; Dr. Rosenbaum makes Benton more interesting than other places—in which case his residency is not "inconsequential," at least as far as the college community is concerned. Gertrude's other concession about Gottfried is equally grudging: "[H]e was the one thing at Benton that couldn't be dismissed with *of course*. Gertrude felt that nothing she said even shocked him. He behaved, pretended to behave, as if he had heard it all before, and treated her with playful good-humor" (68–9). Has he heard it all before, or is he merely pretending? The doubt is always there, the truth always elusive. But either way he is the only match at Benton for the formidable Gertrude; he takes her in his stride, whereas she for her part both resents and welcomes his presence.

A warmer response to the Rosenbaums comes from the younger people at Benton; more open-minded and not in competition with them they are receptive to the foreigners as an exciting novelty. " 'You just haven't *lived* till you've had Dr. Rosenbaum for a teacher,' " the narrator's wife hears one girl say to another (137). It is tempting to read this strong statement as a hearty endorsement of Gottfried's consequentiality to Benton and to attribute the hyperbole merely to an adolescent tendency to exaggeration. But as this tone of excessive adulation persists it becomes apparent that it amounts to an ironic undercutting of Gottfried's importance. Because of their otherness, their exoticism in this environment, the Rosenbaums are turned by the youngsters into symbols for avoiding the dull, conventional existences into which they have been socialized.

This is most apparent in the persona of Constance, whose relationship to the Rosenbaums exposes one side of their potential impact at Benton. For her the Rosenbaums are a "great find" (143). After graduating as a music major the previous spring "(at a plain old-fashioned college not a bit like Benton)" Constance had taken a job at Benton as assistant to the president's secretary as a stopgap "until she made up her mind about what she was to do" (147). At this crossroads in her life the Rosenbaums seem a revelation of a whole other world beyond the limits of women's colleges, either plain or fancy. The very "confusion and richness" of their house make Constance feel "that it was in some strange way the world: that just as there are Sea-Cucumbers and Sea-Anemones and Sea-Horses, so there was at the Rosenbaums the shadow of anything in the world" (143). The profusion of European books, paintings, photographs, scores, and manuscripts gives Constance a glimpse of wider horizons completely beyond her ken till then. At first, as she sits in their house, she can hardly believe what she sees: "everything would seem to her a dream," but then she exalts in what she considers its "reality":

> a real Russian, a real Austrian, a real opera-singer, a real composer, a woman who had really sung with Chaliapin, a man who had really been a friend of Alban Berg's—Constance could barely see the Rosenbaums past so much reality; what would she not have given to be, as they were, a part of that reality! (144)

Constance's gushing expression and her reiterated invocation of reality are clues to the ironic irreality of her perceptions. Throughout this passage and indeed throughout Constance's dealings with the Rosenbaums, the details, the asides, and above all the exaggerations are the key to such a reading. For example the observation that "Constance could barely see the Rosenbaums past so much reality" suggests that she could not truly see them at all. When she begins under their spell to learn German it is "from a paper-bound *College Outline . . .* and from Heath's *Graded Readers*" (144). She "stumbles" along "with such excitement" that she doesn't eat dinner till ten o'clock:

> Constance felt that she was learning the language almost as well as a German child does: at the end of her first year she'd be able to say a few words. But she tried to say them exactly as Dr. Rosenbaum did, and this was, if there is such a thing, a Pyrrhic defeat (144).

The concept of "a Pyrrhic defeat" through its inversion of the norm invites an extended reading otherwise which points to the ridiculousness of Constance's endeavors. The revelation of her immaturity casts an ironic light on the narrator's claim that "she was a girl ripe for the Rosenbaums"—ripe only for a kind of unintentional victimization (147). Her lack of ripeness leads to her being dazzled by the Rosenbaums' appearance of glamor. When Constance sings an aria from *Der Rosenkavalier* it is "in the voice of a soiled dumpling with dreams" (145). This deflating description aptly summarizes the shortfall between her aspirations and the reality of her accomplishments. As with her German, so with the music: "before she had known Gottfried for six weeks she had become—need I say it?—a composer of the twelve-tone school" (148). The narrator's interjected "need I say it?" conveys the inevitability and sad comedy of Constance's pathetic imitativeness. Her encounter with the Rosenbaums is the catalyst for the release of "her form of optimistic assertiveness" (148) rather than for the definitive transformation she seeks. At the end of *Pictures from an Institution* she becomes Gottfried's secretary and goes to Cape Cod with them for the summer. For her development the Rosenbaums are decidedly consequential, but more in fostering her illusions/delusions than in a lasting, positive direction.

Most of the Benton community inclines to a greater skepticism than Constance. At best Gottfried is perceived as "a nice old guy" (139). He appears to be good-natured, for instance in assenting to the requests of Benton's choreographer to write dances for her students' recitals. But in dashing off a dance in fifteen minutes he gives rein to his penchant for mischievous subversiveness:

> The rhythms of his dances made any motions that accompanied them seem timid and constrained; and he specialized in long unexpected rests during which the dancer would stand with one foot in air, waiting, while Dr. Rosenbaum looked at her with twinkling eyes. He himself liked ballet (138).

So the dances he writes with such alacrity actually undermine the effectiveness of the performances by their unsuitable rhythms and long pauses embarrassing to both dancer and audience, though obviously a source of delight to Gottfried, to judge by his "twinkling eyes." The final sentence raises the suspicion that it is precisely his own liking for ballet that prompts him to impair Benton's amateurish efforts. "He was one of the best-humored of men," the narrator assures us, "but sometimes his humor got out of gear" (170). His dances for the ballet are one such instance.

Ambiguities and contradictions of this type abound throughout *Pictures from an Institution*, growing increasingly pronounced the more we see and hear the Rosenbaums. The unreliability of the evidence through its status as hearsay greatly complicates attempts to assess their position: " 'They're an absurd couple,' " the narrator overhears a woman say. This verdict "vexes" him, but he has to admit, "of course they were: Irene occasionally and willfully, Gottfried systematically" (169). This "of course" simultaneously echoes and queries Gertrude's contention that Gottfried is the one thing at Benton that couldn't be dismissed with such a facile phrase. This of course occurs a third time when Constance concedes that "most of Gottfried seemed to be *beyond* her, of course." She then adds: "but the rest of him she understood, or didn't even need to understand" (168). What is left after the "most" that is "*beyond* her"? The chain of ideas from "absurd" to "understand" helps to explain Benton's perception of the Rosenbaums: they appear absurd because they defy understanding in their willful or systematic disregard of conventions. They are a law unto themselves, and for that very reason fascinating and attractive to some, and irritating and disturbing to others. Even Irene acknowledges in answer to Constance's question whether she understands Gottfried: " 'Understand Gottfried? I have never understood him, but then I have never needed to understand him' " (168). The narrator reaches the same conclusion:

> (A man as open as *this* must be hiding something; and something as big as Gottfried, even, could have been hiding behind something as big as Gottfried). But then—you felt just as Irene did—you did not need to understand him (169).

The intuition that Gottfried is hiding something beneath his openness is a reformulation of the pervasive suspiciousness toward him as well as a further illustration of narratorial irony, a certain teasing of readers. If Gottfried has remained an enigma to both his wife and the narrator, no wonder then that Benton (and readers) faces the same predicament.

Benton's incapacity to understand the Rosenbaums is—of course!—a direct product of their alienness in this provincial environment. Benton has apparently never experienced escapees, let alone escapee creative artists to boot, and therefore has no yardsticks by which to measure them, no way of distinguishing personal eccentricities from European norms of behavior. The most remote place and culture on Benton's horizon is New York. Thus, the narrator alleges, if the Rosenbaums had burned their house down on Midsummer Eve and told people that Austrians do this, the act would have been stored in the filing system in the Bentonians' heads under Austrian, Customs of: "[I]t was a strange thing to do, but they were strangers" (176). Now it is the turn of the Bentonians to be unmasked as absurd. Their bewilderment at the Rosenbaums' peculiarity is stressed repeatedly; they simply do not know at all what to make of them. Irene's clothes are a good example of their confused assumptions: "She dressed in no style to which faculty wives were accustomed . . . but they felt that her clothes were very foreign, very characteristic, and must have been once, to foreigners, very impressive" (139–40). Are Irene's clothes as weird to foreigners as to those at Benton? The judgment "very impressive," though likely to be taken as a compliment, opens up an aperture of doubt. The Rosenbaums cannot be extricated from ambiguity.

This ambiguity extends also to Gottfried's status in the realm of music. He is designated as "a respected and fairly ill-known composer" (140). Again ironic undercutting is quite implicit in the students' talk:

> "Is he really famous?" her roommate asked. "I never heard of him before I got here."
> "I'm pretty sure he's famous—anyway, famous in Europe," the girl replied. Then her eyes brightened and she exclaimed, in scorn at her own forgetfulness: "Of *course* he's famous! He's in the *Britannica*, in the article on Schönberg" (139).

This of course signals another irony supported by the message that he is famous not in his own right but only as a follower of Schönberg's twelve-tone system. His is thus a secondary reputation, dependent on another's innovativeness. The narrator himself harbors doubts about Gottfried's current standing. In his thoughts on lines from a poem about the call a bird gives

> *The question that he frames almost in words*
> *Is what to make of a diminished thing.*

he is forced to remain in uncertainty: "But what was the thing that had diminished? The world? Gottfried himself? I did not know" (171). Have Gottfried's fame and his compositions suffered as a result of his uprooting from his native soil, his isolation from the European cultural mainstream, which had nourished his creativity? The incongruity between Benton and Gottfried cuts both ways: just as the Bentonians cannot figure him out, he cannot thrive in a milieu that offers him no spiritual nourishment. The American provinces and the European escapee are a mismatch. Extrapolating from Gottfried's body language the narrator sees him as "saying in half-humorous, half-rueful astonishment: 'What am I doing *here*?' " (171).

The equivocation between Benton and the Rosenbaums is reciprocal. If Benton is often taken aback by them, they for their part "did not like America as well as one would have wished them to like it; they were used to different things" (179). Irene is irked by the pronunciation of her name as "I REEN" whereas she was accustomed to "i RA ne" (179). This mispronunciation strikes her as "a little mocking symbol" of Benton's inability "to perceive her aright" (179). Her rigidity is partly a product of her age, a major factor to her resistance to change. That Irene is "an old woman" (165) is mentioned several times, and although Gottfried is ten to fifteen years her junior, he too is well past middle age. Their relatively advanced age has positive and negative implications. On the one hand they do not suffer from identity problems; through their self-assurance "they had come to accept things, and themselves too, for what they were" (179). So, unlike Gertrude, they never have sleepless nights. On the other hand they lack the adaptability that enabled younger escapees to learn the language better and to adjust to altered circumstances. But apart from the capacity to adapt the Rosenbaums also lack the willingness. In her disdainful evaluation of America Irene "believes in . . . some of the most familiar clichés of European settlers in America" concerning the quality of vegetables, the disproportionate admiration for youth, and attitudes toward education (180). Gottfried, likewise, generally more polite and devious tells Constance:

> Here in your country Art and Commerce and Life are a bitter—no, a sweet pill covered all over with sex; if Moses had lived among you he would have returned to find you worshipping not a Golden Calf but a Golden Girl, and he would have engraved his commandments on her stomach (156).

But then in a manner characteristic of *Pictures from an Institution* Gottfried's ironic comments about America are undercut by a further level of irony at *his* expense. Immediately after boasting of his knowledge "on three continents for six decades," he confuses Henry James and William James, thereby disclosing that his ignorance of American culture is as great as that of the Bentonians about European culture. Gottfried's music is also the object of barbed satire:

> His first American work, a secular cantata that used "The Witch of Coös" as its text, had in it the most idiomatic writing for skeleton that I've ever heard—one *ostinato* figure, half glissando xylophones and half violinists hitting their sound-boxes with their bows, seemed to me particularly notable (135).

The mock-serious, mock-heroic tone of the music buff is capped by Gottfried's own "tremendous understament: 'I knew idt. Idt was de *bones!*' " (135). The interface of overstatement with purported understatement is as seamless—and powerful—here as that among the comic, the ironic, and the elegiac in *Pictures from an Institution*.

The ultimate caricature of the Rosenbaums' critique of America comes in Else, their cook. Contravening the narrator's overt comment that "she couldn't think of anything to say," she discourses volubly on all the wonderful foods that are not to be found in American stores and kitchens, and voices her opinion that Americans are "immoral, though childish, and drunk half the time" (141). She is the proud possessor of a leather-bound copy of Goethe's domestic verse saga, *Hermann und Dorothea*, which she had received as a confirmation gift; when she sees that no Americans own this volume she brands them "uncultivated" (141). The sheer ludicrousness of this sweeping verdict on such a narrow and idiosyncratic basis shows how escapees' prejudices can lead to fundamental misapprehensions as a result of their entrenchment in their own culture. Though exaggerated and—of course—comical Else's reactions point to the potential dangers of cultural misjudgments, particularly on the part of people of limited experience such as Else—and perhaps also many at Benton.

This example more than most others shows the dark underside of the comedy that is *Pictures from an Institution*. The humor is invariably suffused with an irony that is satirical even when it is jocular. Playing the cello, for instance, Gottfried looks as good as—no, better than—the cellist in the Budapest Quartet, high praise indeed. Yet the narrator continues:

> And he looked more like an orangutan, too. He had that animal's fixed, sorrowful, bottomless stare—though the little incidents of the score would lift his spirits immeasurably, and bring a fleeting smile to his lips, as if his keeper had just brought him a banana (168).

The same sort of ridicule is evident when the narrator visits the Rosenbaums in their home to seek advice on his translation of Rilke:

> the phonograph was playing, as usual—this time it was a piece that sounded as though it might have been called *Pages from a Dentist's Life*; there was a score

on the floor, as usual, with two teacups beside it. (The house floated on tea and
Rhine wine.) Constance kissed me, Irene and Gottfried shook my hand; like
most Europeans, they gave the impression of wanting to shake hands with the
cat whenever it came into the room—to shake hands and utter a short formal
sentence that would express their genuine pleasure at getting to see Frau Katze
again (149).

The European habit of shaking hands as a greeting is here derided through
extension to the cat.

An element of the grotesque is apparent here as in Gottfried's pronunciation,
often conveyed phonetically. But whereas in Malamud's *The German Refugee*
the difficulty of acquiring the new language assumes a tragic dimension, here
it is constantly the object of fun. The notoriously tricky "th" is his prime
stumbling block:

> He said *d* a third of the time, *t* a third of the time, and *z* a third of the time, and
> explained, smiling, that after a few years, ass zhure ass Fadt, these would merge
> into the correct sound. It is true that his *d* and *t* and *z* were changing, but not
> in the direction of any existing sound: his speech was a pilgrimage to some
> *lingua franca* of the far future—"vot ve all speak ven de Shtate hass videret
> avay," as he would have put it (13).

However Americans are equally made a laughingstock in their naive linguistic
assumptions: "didn't Adam and Eve and the snake speak to each other in
Standard American?" (175).

This debunking of Americans as well as of the Rosenbaums indicates the
complicated game that Jarrell is playing in *Pictures from an Institution*.
Nothing is immune to the corrosiveness of an irony that is at once humorous
and sardonic. This stratagem pervades every detail. For instance Gottfried
looks "remarkably funny" in his new Simca convertible "since he had bought
it a size too small" (139). The symbolism is transparent: the larger than life
composer doesn't fit into his new car any more comfortably than into his new
environment. The ramifications of the car's miniature size for passengers are
carefully elaborated too: the vehicle has space for only one passenger so that
the second has to sit on the lap of the first, holding the cat too on longer trips
as when the Rosenbaums set out for Cape Cod with Constance. The farcical
here conflates with a dogged realism in the insistence on estranging details.

Nor is *Pictures from an Institution* itself exempt from such ironic
deflation. Gertrude, who has taken the position at Benton because she is
"between novels" (14), embarks in the course of the year on a novel about
the college. The narrator, since he himself a writer, is the first to realize what
she is doing: "She listened only As Novelist" (131); later Irene astutely also
catches on: "Of *course* she is going to write a book about Benton" (152).
The writing of a book about Benton within a book about Benton introduces
a distinctive self-reflexivity as a facet of the ironic comedy of *Pictures from an
Institution*. These dual attempts to write a book about Benton emerge as
even more ironic in light of the fact that "nothing ever happened at Benton,"

as the narrator points out to Gertrude after asking her whether anything had happened to her since her arrival. No more than Benton itself is the action progressive. The narrator's (and Jarrell's) book, a set of descriptive sketches, literally "pictures," has a dearth of action in the sense of plot or character development. The stasis at Benton in part shapes the Rosenbaums' stay there as "an appendix or a coda" to their lives, devoid of dynamism and thereby echoing the college's tendency to subvert progression into retrogression.

Retrogression typifies the Rosenbaums' lives at Benton. Confined to the microcosm of the college they still, as Irene tells Constance, "at least have the memory of having had a world that respected us" (181). After all its boisterousness the section "Constance and the Rosenbaums" closes on a melancholy note: Irene "was a bow waiting, in dust and cobwebs, for someone to come along and string it; no one came, no one would ever come" (183). Compared to the artistic circles in which the Rosenbaums had moved in Prague, Dresden, Salzburg, and Vienna, Benton and its faculty represent "dust and cobwebs," an inconsequential appendix and coda to their lives. They are fortunate to have escaped, but the price of their escape is their radical diminishment in this backwater. When Gottfried asks "the Lord what land He had brought him into," he purports to be citing Mahler, but he also adds the ominous phrase that Mahler "had *also diedt from America*" (139).

Only from such comments are we able to surmise the Rosenbaums' innermost thoughts. Unlike many fictions about escapees *Pictures from an Institution* uses no indirect discourse so that we have no insight into their minds. They are focalized almost exclusively through the narrator's perceptions, and to a lesser extent those of Constance and Gertrude. The effect is a kaleidoscopic mosaic of impressions derived from their appearance, their behavior, and their utterances. They *seem* open, in the case of Irene even tactlessly outspoken at times, yet we share the narrator's sense of never fully knowing, let alone understanding them. Despite the narrator's stay in New York (for how long and when?) he is subject to most of the same limitations as the Bentonians in regard to these European eccentrics. He feels that Gottfried "must be hiding something; and something as big as Gottfried" (169) but we are left to guess what: his contempt for Benton? His alienation? His mourning for the past? Gottfried remains a mystery, a subject for speculation, a figure that elicits a mixture of fun and respect, a presence alternately irritating and welcome at this small Southern college.

Pictures from an Institution presents a predominantly comic view of escapees—perhaps the only fiction to do so. The Rosenbaums come across as eccentric and droll because the perspective is that of the host environment, which is at a loss what to make of them. In keeping with this emphasis on the comic the Holocaust is brought up only once, again a rarity in fictions on escapees. Gottfried's startling words are contextualized in the narrator's observation that "sometimes his humor was out of gear":

About the killing of six million European Jews, even, he spoke with detachment. He said to my wife and me: "I can understand killing them. We have our faults. Six million Jews are, after all, six million people." But then his face distorted itself into vivacity, and he exclaimed: "But those poor *gipsies*! What have *they* done?—told people's fortunes, stole people's cows" (170).

Gottfried's harshness is estranging; anti-Semitism in a Jew is always ugly. Although he uses the first-person plural "we," he appears, perhaps as a creative artist, to identify more with the gypsies. Yet they too have their faults (stealing cows). Gottfried's removal from his Jewish heritage leaves him even more rootless and destabilized.

In the last resort the image of the Rosenbaums is a sad one as the elegiac closing suggests. While we join the narrator and Bentonians in their amusement at their peculiarities, we realize at the same time that their isolation in this remote Southern college is just an inconsequential appendix and coda to their previous life. Materially they are comfortable enough, but intellectually and spiritually they are utterly displaced. The comic surface of *Pictures from an Institution*, through its ironic brittleness, conceals an undertow of dejection.

India

11

"Accepting—but not Accepted"

Anita Desai, *Baumgartner's Bombay* (1988)

"Accepting—but not accepted; that was the story of his life, the one thread that ran through it all. In Germany he had been dark—his darkness had marked him the Jew, *der Jude*. In India he was fair—and that marked him the *firanghi* [foreigner]. In both lands, the unacceptable" (20). Having come to India from Berlin in his late teens, fifty years later Hugo Baumgartner is still "acutely aware of his outlandishness" (20). Not only was he persecuted in Germany as a Jew; in India he is shunned as a foreigner, and also, ironically, cast not just as a German but often assumed to be a Nazi. He has to explain that he is a Jew.

Baumgartner's gloomy assessment of his situation is an accurate reflection of the historical position. Only about 1,000 escapees found refuge in India where they were definitely undesirables. The reasons for the poor reception they were given, apart from the innate suspicion of strangers, were connected to internal Indian politics. Besides being anti-Zionist the Congress Party feared that the arrival of even a small number of refugees would provoke the Muslim population. As Laqueur points out, "there was little logic in Indian attitudes" for those who came to India were not Zionists; he concludes that "whatever the reason, Jewish refugees were not wanted."[1] The suspicion of them as Germans is more understandable since India was then part of the British Empire at war with Germany. So, as *Baumgartner's Bombay* shows, the escapees were interned alongside German nationals who were in fact Nazis. The novel's fictive plot has an authentic historical backdrop in its portrayal of the rise of Nazism in Germany, the internal tensions, religious as well as political, attendant on the partition of India and Pakistan, and India's struggle to emerge as an independent nation. Desai, who was born in 1937 to an Indian father and a German mother, would have personal knowledge of recent Indian history.

Although Baumgartner's statement is made in the novel's opening chapter it is a retrospective evaluation on the basis of his lifetime's stay in India. For *Baumgartner's Bombay* is circular in shape. Its first chapter begins, as it were, after its last one, after Baumgartner has been murdered by a young German drug addict to whom he had given shelter. The circle is completed as Lotte, his German friend, contemplates in the closing paragraph the cards Baumgartner's mother had sent him between 1939 and 1941, a packet she had come upon in his room in the initial paragraph. The novel's design is ingenious, introducing readers to the exotic location at the outset, and building suspense by its foreshadowing of the plot in references to "stealing" and "murdering" (16) by young hippies. Further time shifts between the present and the past occur as Baumgartner's history is unfolded. Following the dramatic start on the post-murder scene the second chapter harks back abruptly to Baumgartner's origins in Berlin in the 1930s. The third shows his arrival in India, while the fourth centers on the war years and his internment. The fifth chapter reverts to the more immediate past as Baumgartner meets the boy and takes him home. The sixth, another return to a further past, fills in the gap between the end of the war and Baumgartner's current life, including his move to Bombay, his friendship with Lotte, and his adoption of the umpteen stray cats that swarm about his room. The enactment of the murder forms the final chapter.

The novel's overall pattern is reminiscent of the picaresque in the successive challenges that Baumgartner faces, though with one fundamental difference. He does not seek out adventures, either dragons to slay or windmills to tilt at. On the contrary he tends to passivity ("accepting"), merely trying to cope with what happens to him through the vicissitudes of historical events. His typical reaction, illustrated as he is on his way to India by boat from Venice, is "a lurch of fear," but as on later occasions he finds that "he had to accept it" (57–8). The nature of the "it" in question varies: expulsion from school, loss of home, emigration to India, internment, rejections, insults, and indignities in the pursuit of a means to support himself. In every instance Baumgartner has little or no choice; he is driven by necessity to an enforced acceptance of what befalls him.

If acceptance becomes a habit for Baumgartner not being accepted is far harder for him to take. His first experience of his differentness comes at school in Berlin at the Christmas celebration when his parents have not sent a gift for him because they did not know that they should. The teacher benignly tries to save the situation by handing him the glass globe off the top of the tree, but he won't take it as he knows it doesn't belong to him. He

> collapse[s] into the dark ditch of his shame. What was the shame? The sense that he did not belong to the picture-book world of the fir tree, the gifts and the celebration? But no one had said that. Was it just that he sensed he did not belong to the radiant, the triumphant of the world? (36)

This incident prefigures his entire future life. In Germany during the rest of his time there under the Nazi regime, as a Jew he certainly cannot belong among the Aryans' uniformed parades and other more nefarious activities.

Nor does he ever feel a belonging in India. He had at first thought of his emigration as a temporary measure; in the course of the war he comes to realize that there was "no possibility of returning, so that he would have to accept India as his permanent residence" (132). A place of "residence," even if it is "permanent," is not the same as a home. He recognizes that he is "a man without a family or a country" (133). The impossibility of a return to a Germany devastated morally as well as physically is the most difficult insight for Baumgartner to accept. Even as he takes in every morsel of information about the situation of the Jews in Germany, another part of him

> frantically built a defensive barrier against it. It was as if his mind were trying to construct a wall against history, a wall behind which he could crouch and hide, holding him to a desperate wish that Germany were still what he had known as a child and that in that dream-country his mother continued to live the life they had lived there together (118).

When he had been forced to emigrate he had imagined that his mother would join him and that they would resume their life together. Acceptance of his mother's extermination is the hardest hurdle for him. But he cannot "live, ostrich-like, under the sands of this illusion" (118), maintaining a radical, self-protective denial; he has to face the fact that "there was no return. No return. No return" (119). When Lotte or other German acquaintances lament " 'why did we not go back? We should have gone back long, long ago,' " he withholds the response " '[G]o back *where?* To what' " (211) because it was "against the rules" (211) of the escapee community to utter such thoughts. While Lotte wails, " '*[L]iebchen*, there is no home for us' " (80), Baumgartner repeatedly acknowledges "that a return to Germany was out of the question," and he feels "himself growing tense, his muscles, hands and knees all bunching together in a knot as if he were on the edge of an abyss and about to leap" (167). The abyss is one of the favorite images for the treacherous, uncharted territory into which the escapee is launched.

India is indeed an abyss that swallows Baumgartner up. For a time after the war, living in Calcutta, he manages to do reasonably well, but the growing political turmoil disrupts such connections as he has made. The rising generation, in its patriotic fervor, is ever more antagonistic to *firanghi*, foreigners. So Baumgartner is again undone by political forces totally beyond his control. In a powerful vision he perceives himself as "indigestible, inedible . . . spat out . . . Out. He had not been found fit. Shabby, dirty, white man, *firanghi*, unwanted. *Raus* [out], Baumgartner, *raus*" (190). In this kind of epiphany he makes a bridge between his rejection in Germany as a Jew and his similar fate in India as a foreigner. He had never, he concludes, "been a part of the mainstream" (211); he is the eternal outsider. He accepts this role perhaps because he has no viable alternative, just as he accepts without flinching the squalor and the vile odors in the heat in the slums, odors that are evoked with such visceral intensity in this novel:

> debris was piled everywhere—banana peels, coconut husks, ashes and cinders from the fires the householders lit in their small brick-stoves with cakes of

cowdung soaked in kerosene, a lethal substance that let out billows of choking yellow smoke. In the evenings the smoke rose to meet the mists that descended from the river and the swamps and mingled to form an impenetrable quilt that made one gasp for breath and cough (171–2).

This is surely the abyss into which Baumgartner leaps in his acceptance of India as his permanent residence. He never has a home after leaving Germany. He lives in a succession of dingy rooms in decayed houses at the end of narrow passages. His last habitat in Bombay bears the ironic name Hira Niwas, House of the Diamonds, on account of its balconies, but Baumgartner's balcony "overlooked nothing but the narrow, enclosed lane and the blank wall on the other side" (213). He has reached literally a dead-end. His ever more decrepit housing is the visible symbol of his decline. He accedes with resignation to his transformation as a manifestation of an inevitable historical process. From being a cultivator of trees (Baumgartner), a constructive occupation rooted in the soil and conducive to upright, productive growth, he becomes the Madman of the Cats, as he is known in the district. His cats, far from being domestic pets, are wild, ferocious, demanding, overwhelming, and destructive. He retains just enough pride "to remain a customer, not to slip down to being a beggar" (10) by buying tea (although he cannot afford it) at the café where he is given scraps to feed his colony of cats.

The cats are the only creatures who accept, want, and welcome him. Starting with one "cruelly maimed cat dragging its broken leg and halved tail along a gutter" (195), Baumgartner has amassed a "cat family that grew and multiplied under his roof. . . . The more crowded and messy it grew, the more comfortable Baumgartner felt in it" (196). The cats, homeless strays, unwanted like himself, are obviously a substitute family: "[N]ow there was a reason, even a need, to hurry back to the flat" (196) for some living beings await his return. The mess the cats make in his room is rather disgusting, yet also indirectly highly revealing of the pathos of Baumgartner's terminal existence. The contrast is crass between his willing acceptance of the dishevelment represented by the cats and his mother's propriety in disapproving of the hedgehog he brings home in his childhood in Berlin: " 'How can we keep that smelly thing in Berthe's [the maid's] beautifully cleaned house?' " (28). Nothing more succinctly captures the distance between his beginning in Berlin and his end in Bombay.

Baumgartner's youth in Berlin and the period of deteriorating conditions for Jews up to his departure for India are graphically portrayed in flashback in the novel's second (and most extensive) chapter. The disjunction between chapters 1 and 2 arouses readers' curiosity about the mystery of how the well-brought-up little Hugo Baumgartner of Berlin had turned into the neglected down-and-out who ends up being murdered. The focalization in the second chapter is through the eyes of the boy and then the teenager as he experiences the bewildering changes that hit him and his parents. The only child of a thoroughly assimilated family Hugo starts by recalling

> his father. When he walked, there was no obstacle, and no hesitation. He strode, he paraded—his head held high, his hat gleaming like the wing of an airborne beetle. His waistcoat gleamed too, now black, now green, like a bottle of dried ink, and the spats on his shoes were like the ears of a soft animal laid close against the leather. His walking-stick with the ivory knob tapped the Berlin streets with authority—pleasantly, lightheartedly on a Sunday afternoon, but still with authority (23).

This almost arrogant self-confidence, this mastery of his milieu forms a painful baseline to the subsequent fates of father, mother, and Baumgartner himself. The father's fervent patriotism is denoted by the "Prussian helmet ashtray" beside his favorite chair (44). In a series of episodic scenes, which open up in Baumgartner's memory, Desai sketches the catastrophic upheavals in the family's life with masterful vividness and economy. It is a well-known story, rendered poignant by its perception through a youthful, barely comprehending intelligence as well as by the contrast to the Baumgartners' initial level of physical, emotional, and spiritual comfort in their homeland. Their orderly life is disrupted and eventually destroyed as the maid has to leave, Hugo is sent to a segregated school for Jewish children, his father's furniture showroom is vandalized and the word "JUD" painted on the window, the business is confiscated, the father commits suicide, the apartment too has to be surrendered to the new German owner of the business, the mother moves into a small room, while Hugo beds down in a corner of the showroom, courtesy of Herr Pfuehl, the new German owner from Hamburg. He grasps the danger more clearly than the Baumgartners who remain in a state of denial and shock. It is Herr Pfuehl who urges Hugo to emigrate to India, and is irked at his and his mother's hesitancy, comparing them to "obstinate mice who turned up their noses at the cheese" (54).

This is one of many incisive turns of phrase that sharpen the stark chronicle of the Baumgartners' agony. "The whole flat filled with quiet like a well in which they sat drowning" (34). In lieu of direct narratorial comment Desai resorts to images, which convey their debasement and the paralysis of their willpower. A metaphoric subtext runs through the entire second chapter, particularly its first half, centered on references to sweetness. At the outset, when Hugo goes out with his father on Sundays, the medley of Strauss waltzes in the café sifted "through the sunlight like honey circulating through the hive" as the waiter brings the boy "a mug of chocolate" (24). It is as if the Baumgartners were literally ingesting the sweetness of their pre-Nazi lives. Later, in their diminishment, Hugo is reduced to sucking a stick of barley sugar on his way home from school, for "there was no dark expensive chocolate to give him instead" (39).

Another recurrent trope is that of mirrors, which give access to normally hidden or ignored sides of existence. Hugo is alarmed and mystified by the three-piece mirrors on the dressing tables in his father's furniture showroom because "they showed you unfamiliar aspects of your head, turning you into a stranger before your own eyes as you slowly rotated to find the recognisable" (26). Before Hugo's own eyes the known surface is giving way to disturbing appearances. His father's "rococo mirrors, gliding as they did upon the shining gloss of their reflections in the still water" silence Hugo "by the knowledge of their transience" (46). Subsequently Baumgartner will characterize India as "revealing the world that lay on the other side of the mirror," flashing "in your face, with a brightness and laughter as raucous as a street band" (85). The mirror functions as the symbol for Baumgartner's progressive alienation from his once familiar world, an alienation that reaches its climax in India.

An even more striking and still more oblique means of conveying the boy's mood during those darkening days in Berlin comes in the intercalation of snippets of common German nursery rhymes and songs. Since they are not translated their significance is likely to be lost on English-speaking readers. Often they form a seemingly naive but actually sinister gloss on the narrative. For instance in the early phase when the father plays with the child he sings a song about a horse, "Hopp, hopp, hopp" that contains the warning "Aber brich dir nicht die Beine!" (25; but don't break your legs!). The folk song about a bird that brings a greeting from mother ends with the child's inability to go along back to its mother; it has to stay where it is. This clearly foreshadows Baumgartner's situation in India where for a time he receives messages from his mother but remains separated from her. Hugo shivers as he recognizes that something is amiss: "the sweetness always ended in a quaver" (28). The popular ditty, "O du lieber Augustin" has as its refrain "alles ist hin!" (32; everything's gone) as it tells of the loss of Augustin's bag and money, and his end lying in the mud. All the songs cited contain threats, generally open, of the ills that may befall a child without its behavior being especially risky. The songs therefore suggest the dangers lurking for Hugo.

They also add a mythical dimension in their allusions to the German culture in which the Baumgartners are so deeply embedded. They accept it wholeheartedly without realizing how little they themselves are accepted. When Hugo's mother has to move out of the family's apartment into a small room, one of the few possessions she takes with her are "her volumes of Goethe" (57). As she begins to contemplate the possibility of her son's emigration to India, she sings "Kennst du das Land / wo die Zitronen blühen?" (47; Do you know the land where the lemons flower?), the famous expression of nostalgia from Goethe's *Wilhelm Meister*, although here it is an inverted nostalgia, the longing to stay at home. The Baumgartners' cultural frame of reference is always pronouncedly German. In India Baumgartner envisages the impossibility of a return as his being in a state of "*Nacht und Nebel*" (119; Night and Fog), the scenario for an episode in Goethe's *Faust*. Desai assumes a reader steeped in German culture, able to pick up these multiple references. Some are obvious, such as Baumgartner's longing for German food: herrings, rollmops, and gherkins, *Wienerschnitzel, Leberknödel, Kartoffelpuffer* (118). Similarly when he sees and hears a young German missionary in the internment cap playing "Backe, backe Kuchen" (Pat a cake) with her small children it seems to him "that Deutschland, the *Heimat* [home] was alive here, on this dusty soil, in the incredible sun" (127).

It is this attachment to German culture that ultimately proves as lethal to Baumgartner as it had been to his parents. They had died on account of their unwillingness to accept their otherness and to leave their home; he is murdered as a result of his need to reconnect with Germany. When the young hippie comes into the café where Baumgartner normally collects scraps for his cats, he speaks to him "unconsciously, without forethought, in German" (141). He immediately recognizes him as "a fair Aryan German," and his rational part "wanted nothing to do with him" (141):

> That fair hair, that peeled flesh and the flash on his wrist—it was certainly a type Baumgartner had escaped, forgotten. Then why had this boy come after him, in lederhosen, in marching boots, striding over the mountains to the sound of the *Wandervogels Lied*? The *Lieder* and the campfire. The campfire and the beer. The beer and the yodelling. The yodelling and the marching. The marching and the shooting. The shooting and the killing. The killing and the killing and the killing (21).

Baumgartner's love/hate relationship, the attraction of the deepest core of his being to things German makes him overcome this revulsion as he tells himself that the boy was "not so different from a sick cat" (142). Extending his pity for sick cats to the boy is his undoing. In the boy, the ruthless, intoxicated, irresponsible German, Baumgartner meets the extinction he had escaped through his flight from Germany. In this ironical twist to the plot his fate is fulfilled.

Baumgartner's conflicted feelings toward his native land combine with his continuing alienation in his host country to impede the development of his identity. As a child he had always felt himself simply to be a German, but this option is taken from him. He had never been given any consciousness of his Jewishness, let alone any Hebrew education. When he is forcibly transferred to a Jewish school he is completely bewildered and repelled by what he sees and hears. The school is shown through his perceptions in a negative, repugnant light. It is situated in

> a warehouse with no windows or lights, only a mass of squirming, frantic children and a teacher who had a face like curdled milk in a pan and was called Reb Benjamin; Hugo recoiled from the grease-lined collar and patched and odorous jacket; strange, large volumes lay open on his desk from which he read in a harsh and melodramatic tone in a language Hugo had never heard before (37).

Hogo's reactions are those of a thoroughly German child who is suddenly thrust into an environment wholly unknown and repulsive to him. To be Jewish is never envisaged in *Baumgartner's Bombay* as a matter of religious belief; much rather it is an ethnic or racial category. Robbed of his secular beliefs in propriety, order, and cleanliness, beliefs innate to German culture, Baumgartner finds no replacement beyond surviving and tolerating whatever situation he is placed in.

In Venice on his way to India his attitude toward Jewishness does undergo a change, at least temporarily. In a café he gets into a conversation with a young woman who is reading a Hebrew newspaper. He learns that she is a painter who has a studio in the Jewish quarter. She presents, of course, a far more attractive image of Judaism than the school had done so that Hugo (who has to wait a few days for his boat) goes in search of her in the Jewish quarter:

> Jews. Strange, in Germany he had never wanted to search them out, had been aware of others thinking of him as a Jew but not done so himself. In ejecting him, Germany had taught him to regard himself as one. Perhaps it was important to find what she had called their "quarter." Perhaps over here he would find for himself a new identity, one that suited him, one that he enjoyed (62–3).

But this is no more than a passing, youthful fantasy, inspired by a comely young woman.

In India being Jewish has quite a different connotation; it serves primarily as a means of distinguishing Nazis from other Germans. When he is interned Baumgartner is subjected to sharp interrogation because his passport designates him as "German, born in Germany" (105). His efforts to mumble something about his Jewishness, about being German " 'but of Jewish origin, therefore a refugee' " (105) are ignored. The internees complain that their guards " 'don't understand a thing . . . They don't even know that there are German Jews and there are Nazi Germans, and they are not exactly the same' " (107).[2] Eventually the Jews in the camp are separated from the Nazis, and excluded from the morning assembly and most other duties as the Nazis run the camp for and with the British. The Nazis express their willingness to have the Jews do the menial work for them, but this the Jews decline.

Only once more does the question of Jewishness come up in *Baumgartner's Bombay* when Baumgartner meets Sushil, an Indian clerk who lives in the same house as he in Calcutta. Sushil is violently anti-British, has been imprisoned for his part in a bombing attack, and has in prison read Marx, Trotsky, and Lenin.

> The day he discovered that Baumgartner was a German, he lit up with admiration as if in the presence of a war hero. "But a Jew, a Jew, not a Nazi," Baumgartner tried to deflect his misplaced ardour but this meant nothing to Sushil who had renounced religion for politics and had no interest in Judaism; nor would he entertain any criticism of the German regime (177).

This tragicomic encounter is an ironic footnote to Baumgartner's sporadic attempts to fashion an identity. In the end he is simply the Madman of the Cats, an apposite but demeaning identification.

Among the foreigners in Calcutta, where he lives in reasonable prosperity for a while after the war, and later in Bombay no mention is made of their Jewishness. Mostly episodic figures who flit in and out of the narrative they are not endowed with in-depth personal histories. They form a segment of the host of characters who cross Baumgartner's path occasionally but, with one exception, play no significant part in his emotional life. Julius Roth, whom Baumgartner meets in the internment camp, is probably a Jew, judging by his name, but as for Baumgartner this circumstance appears to be of no importance to him. Trading in anything and everything he rises to considerable affluence, although later he too falls onto bad times. Other Germans may have stayed in India because they had been Nazis and were afraid to go back after the war. Baumgartner has no congenial subcommunity to turn to. This may be due partly to the small number (1,000) of escapees in that huge land. However it could also be interpreted as a consequence of his character; as a result of the rejection he had suffered in Germany he becomes a loner, distrustful of others, and averse to relationships lest they may lead to further hurt. After his experience of communal living in the internment camp, he becomes more inclined to solitude than ever, not caring to seek out Europeans when he moves to Bombay. Cats are safer companions.

The sole exception is Baumgartner's friendship with Lotte. She had long ago come to India as an exotic nightclub dancer, but by now she is so far beyond her best as to verge on a caricature of her former glamor. Although heavy, with thick, purple-veined legs, she teeters about on high-heeled red shoes, which make her wobble as if she were drunk. It is their common German background that draws Lotte and Baumgartner together as they reminisce and share their miseries with each other, freely interweaving German words and phrases into their conversations. Baumgartner's association with Lotte, despite his reservations, is yet another expression of his lasting devotion to his German origins. However it also has a further dimension insofar as she too partakes of his uprootedness: "[H]e saw Lotte not because she was from Germany but because she belonged to the India of his own experience; hers was different in many ways but they still shared enough to be comfortable with each other" (150). He disapproves of her hair, dyed a livid, foxy red, of her gin drinking, and "her disreputable ways." "But," he reflects, "what did it matter—she spoke German, had his language, *nicht wahr?*" (66). He enjoys "spending a little time with Lotte, perhaps drinking a cup of coffee with her, listening to a little German, however foul her accent, coarse her expression and jarring her voice" (66). He is closer to Lotte than to any other human being so that it is fitting that it is she who takes possession of the package of his mother's messages after his death. To some extent she is a grotesque substitute mother to Baumgartner. Nevertheless his friendship with a superannuated nightclub dancer with a dubious past is another sign of his degradation, measured against the staid, bourgeois standards in which he had been raised. He fully realizes "the absurdity" of his keeping company with a woman who would have been considered "disgraceful" (65) in his parents' circle in Berlin. It would have been "unthinkable" (65), yet it is a fact he is now prepared to accept. It also foreshadows his acceptance of the boy, again in contravention of his revulsion. Like Lotte he is German, and this remains a persistent magnet for Baumgartner.

His intimate rapport to the German language, a major factor in his link to both Lotte and the boy, has a negative effect on his dealings with other people. At first on his arrival in India, contacting the man to whom Herr Pfuehl had recommended him, he tries out "his new and hesitant English . . . dragging it off his tongue with a reluctance bordering on paralysis" (86). Although he is young and should therefore learn fairly easily Baumgartner appears to have a scant gift for language acquisition. In any case India presents peculiar linguistic problems:

> He found he had to build a new language to suit these new conditions—German no longer sufficed, and English was elusive. Languages sprouted round him like tropical foliage and he picked words from it without knowing if they were English or Hindi or Bengali—they were simply words he needed: *chai, khana, baraf, lao, jaldi, joota, chota peg, pani, kamra, soda, garee.* . . . what was this language he was wrestling out of the air, wrenching around to his own purposes? (92)

It is not a matter just of mastering a new language but of negotiating among a multitude of idioms and dialects as if he were making his way through a tropical jungle. This linguistic perplexity greatly intensifies Baumgartner's sense of remaining a confused outsider in India. His linguistic exclusion is a symbol of his existential status as a nomad.

The language problem offers another instance of Baumgartner's proclivity to acceptance, as does his shrinking from cogitating on the reasons for the bizarre shape his life has taken. His is not a reflective character nor an active one. He tends always to accede and to buckle under with a passivity that suggests a mixture of fatalism and depression: "[D]efeat was heaped on him, whether he deserved it or not" (135). His submissiveness may well be an acquired trait inculcated into him by events in Berlin such as his enforced transfer to a Jewish school and the necessity of acquiescing in Herr Pfuehl's plans for his emigration. By the time he reaches Venice he has already learnt to accommodate to inevitabilities. His boat, he is told brusquely by the clerk at the shipping company office, has been delayed for at least a week. Though frightened by this setback, "he had to accept it" (58). He reacts by addressing "the most urgent and immediate problem" (58), that of stretching his scant money to cover this unforeseen week. He solves this problem by sharing a bedroom in a cheap lodging house with a medical student who is out all night and claims the bed in the morning. This experience teaches Baumgartner a lesson that will be his guiding principle throughout his life: to deal with the most pressing difficulty without looking either too far forward—or back.

So he keeps the fact of the Holocaust pretty well buried in the back of his mind most of the time while coping with the exigencies of his day-to-day life.

After 1941 the cursory, occasional messages from his mother cease abruptly. She had refused to go to India with him, not taking seriously the admittedly "clumsy" and "crude" picture he had tried to paint of "their new beginnings in the East . . . all tigers and palm-trees and sunsets" (55). She had been quite interested to hear friends talk about the work of Tagore, but why, she asks her son, " 'should your mother read a *bengalische* poet' " when she has her Goethe (56). In a "half-jocular, half-petulant manner," she challenges Hugo how he will protect her from the snakes and tigers when she is frightened even of little German mice. " 'We are not talking of little German *mice*, you know,' " he responds with unusual acerbity (56). It is a mixture of fear and Germanophilia that holds her back from the decision to emigrate and so condemns her to death.

On Baumgartner's side it is a matter of survivor guilt, that is, guilt at having been unable to persuade his mother to come with him. While still in the internment camp the fears he has about her and "about what was happening in Germany . . . become a dark monstrous block" in his mind (109). This block turns into a roadblock in his life; it fosters his withdrawal, his self-containment, his passive acceptance of everything except perhaps the one fundamental fact of his failure to save his mother. He has been traumatized into a belief in his own powerlessness to direct his life in any way. Desai shows the utmost discretion in her handling of the Holocaust, yet at the same time she succeeds in evoking the potency of its impact on this escapee. In a striking image the incursion of the German boy is likened to "picking open a scab long formed, revealing the rawness, the ugliness underneath" (151–2). *Baumgartner's Bombay* is such a painful novel because it depicts the rawness and ugliness of the Indian slums and beyond this surface it is infused with the rawness and ugliness of the Holocaust. It opens the wound beneath the scab.

The sense of doom that hangs over *Baumgartner's Bombay* emanates largely from the covert presence of the Holocaust, the cause of Baumgartner's residence in India. But it is also a product of the novel's adroit design, which allows readers to learn in the opening chapter of Baumgartner's death by murder. He thus appears from the outset as just as doomed as his parents. Many details in the plot foreshadow its conclusion. For instance both Lotte and Baumgartner live in constant fear of murder by thieves; she has solid gold bangles given to her by a rich former lover, and he has on display the trophies won by a horse he co-owned in the days of his prosperity in Calcutta. The "long thin kitchen knife" (218) he uses to prepare his cats' food will be the murder weapon.

Baumgartner's Bombay is perhaps the bleakest among the fictions about escapees. The possibilities for being accepted are scant in a country as remote and culturally different from Europe as India. Despite Baumgartner's youth on his arrival he is never able to gain a firm foothold. The ingrained hostility at that time of many Indians to Germans, indeed to all foreigners, forecloses any chance he might have had to settle into a stable situation. India's internal strife is brought out by another enforced move, parallel to Baumgartner's, that of Habibullah and his family; the only natives open to working with him in Calcutta; they in turn become outcasts who have to flee because they are Muslims. The unpropitious conditions in the host country, the medley of languages, the fundamental alienness: all these factors combine to prevent Baumgartner's adaptation to his new environment. In contrast to his family's assimilation in Germany he remains forever a lonely, increasingly eccentric stranger in India.

Baumgartner's progressive decompensation during his years in India bears all the negative effects of migration enumerated by the Grinbergs in their *Psychoanalytic Perspectives on Migration* (1989):

> Migration is a change; but it is a change of such magnitude that it not only puts one's identity on the line but puts it at risk. One experiences a wholesale loss of one's most meaningful and valuable objects: people, things, places, language, culture, customs, climate, sometimes profession or economic/social milieu. To all these memories and deep affections are attached. Not only does the emigrant lose his attachments to these objects, but he is in danger of losing part of his self as well (26).

These multilayered losses and deprivations lead to the "ego impoverishment" (Grinbergs, 88) that characterizes Baumgartner.

At the close Lotte spreads out on her table and orders all the affectionate cards from Baumgartner's mother, each stamped with the number J673/1, "[A]s if they provided her with clues to a puzzle, a meaning to the meaninglessness" (218). That is the final phrase of *Baumgartner's Bombay*, and since there are patently no clues to the puzzle it serves only to underscore the meaninglessness of what has happened. The imperative of acceptance without the possibility of comprehension is Baumgartner's—and Lotte's—dismal destiny.

12

The "Hanger-On"

Ruth Prawer Jhabvala,
"An Indian Citizen" (1968)

" 'Most of my friends are Indians,' " Dr. Ernst proudly tells Lily, his English neighbor (151). He himself is the titular Indian citizen of Jhabvala's story, while Lily has lived there a mere three years. In her thirties, she is outspokenly soured, negligent of her appearance and even her hygiene. She had come to the country to follow a young Indian she had met in London who had promised her marriage. Nothing had come of this or of the succeeding relationships so that she is very disillusioned. Her cynicism seems to motivate her mocking negation of Dr. Ernst's claim to many Indian friends. As he lists a few she interrupts him: " 'You call those friends? Why, you're just their'— she shrugged and said in her careless, rude, English way—'their hanger—on' " (152).

Which of them is right? That is the question animating this twenty-two-page story in Jhabvala's second collection, *A Stronger Climate* (1968). All its nine stories are set in India where Jhabvala lived from 1951 to 1975; they are divided into two sections, "Seekers" and "Sufferers," which comprise six and three stories, respectively. "An Indian Citizen" is the first among the "Sufferers." Neither the location nor the year of the action is given, but Bombay is mentioned as one of the places where Dr. Ernst has lived (or currently lives?). The scene is certainly a major city with government offices. The time can be deduced as the early 1960s from Dr. Ernst's reference to his start on his "enforced travels almost thirty years ago" (148). He is an escapee from Vienna, which he likely left in the late 1930s. The internal time, however, is well defined, spanning from the morning when he leaves his room just as the office employees set out for work to the mid-afternoon heat when he takes a nap. During those hours he looks in on Lily, calls on Mrs. Chawla, has lunch in a coffee bar, and finally visits another friend, Maiska. The story is thus episodic, consisting of the picaresque series of stations in Dr. Ernst's day. Taken together his experiences lead to an answer to his initial disagreement with Lily.

Dr. Ernst is presented from both the outside through the narrator's eyes and from within his mind in his reactions and thoughts. Yet in some respects he remains curiously unknown. For instance is Ernst his first or his last name? Probably the former since most of the foreign characters have only a first name (e.g., Lily, Maiska, Herman) as though they lacked a complete identity, while the Indian one (Mrs. Chawla) has only a last name to suggest her lofty position. Yet he is dignified by his title, "Dr.," a mark of social status so important in Central Europe. Ernst, meaning "earnest" or "serious" in German, is a fitting name for him and for his attitude to life.

We first encounter him in a narratorial description of his appearance and deportment. The opening word of the story is "neat": "Neat in his person," and as if to emphasize this cardinal trait, the word is immediately repeated in "just as neat as the room he left behind him" (145). With his panama hat, "worn as much for decorum and decoration as to shield him against the sun" (146) he makes the impression of being a dapper figure. Unlike Baumgartner in Desai's novel he has lost none of his pride in his appearance and with it his self-respect. Raising his hat "in a greeting that was courtly but at the same time unobtrusive" (146) he makes the impression of being rather prim and proper, intent on observing social formalities and being agreeable. Yet in contradiction to this seeming bourgeois solidity we also learn that he is engaged in an elaborate pretense since he is actually unemployed, having lost his temporary job at the Ministry of Information to "a genuine Indian subject" (146). So the basic issue in this story of Dr. Ernst's acceptance by and acceptability to his host country is raised indirectly in the first couple of pages. Although he acknowledges that he has been rejected for government employment he still believes he has many Indian friends, and one of his reasons for going out every morning is to keep up the "contacts" (153), which will, he hopes, enable him to find a position. Also going out regularly, as if he were employed, makes him feel better, "not left out of anything but part of a busy world" (145–6). He aspires to be integrated into the modern India he admires even more than to acquire a regular income. For his lack of function makes him an outsider. The issue of his employment/unemployment is symbolical of his belonging/not belonging. So is his having acquired Indian citizenship. While to Lumbik in "A Birthday in London" (1963) to become British is a measure of security, to Dr. Ernst citizenship is a declaration of allegiance, "an act which marked one of the most significant steps in the break with the old 'Heimat' [home] as well as in coming to terms with the new situation."[1] But for Dr. Ernst, as the story reveals, it has not worked out in this way.

From little fragments of information scattered throughout the story Dr. Ernst's personal history can gradually be pieced together. He is sixty and single because he has never found a partner who met his one condition, namely, that she should be "a paragon" (150). This stipulation of perfection suggests that he is, beneath his show of courtesy, quite arrogant and unrealistic. On the surface "mild and friendly" (152) at heart he is "fastidious" (149) and somewhat snobbish. How he had landed in India is not explained. He had been a student of philology in Vienna, had embarked "on his enforced travels, almost thirty years ago" (148), had suffered "hardships" (149) in a life "full of setbacks" (153), and had been in Amsterdam, Beirut, and Bombay. Now he imagines that his friends will refer to him those who want to learn German, French, or Latin; "(he was willing to teach anything, even Viennese, he often joked)" (154). The thin joke conceals a certain desperation. Despite his problematic situation he voices his sense of gratitude to his host country: "Indians had always been kind to him, and he owed them so much: a place to live, a nationality, friendship, respect—all this they had given him" (151).

On this question of belonging to India Dr. Ernst clashes headlong with Lily. His visit to her is not of his own volition; as he is about to leave the house she calls out to him and asks him to inform her supervisor at All India Radio that she is too sick to work that day. The fact that she is employed whereas he is not creates a fundamental tension between them. The disparity is aggravated by the contrast between his neatness and her bedraggled state: "Lily sagged on her couch in a crumpled flowered wrap, her face too white and a bit puffy, and her hair a tangled, clotted nest" (148). Dr. Ernst is disgusted by the smudge of lipstick on the rim of the coffee cup handed to him by her servant. The sordid messiness of her room makes him feel uncomfortable, and he disapproves of her unwillingness to work. But it is in their views of the relationships of Indians to outsiders that they disagree most violently. Lily asserts with all the passion characteristic of her nature that they " 'hate and *despise* us' " (151), an accusation that Dr. Ernst rejects with almost equal vehemence. Their encounter comes to a head with his affirmation that most of his friends are Indians, and her verdict that to them he is no more than "their hanger-on." So Dr. Ernst's first visit of the day opens up the central issue in "An Indian Citizen."

After this grating start to his day he decides to call on one of his "many, many good [Indian] friends . . . whose doors were always open to him and who would be delighted to see him any time he cared to call" (156). This statement sounds like a citation from one of those friends, but is it really intended to be taken literally, or is it just a conventional formula of polite social ritual? Dr. Ernst's discomfiting visit to Mrs. Chawla supports the latter interpretation, and thereby projects the possibility that he is altogether misreading the signals customary in this country because he simply doesn't understand its conventions and practices.

Dr. Ernst's innocence—or ignorance—becomes quite evident in his call on Mrs. Chawla. Like the story's opening this incident is focalized through both the narrator's and the central protagonist's perceptions. Paralleling the omniscient narrator's statement "neat in his appearance" (145) is the initial declaration to this episode: "Mrs. Chawla was not in a very good mood" (156). Disappointed that her singing master had once again not shown up, she had "retired in a huff to her bedroom" (156) to do her yoga exercises. As she returns to the drawing room the viewpoint switches to that of Dr. Ernst. It would not take great sensitivity on his part to grasp the situation. Her "stiff and uncordial" smile makes his heart sink for, as we learn in an apparently casual parenthesis, "he had often been an unwelcome visitor" (157). Furthermore "he had learned long ago that the trouble with dropping in on people was that, unless they were as pleased to see him as he was to visit them, the atmosphere tended to be strained" (157). His previous experiences thus seem to refute his earlier confident assertion that doors were always open to him. It now begins to seem as if he were not just unfamiliar with Indian ways but inclined to self-deception too. Although he does his best to be charming, kissing Mrs. Chawla's hand in the Viennese manner, a greeting that usually flattered her, today she responds ungraciously, withdrawing her hand quickly and wiping it on her sari. Things go from bad to worse; at first "sulky and bored" (157), she grows "quite snappish" as she inveighs against foreign imperialists who had sought to rob India of its cultural heritage. She puts Dr. Ernst among them, and doesn't listen when he tries to make clear that he is on her side. He hopes in vain "for some reassurance that she accepted his allegiance" (158). Such "acceptance of allegiance" to India is his central aim, and here it is shown to be complicated by the country's troubled political history, which had resulted in prejudice against Europeans and so forms another factor in Dr. Ernst's difficulties. His discomfort in Mrs. Chawla's drawing room is summarized in his dislike of sitting on a floor-level seat, shifting from one leg to another, whereas she is "perfectly at ease, leaning with her elbow on the bolster behind her, one hip pushed out, and her large legs folded effortlessly beneath her" (158). The physical position stands for and encompasses the emotional tension to express the gulf between the new Indian citizen and the native born.

The motif of sitting forms a continuity when the singing master, a young man with curly hair and a fine pair of shoulders, finally arrives. He is, of course, adept at sitting on the floor so that he and Mrs. Chawla are "grouped like lovers" (160). "Passive" and "yawning" in Dr. Ernst's company she is energized by the young man's presence: "all that inert mass throbbed with animation, and her sleepy eyes opened wide" (159). In the singing lesson the two Indians are literally in harmony, while Dr. Ernst is more than ever the outsider. His shout of " 'Encore!' just as if he were at the opera is Vienna" (160) is barely heeded, and when he once more interjects a compliment he is bluntly rebuffed: " '[I]t is very difficult for me to concentrate on my singing when others are there to create a disturbance' " (161). This brusque dismissal makes Dr. Ernst realize that "it was time to go" (160) but not to acknowledge that he has been cherishing illusions. He was "foolish," he tells himself, "to feel hurt or slighted . . . It was kind enough of her to let him stay as long as she did. She was his good friend and esteemed and liked him as much as he did her" (161). With these thoughts he insists on denying the evidence staring him in the face.

Since he has not been lucky enough this morning, as on some other days, to have been offered lunch, he stops next at a coffee bar. Although he knows the menu by heart and it is on a very dirty sheet of paper despite its cellophane cover, he reads it carefully because he remembers that studying the menu is part of restaurant going. This is the only point in "An Indian Citizen" when Dr. Ernst draws on his memories of his childhood in Vienna. He recalls his parents "leaving their comfortable home and dressing up in going-out clothes, all of them on special behaviour, ready for an evening of elegance and entertainment" (161–2). The comedown from that former, European style of restaurant going and his current one is sharp. The place is "somewhat shabby" (162) but its patrons, students or recent graduates indulgently looked after by rich parents, are flashily dressed. The jukebox blares out last year's American hit-tunes, loud, shrill, and tinny. Yet Dr. Ernst likes being there, even though he sits alone in a corner, just watching the other customers. Maybe he enjoys being anonymously among young people. He notices "how well they fitted in with everything . . . it all, all belonged to them, and they to it" (163). Their fitting in prompts the reflection that "he and Lily and Maiska and Herman and the rest of them would remain only pale, stray strangers" (163).

As Dr. Ernst begins to touch on the truth, "a great oppression took hold of him" (163). But maintaining his customary habit of keeping his head in the sand he ascribes the "ridiculous sensation" (163) to the noise and the smoke, and prepares to leave. In a reversal of the usual order the coffee bar scene is first presented through Dr. Ernst's perceptions, and only at the end does the narratorial voice supervene. As he reaches the door a party of youths in trendy clothes and expensive boots comes surging in, rudely pushing him aside and ignoring his repeated pleas " 'Excuse me, excuse me please' " as he raises his panama hat (163–4). The subtext of this incident is unmistakable: an elderly European, however strong his allegiance to India, does not fit into this environment.

Dr. Ernst does fit in at the last place he visits that day. Significantly he had thought of going there right after his altercation with Lily, but he had opted to go to Mrs. Chawla instead. The reasons for his decision are pretty transparent. By going to Mrs. Chawla he is trying to implement his belief that he has many good Indian friends whose doors are always open to him. He resists his spontaneous choice to go to Maiska's, a middle-aged European woman, who had been married to a Bengali and who teaches languages at the university. Dr. Ernst visualizes her as "plain, dowdy, yet with a charm born of good nature and sympathy which made her the centre of a whole group of friends" (154). Without hesitation he deems hers "the nicest place to go" (154), and his steps are already turned in that direction when he is stung by Lily's condemnation of him as a "hanger-on" and resolves to visit one of his Indian friends to disprove her accusation. It becomes "a matter of pride" (155) precisely not to go to Maiska's that day, a kind of test to call on Mrs. Chawla instead.

But finally he pockets his pride and makes his way to Maiska's, where he "had spent some of his best hours" for "she really knew how to make one feel at home" (155). Usually a few "members of that band of lonely displaced Europeans" (155) gravitated there, drinking "good, strong, European coffee" and eating such delicacies as potato salad and cheese-cake. As in Jhabvala's slightly earlier story, "A Birthday in London," the escapees congregate in a subcommunity, which continues within the host country to uphold the habits of their native lands. So the music played at Maiska's is Beethoven,

Brahms, Bach, and Mozart, and New Year's Eve is celebrated with sandwiches and beer and the Ode to Joy from Beethoven's Ninth Symphony. In the afternoon heat Dr. Ernst sinks into one of the comfortable armchairs in a room where the curtains are drawn so that everything is shrouded in a soothing dusk. The relaxation in his posture conveys his ease at Maiska's as against his discomfort perched on Lily's disintegrating hassock and his even greater awkwardness squatting on Mrs. Chawla's floor-level seating. Indeed the release from the strains generated by his other encounters that day results in his falling asleep.

The sequence of Dr. Ernst's visits structures "An Indian Citizen" in a picaresque format. Jhabvala makes effective use of such literary devices as contrast and symbolic details to expose the rupture between European and Indian culture. The dichotomy is tellingly exemplified in the recurrent references to the variety of seating arrangements just discussed. Seating plays an important role in the congruity between Mrs. Chawla and her singing teacher when they both settle in Indian style, which Dr. Ernst has not mastered. His status as an outsider is literally embodied in the failure of his ability to accommodate to this local habit.

But the contrasts are by no means always clear-cut so that "An Indian Citizen" proves more complex than it may at first appear. Among both Indians and Europeans the spectrum is as wide as between them; the story does not fall into a simple schematicism. Lily is the foremost instance of a European who cuts across the stereotypes insofar as she seems in many ways to have gone lower-class native. On the other hand the young Indian "intellectual ladies" (145) whom Dr. Ernst watches with admiration on their way to their offices every morning have a stylish elegance. One of them in particular catches his eye—Miss Jaya "walking slim and upright in a green patterned sari, her hair balanced on her head in a shining coil" (146). She represents to Dr. Ernst "the pride of modern India" (145). The discrepancy between her and Lily is underscored by the fact that Miss Jaya is briskly on her way to work, perfectly turned out, while Lily is taking unwarranted time off to laze around, unwashed and unkempt. This crass distinction at the opening of the story forestalls any facile generalizations about the differences between Indians and Europeans. The total picture is quite subtly shaded to show the tensions that arise from divergences in the respective codes of behavior on both sides as well as infractions of them.

Those codes are imbricated in the profusion of symbolic details throughout "An Indian Citizen" as in Jhabvala's novel *In Search of Love and Beauty* (1983). Interiors are especially important in conjuring up at once an external and internal landscape, as illustrated in the juxtaposition of Lily's and Dr. Ernst's rooms. They live in the same building in rooms identical in construction and with the same standard government furnishings, but their places could hardly be more different. Lily's is as repellent as her body because everything is filthy. She has smothered the basic furniture in "curtains, cushions, rugs, hangings, masks, prints—all oriental, all folk-art, and all very dirty" (145). This welter of artifacts is suggestive of Lily's character in a number of ways. She has, according to the narrator, "vivid taste" (147), which could be interpreted as a streak of flamboyance that goes hand-in-hand with her slovenliness. The softness of many of her possessions (curtains, cushions, rugs, hangings) evokes the desire to make a cozy nest in which to bask. Their movable, makeshift nature is typical of those in the early stages of a major displacement before resettlement into homes with more solid, permanent furniture.[2] Lily's room is an idiosyncratic retreat from adult obligations into a private world of fantasy.

Dr. Ernst's room is in its neatness and cleanliness the utter antithesis to Lily's, but it, too, is an oblique means of characterization. He scrubs it every morning with a bucket and soapsuds and a brush, and during the dust storms in summer carefully wipes the yellow duster over everything four or five times a day. Not that there is much to dust, for he has added few things to the minimal necessities already there: a photograph of his parents in an oval frame, a thirty-year-old alarm clock that still keeps excellent time, and two wooden bears from Switzerland that are meant to serve as bookends. Whereas Lily's untidy assortment of folk-art is "all oriental," Dr. Ernst's scant objects are exclusively from his European past. The clock's age coincides with the beginning of his enforced travels, the photograph is the only vestige of his family, and the bears, from a German-speaking part of the world, are perhaps a reminder of the books he used to own as a student of philology. The sparseness of his belongings supports the conjecture that the room is merely a temporary abode. He feels fortunate to have got it in an apartment block occupied mainly by middle-rank officials from the Ministry of Education. It probably dates from his own short stint at the Ministry of Information. Why he doesn't furnish it more could be due to a number of reasons. Its bareness may stem from a lack of funds, or be a reflection of his neat but limited personality, or a reluctance to encumber himself after many years of wandering, or alternatively an expression of his hope of moving to something larger and better if he finds employment. Whatever the grounds for its austerity Dr. Ernst's room projects transitoriness, an unsettled existence at odds with the commitment implied by his assumption of Indian citizenship.

Mrs. Chawla's and Maiska's homes form another contrasting pair. Mrs. Chawla's drawing room testifies to her rootedness in the indigenous tradition:

> it was full of wonderful artistic pieces such as a huge carved chest (once a village dowry chest but nowadays very fashionable in place of a sideboard), a heavy brass tray from Kashmir used as a coffee-table, a delightful old-fashioned urn and bowl made of copper, and a silver rose-water sprinkler. Sticks of incense smouldering from incense-holders gave a richly Indian smell and atmosphere to the room (157).

The luxurious quality and traditional nature of these furnishings place Mrs. Chawla socially, culturally, and economically. Maiska's position at the intersection of the Indian and the European is also conveyed by her home.

She lives near the university in a rather shabby, crowded area, "in a house equally shabby and crowded, with dirty stairs and chocked drains" (154). These sordid aspects of Indian cities are set off against the pleasant interior. Here too Indian elements are present in the cheap Indian handloom materials, reminiscent of Lily's room, although without the excess (or the dirt). Maiska is likewise somewhat untidy, with records scattered over the floor near the still open and humming record player and ashtrays full of stubs. But the records are of European classical music, the pictures on the walls are good, and so are the books in the bookcases. Once inside this flat the "total effect was completely, cosily European" (155).

These interiors also reveal Jhabvala's skill in manipulating viewpoint. Only the description of Dr. Ernst's room emanates from the narrator. The other three places are perceived through his eyes on his visits without narratorial comment. Combined with the constant recourse to symbolical details this technique results in an extraordinarily dense narrative in which even minor elements and gestures are allowed to speak eloquently for themselves: the lipstick smudge on the coffee cup Lily offers to Dr. Ernst; Mrs. Chawla's wiping her hand on her sari after Dr. Ernst has chivalrously kissed it; the absence of hospitality at Mrs. Chawla's and the abundance of European food and coffee at Maiska's. The functionality of the details is often potentiated through recurrence; for instance the very different kinds of music and of food in three successive locations. Dr. Ernst's habit of raising his panama hat also has a dual role; first it denotes his old-fashioned European civility; on its second appearance, however, when he resorts to the same gesture to ask the young Indians thronging into the coffee bar to let him pass, it reveals his pathetic powerlessness as an elderly foreigner. It is the selfish, pushy young-sters who are in control, and they have neither respect nor manners. These spoiled, arrogant youths counterbalance Miss Jaya and the elegant, intellec-tual ladies, the pride of modern India. The outcome of Jhabvala's narrative strategies is a story that hints much more than it actually states.

So ultimately the seeming transparency of "An Indian Citizen" proves misleading. Beneath its focus on the discord between East and West it conceals another conflict within its pivotal figure. Dr. Ernst aims for integration into his Indian surroundings by finding employment and friends. Out of gratitude for the haven India has afforded him he is very favorably disposed to the country. But his experiences on the day depicted in this story repeatedly uncover the illusion he harbors that to have become an Indian citizen signified his inclusion in Indian life. His citizenship proves no more than a legal doc-ument, an important one certainly, but no passport to his full acceptance in the host country. His continued unemployment is a cipher for his exclusion, marginalization, indeed rejection.

Because of his devotion to India Dr. Ernst refuses to admit the reality of the situation. The only place where he feels at home is among the displaced, lonely Europeans at Maiska's. For his cold reception at Mrs. Chawla's he takes the blame, scolding himself: "[Y]ou silly old Ernst . . . always so touchy, that was his trouble, looking for offence where none was meant. It was a very bad trait in him" (161). The contrary is true; the really bad trait in him is his unwillingness to register the offense. His deepest need is for a sustained self-deception, which drives him into the cultivation of a false optimism, summarized in his insistence that he has many good Indian friends whose doors are always open to him. As the story is told predominantly from his angle readers are disposed, especially at the outset, to go along with his beliefs. Moreover his neatness, cleanliness, and courtesy make him an appealing character who seems deserving of success in attaining in India the security associated with citizenship.

Only gradually do the ironies implicit in the story surface, beginning with its title. Dr. Ernst is technically an Indian citizen, but is not considered a genuine one. It is to "a genuine Indian subject" (146) that he had lost his position. The opposite of "genuine" is "ersatz," a German word that has—like Dr. Ernst!—been naturalized into English although it has to be placed, with evident self-consciousness, into inverted commas for—again like Dr. Ernst—it is not a natural, fully accepted term. *Ersatz* means substitute, yet it also carries an undercurrent of inferiority, even phoniness as if a substitute were pretending to be, or mimicking, something else, something genuine. Certainly it implies a second best. In "An Indian Citizen" *ersatz* appears not only in inverted commas but also within parenthesis: "(and not an 'ersatz' one, as he liked in fun to call himself)" (146). Is Dr. Ernst really speaking "in fun" when he designates himself an *ersatz* Indian citizen? Or is this, like his other wry, self-deprecating joke about his readiness to teach even Viennese, a rare glimpse of his despair? In the word *ersatz* he concedes for a moment the deeper truth that he will never be a genuine Indian citizen.[3]

To what extent then is his entire existence *ersatz* in the sense of substitute and not quite genuine? His life in India is an ironic substitute for what he would have had in Vienna; if he had graduated in philology he would likely have obtained a position as a high-school teacher, have lived in a nice apartment, and more or less continued his parents' lifestyle. The causes for the thwarting of this normative, expected path are never mentioned in "An Indian Citizen." Rich as the story is in material detail it is strikingly elliptical in making any mention of events in European history. That Dr. Ernst's travels were "enforced" is as close as we come to the upheavals of the 1930s. It is taken for granted that readers will understand how Maiska's friends with the foreign names—the Linskys, Anna Shulka, Herman—had come to be "displaced" (155). Perhaps one indirect indication is in the placement of "An Indian Citizen" as the first in the collection's section "Sufferers."[4]

But Dr. Ernst's life as an Indian citizen has a dimension of inauthenticity too. His determined optimism allows him to cherish illusions (of the open doors of his many good Indian friends) and to deny unpleasant realities. Occasionally his intuitive recognition of the situation does break through, as, for instance, in his acknowledgment that "he and Lily and Maiska and Herman and the rest of them would always remain only pale, stray strangers" (163). Mostly, though, he protects himself through an innocence, which is the cover (in fact, an *ersatz*) for a willed not wanting to know.

Seen from this perspective Dr. Ernst becomes a more troubled and troubling figure than the neat person in the panama hat we first meet. That compulsive neatness itself assumes a rather sinister aspect as an attempt to keep at bay "that chaos which seemed perpetually to lie in wait for him and had done so ever since he had started his enforced travels almost thirty years ago" (148). Any dust or disorder in his room "was to him like giving in to that chaos" (148). A strong streak of anxiety and compulsiveness is in evidence here. "Giving in" is tantamount to letting go in the endless struggle to maintain the image of himself he has so strenuously cultivated. That fear of giving in is on his mind again when he takes a nap at Maiska's:

> a nap in the afternoon was nothing to reproach oneself with—good heavens, at his age and in this climate!—but one also had to know when to cut it short. Otherwise there was the danger of sinking too deep and giving way to the desire to sleep for ever and not have to get up at all any more and walk around and meet people (165).

The life he leads as an Indian citizen is here unmasked as a calculated effort not to let himself sink into the depressiveness of prolonged sleep, sloth, or even death but to keep going and to keep up the pretense of a rosier future when he finds employment with the help of those many good Indian friends.

Whether Dr. Ernst has such good Indian friends therefore becomes the crucial question in this story. Mrs. Chawla's annoyance at his unannounced visit points to a negative answer. But it may be dangerous to extrapolate from a single instance. On the other hand Dr. Ernst chose to go and see her precisely because he expected a warm welcome from her. In the past she had been flattered by his hand kissing; this time she recoils from it. Perhaps her attitude has changed with his worsened circumstances; as an employee of the Ministry of Information he warranted greater respect than in his current unemployed status. Such a hypothesis creates a vicious circle since it is employment he hopes to achieve through his Indian friends.

Dr. Ernst's persistent self-deception is confirmed by his exchange with Lily at Maiska's later in the story. " 'I spent a very nice morning with Mrs. Chawla,' " he tells her, " 'she asked me to come again very soon' " (165–6). We know this to be untrue, a kind of *ersatz* for the way he had actually been treated. Lily is as harsh on Mrs. Chawla as she had been on Dr. Ernst earlier on: " 'I can't stand her . . . A conceited stupid cow' " (165). Lily's judgment is corroborated by what we have seen of Mrs. Chawla. So in retrospect we are obliged to reconsider her assessment of Dr. Ernst as a hanger-on. What had seemed like an expression of her cynicism, born of her personal disillusionment with India, now appears instead as realism on her part. At the outset readers are inclined to give more credence to Dr. Ernst than to her because he is neat, clean, and conforms to social proprieties. By contrast her scruffiness and laziness throw a bad light on her, which undermines her credibility. She lies about being too sick to work that day. The ironic twist to this story is that we eventually come to believe her verdict that Dr. Ernst is a hanger-on as we see through the mixture of forced optimism and desperation, which inspire his self-deception.

In the story's closing paragraph, however, Dr. Ernst gives up the pretense. Under the spell of the magical sounds of Mozart's flute concerto, "graceful and happy," emanating from Maiska's record player he changes his own tune: "it was much much nicer than Mrs. Chawla's singing," he avows in a burst of honesty. Suddenly he feels "proud and European" as he remembers his "wondrous heritage—Mozart, Versailles, Goethe's Weimar" (167). He is so elated at shedding his false identity as an Indian citizen and reverting to his genuine one as a European that he breaks into a little dance, "getting up on his toes as if to reach with the music up to heaven" (168). In these concluding words the *ersatz* has yielded to the authentic in his spontaneous response from the heart to the Mozart music.

"An Indian Citizen" is a poignant story about an escapee whose life has been disrupted beyond repair. At sixty he is unlikely to find the employment he needs to reestablish himself socially as well as economically. He has been unable to assimilate, let alone to integrate into a culture very alien to a Central European. The more remote and exotic the country of destination, the harder the task obviously was. Dr. Ernst's dogged self-deception is his primary means of self-preservation.

Conclusion: "A Bit in the Middle of Nowhere"

" 'I'm not an Englishwoman, I don't think I am. On the other hand, I'm not an Austrian either; I'm not a Jewess either because my religion doesn't come into it. So I'm a bit in the middle of nowhere.' "[1] This is the ultimate self-assessment of Gertrud Wengraf, who was born in 1915 in Ludenburg, Moravia, and who grew up in Vienna after her family moved there when she was thirteen. Her father was an industrial chemist, and she herself studied at the university, where she was active in a Socialist youth movement; there also she met her husband, a Jewish art dealer. Right after Austria joined Germany they left for England, settling in London, where she still lives. Her husband's picture dealing prospered so that he was able to open an art gallery, and they have a son, born soon after their arrival in England.

Wengraf is clearly among the most fortunate of the escapees. She left Vienna together with her husband in the early days of Nazi rule, probably because her previous activity in a Socialist youth movement made her particularly vulnerable. She moved directly to London, where she has stayed ever since without the lengthy phase of disruptive wandering that was the fate of so many escapees before they were able to resettle on a permanent basis. Her immediate family remained intact, she has a son, and is financially secure. Hers is almost an escapee fairy story.

Yet even under these most propitious circumstances something is amiss, for Wengraf feels herself to be "a bit in the middle of nowhere," not belonging to her homeland or to her adopted country even though she has spent the major part of her life there. She has ceased to be a part of the world she left, but is not part of that in which she now resides. The fact that she has no sense of religious commitment, coming as she does from a secularized family, aggravates her identity problem. It is significant that she can define herself only negatively in terms of what she is *not* without any positive replacement. She does not express overt allegiance to the category of escapee despite her admission that most of her friendships are with the likes of herself: " 'It wasn't my intention and I certainly haven't done it deliberately, but somehow that's how it happened—I feel more comfortable with them.' "[2] Wengraf's observations evoke the subcommunities that appear in so many of the fictions: in "A Birthday in London" (1963), *Shadows on the Hudson* (1998), *In Search of Love and Beauty* (1983), *The Flood* (1987), "An Indian Citizen" (1968), and in an attenuated form in *Baumgartner's Bombay* (1988) in Hugo's friendship with Lotte. The bond represented by the common experience of expulsion and radical dislocation, together with the continuing awareness of remaining an outsider, draws the escapees involuntarily to each other.)

The spontaneous formation of these subcommunities is one telling indication of the lingering sense of "otherness," which besets many escapees, even those who made the transition from their first to their second life at an early age. The comment that Hass makes of concentration camp survivors applies with almost equal force to escapees: that the Holocaust did not end for them in 1945, that it has "ongoing consequences," mainly psychological in nature but also concrete, for instance, in the loss of family.[3] While most people view the Holocaust from a historical perspective as an event that occurred between 1939 and 1945, one more episode in the Jews' tragic story, for those immediately affected by it, it proved to be *the* central happening in their lives, which altered everything that came thereafter. Having been so brutally uprooted many of the escapees, like Wengraf, never felt completely rooted again. As George Weidenfeld, the prominent British publisher, put it, he saw himself as being " 'with the English but not of the English.' "[4] To the fundamental question that Laqueur poses, "Where do we belong?" there is simply no answer.[5] Escapees can never belong as deeply as those who have spent their entire lives in one place or even in one country; they may belong a little in many places, yet never whole-heartedly because vestiges of the former existence cling to them for better or for worse, giving them a broader horizon than their neighbors as well as a measure of detachment. Their lives are, as it were, doubled with remnants of the past ingrained in the present. While the escapees may not be "marked men,"[6] like those who were in the camps or in hiding, they do become different through their early forfeiture of security, illusions, and mother tongue.

Being a bit in the middle of nowhere does not, however, preclude the kinds of stellar achievements so much to the fore in the sociohistorical studies of this group. On the contrary a certain degree of marginalization may even spur above average attainments as a form of compensation. None of the fictions shows the outstanding successes recorded in the chronicles of "generation exodus," as it has aptly been called.[7] Still many of the fictional escapees do make a modest success of their lives professionally and economi-cally. Hartmann and Fibich in *Latecomers* (1990) do well enough in their greetings card and xeroxing business to live more than comfortably; in mid-dle age they are even able to consider acquisition of a vacation home in the South of France. Similarly Joe Beech in *To the City* (1987) has established himself in publishing. Max Ferber in Sebald's story has become an eminent painter. Boris Makaver in *Shadows on the Hudson* remains quite a wealthy man despite his losses in the shipping salvage venture. The Sonnenblicks, too, in *In Search of Love and Beauty* enjoy prosperity through all three generations. David Hoffman in *The Flood* is a psychiatrist at the prestigious Menninger Clinic. Gottfried Rosenbaum in *Pictures from an Institution* (1954) has also found a niche, albeit not a very appropriate one, at Benton College. Although none of the fictional characters rises to the astonishing heights of the exceptional escapees featured in the sociohistorical works, most of them show the capacity to rebuild their lives on the practical level.

But by no means all the fictive escapees thrive to this extent. Oskar Gassner in "The German Refugee" (1964) commits suicide, ironically after he has managed to deliver his crucial lecture. Hugo Baumgartner in Desai's novel declines into squalor before succumbing to a murderous thief. The future of Tilde in *Change* (1987) is left open; at the end of the war she is still in a lowly situation and in a depressed state, yet there are some grounds for hope in her youthfulness. For the older escapees the prospects are less good. It seems unlikely that Dr. Ernst in "An Indian Citizen" will ever find employment again. As for Sonia Wolff in "A Birthday in London," while she suffers no physical discomfort, she misses the social position she had enjoyed in Berlin. Perhaps the most pathetic casualties are Otto Wolff and Bruno Sonnenblick, both too old and defeated to start anew.

However even those who make the optimal adjustment continue to experience a residual malaise that is generally, it would seem almost programmatically, bypassed by the sociologists who focus on the positive contributions made by the escapees to their host countries. As to the value of these contributions there can be no question. But what the escapees do, that is, how they fare outwardly, and how they actually feel inwardly are two different matters. Wengraf is, from a realistic perspective, well settled, but she herself admits that she is not assimilated, let alone integrated into her current environment. *traumatized*

This, indeed, is the trickiest issue. To "assimilate," a term derived from the idea of similarity, means to assume a resemblance, that is, to blend in, becoming absorbed and amalgamated into the social fabric. To "integrate" goes a step further still, denoting a wholeness derived from unification of the constituent parts. The fictive characters stand at diverse points along the spectrum of assimilation. At one end Hugo Baumgartner in *Baumgartner's Bombay* finds himself in a culture so alien that he cannot hope ever to be anything other than an outsider. His European appearance, the profusion of India's languages, the complexity of its political and religious tensions combine to condemn him to lasting exclusion. At the opposite extreme is Joe Beech in *To the City*: he has changed his name, married an English Protestant, acquired English friends, and brought his children up without heed to the European strain in their parentage. But even the apparently quite assimilated Joe proves to have a deeply fractured personality. His marriage is falling apart, he is strongly drawn to Anna, a fellow escapee, and his closest friend and surrogate father is Ted, who, like Anna and himself, is originally from Vienna, the novel's titular city to which he returns and where he meets his end.

The ambivalences that become increasingly evident in Joe are characteristic of many escapees. What the literary critic Geoffrey Hartman, himself an escapee, denotes as "an organic relation to place" is lacking, and according to him, irrecoverably so.[8] He argues that we underestimate the importance of such a feeling for place not only as a physical memory but also in its connections to love "which fuses person to place" (20). The randomness of the escapees' destinations, far more frequently the outcome of chance than of

psychic connection as
integration / connection as
goal of psychotherapy
of the traumatized

choice, is surely a potent factor in the conflicted feelings they often have toward their host country. Gratitude for refuge is tempered by a reluctant recognition, at times a barely conceded consciousness of the nostalgia for their lost home, which is inextricably linked to the happier days of the past. Even though Hartmann in *Latecomers* sensibly and rationally urges Fibich to remember that the only fact that matters is that they have survived and created a whole new existence, Fibich nevertheless needs to go back to Berlin to explore his hometown and his inchoate emotions. In the end, to satisfy their metaphorical as well as literal yearning for warmth, they lay plans to return to Europe as if to replace their original home with a third one, which will make restitution by granting them a foothold on the Continent again. But this is a romance ending. The escapee's business remains inevitably unfinished; there is no final closure because the strands from childhood and early adulthood are integrally interwoven into the personality. This accounts for the apparent irrationality of the escapees' tendency to hark back to a country that had not only humiliated and rejected them but would have exterminated them if they had not succeeded in getting away.

Since they carry this psychological baggage, live at the crossroads between cultures, and are essentially dualistic in identity, it is hardly surprising that the escapees should seem self-contradictory in their attitudes toward both their past and their present. All of them show signs of a love/hate relationship to their previous existence; their revulsion at the injustices and cruelties inflicted on them does not override an instinctive attraction to a place and a time in which they were grounded to an extent not possible in their second lives. The culture and customs of their native place are lodged in their psyches. This sense of connectedness to something bygone assumes many guises, some quite open, others more veiled.

One of the most open examples of the maintenance of European culture occurs in *The Flood* where the Hoffmans' liberal, dissenting political and social views drive a wedge between them and their neighbors. Fortunate though they know themselves to be to have escaped arrest and worse in Vienna, they are nonetheless after a good many years in the United States still fish out of water in Topeka, Kansas. Leah, even as she impresses on her daughters the necessity of fitting in, herself continues to uphold values very different from those prevalent in this milieu. David reads, plays the piano, teaches his elder daughter the violin, and finds companionship and consolation in the classical chamber music he performs with fellow escapees. As in this novel music often functions as the cipher and the vehicle for the link with the familiar culture of the past. Thus Tilde, in *Change*, goes to free concerts on her afternoons off. The sound of European music also has a transforming effect on Dr. Ernst in "An Indian Citizen" prompting a spontaneous dance of joy after a rather wretched day as he reconnects with his own tradition. For however hard he works to accept his new home, as is symbolized by his assumption of Indian citizenship, he feels relaxed only at Maiska's, listening to her records of Mozart and Beethoven, drinking strong coffee, and eating potato salad. Maiska's home reproduces the habits and atmosphere of the

Old World, as do Boris Makaver's apartment in *Shadows on the Hudson*, and that of the Sonnenblicks in *In Search of Love and Beauty* with their old heavy furniture. In both these New York apartments the impression of still being in Europe is reinforced by the observation of traditional customs, religious in Boris Makover's case, conventionally German in the birthday and Christmas celebrations at the Sonnenblicks. At her birthday party in London Sonia Wolff unabashedly voices her nostalgia for the privileged life she had led in pre-Nazi days. It is left to Lumbick to redress the balance by pointing out how comparatively lucky they are to have escaped at all. The ambivalence is very pronounced here between loyalty to the host country and longing for what once was. All the escapees know at the rational level that they owe their lives to the refuge they have been given, but this does not stop them from hankering for a past that was both richer and less complicated emotionally.

The preference for that anterior existence is certainly implied by every facet of the Rosenbaums' lifestyle in *Pictures from an Institution*. They positively flaunt their European heritage in Irene's extravagant clothes, the Rhine wine that flows in their house, and their boastful references to the lofty artistic contacts they used to enjoy. As they are focalized through the eyes of an ironizing narrator, who turns them into figures of fun as much as of respect, it is impossible to determine what the Rosenbaums really think or feel, but they alone among all the escapees portrayed in fiction incline to a scantily concealed contempt for their host country rather than to the more common ambivalence.

By contrast the renunciation of the native land is strong in both Desai's Baumgartner and Sebald's Max Ferber. Baumgartner never ceases to feel wounded and embittered at his mother's disappearance. Although his family more than any other in these fictions saw itself as primarily German and not at all Jewish before Hitler, he knows only too well that there is no possibility of return. He is caught as in a vise, unable either to go back or to acculturate to India. That he is nonetheless instinctively still deeply touched by things German is illustrated by the fascination with which he watches a German missionary's wife in the internment camp as she plays German games with her children. This scene must remind him of his own childhood, thereby stirring poignant memories. His affinity to Lotte, despite their social incongruence, is another manifestation of his persistent attachment to remains of Germany; what holds them together above all is their shared language. Max Ferber even virtually loses the language as he consigns most of his past to the furthest recesses of his mind. At first he refuses to speak at all of anything preceding his arrival in England. When he eventually does open up a little more it becomes clear that he is engaging in a self-protective pain containment by largely obliterating, for instance, the scene of his parting from his parents at the Munich airport in May 1939. But gradually he does also retrieve happier aspects of the past such as his visit to Switzerland with his father.

These recurrent ambivalences underlie the conflicted image that escapees present. As they endeavor to grapple with the present and to build a future they cannot help also looking over their shoulders to the past. They are at once irreparably damaged by the dislocations and losses they have suffered, and extraordinarily resilient in coping with emotional difficulties and showing flexibility, tenacity, and assertiveness in overcoming frustrations and disappointments. They have been described as "an unusually gifted and resourceful group of men and women."[9] Since only the more resourceful managed to escape anyway, it is more accurate to argue that what was unusual about them was the challenging situation in which they found themselves after their escape—one in which community and locality did not coincide.[10] In this predicament they were torn between allegiance to their community, that is, to their past, and the obligation to adapt as far as possible to their new locality in the present.

The most striking form that this split takes is the dual pull to remember and to forget. This replicates on a perhaps less conscious psychological level the tensions innate to the escapees' central dilemma of committing to the here-and-now as against thinking back to what had been. But, as Heilbut points out, their "only portable property was [their] memory."[11] However memories can cut both ways: they may bring consoling recollections of happiness or they may become an affliction, further intensifying the sufferer's torment by constant reminders of loss. The inexorable presence of absence haunts escapees like a shadow that hangs over their entire existence. Much as some of them want to forget, to move on (in contemporary parlance), they are unable ever to do so completely because past and present, though outwardly separate, are not discontinuous psychologically. The past frames the present, intruding on it and incessantly reconfiguring it.

This aspect of escapees' lives is particularly well uncovered in fictions because they can imaginatively enter into the characters' minds and reveal the subconscious aftereffects of the traumas they have undergone. The foremost example of such recrudescence of memories believed to be long buried and conquered is Joe Beech in *To the City*. The carefully constructed edifice of his integration into British society collapses under the impact of the absences present in his subconscious, especially those of his sister and of his father who had been exactly the same age as Joe now is when he disappeared off the face of the earth. Joe has sought (fought?) for years to banish these memories just as he has abolished his earlier self, Josef Buchsbaum. What is more for a while he has managed to do so, to keep up the appearance of being just Joe Beech, until the vacation in his native Austria triggers an overwhelming avalanche of memories, which figuratively (as well as literally) destroy him.

Joe is a failed denier of his past. Lumbik in "A Birthday in London" and Hartmann in *Latecomers* remain in better control. Lumbik has an easier task insofar as he has apparently not lost close family members, nor was he yet well established in Vienna. The minimal extent of his losses and the long-drawn-out process of his resettlement combine with the natural buoyancy of his temperament to make him rejoice that he is at last secure as a British citizen. Hartmann is a far more complex case: he has deliberately fashioned a veritable ethos of hedonism specifically designed to maximize the small pleasures of his daily round. But even this program of forgetting does not totally spare him recall of his childhood in Munich, albeit without the flood of grief that engulfs Joe Beech.

Mostly, however, memories are fraught with pain for escapees. Even when they are memories of a happy past, as are Sonia Wolff's in "A Birthday in London," they underscore by the discrepancy with the present the deterioration that has resulted from the enforced emigration. Tilde's repeated thoughts in *Change* of her schoolteacher and her friend cause her acute anxiety as she misses them terribly and keeps wondering what has happened to them. Baumgartner is deeply distressed every time he recalls his mother. Luria in *Shadows on the Hudson* is so profoundly troubled by the extermination of his first wife and their children that he succumbs to clinical depression and drowns himself. Oskar Gassner, too, in "The German Refugee" commits suicide in the wake of guilt as well as grief at the fate of the wife he left behind in Germany. In all these instances the past is not just unmastered but in fact unmasterable.

In contrast to the majority of escapees who are unable to forget, Fibich in *Latecomers* cannot remember. He is plagued by the void about his life prior to his arrival in England. Psychoanalysis does not help him to recuperate more than quite fragmentary images of himself as a small plump boy sitting in a large armchair. The devastating lacuna in his knowledge about his family and his early home makes him feel not merely uprooted but depersonalized. He cannot follow Hartmann's creed that the present alone matters. Only after the crucial recollection of the circumstances of his parting from his parents comes back to him can Fibich achieve acceptance of himself by recognizing his mature role as a father instead of continuing to envisage himself as a stranded orphan. For Fibich remembering, beyond the sorrow it entails, also proves healing.

Like Fibich, Max Ferber has difficulty in remembering, but he seems rather to want to forget. His reticence is a manifestation of his desire to repress excruciating memories. Again as for Fibich his amnesia centers on the agonizing moment of his final parting from his parents. He eventually has partial recall of the scene, but it is flat and silent, as if it were a still life in which he intuitively perceives his parents as if they were already dead, sitting like wax figures in the rented car that is to take them back from the airport. Ferber's idiosyncratic method of painting, constantly erasing and turning the paint to dust, comes to appear emblematic of the way he handles the processes of his memory, simultaneously effacing even as he recollects. It is as if he wished to abrogate the reality of what he has created and with it that of the past.

The fictions thus present an image of escapees that differs in crucial respects from that predominant in the sociohistorical studies. Aiming as they do for objectivity, sociologists and social historians approach their subjects from an external angle, which relies on factual information. They therefore spotlight the escapees' doings, that is, the outer events of their careers. As many of them have the barely concealed agenda of demonstrating how valuable the newcomers were to their host country (rather than the burden it had been feared that they might prove to be), they inevitably underscore selectively the achievements, the successes, the contributions, that a considerable number of them have undeniably made.

The fictions have no such political axe to grind. While they include specifics of their protagonists' second start in life, sometimes rather fully, at other times more sketchily, they tend to center primarily on the psychological aspects, on the characters' responses to the new situations and challenges they face. So in contrast to the escapees' visible activities, recorded in the sociological works, the fictions expose their underlying feelings. For the particular strength of fiction lies in its capacity for a perspective that is at once external and internal. This dual perspective is especially valuable in regard to escapees because the difficulties they have to overcome in starting life anew are as much emotional as economic and social. The feelings involved remain beyond the purview of sociology, or at best marginal to its surveys except those that privilege personal testimony, which, however, as in the memoirs, runs the risk of unchecked subjectivity. In the fictions, on the other hand, it is the characters' emotional dramas and traumas that are of absolutely cardinal importance. These are imaginatively conceived by the writers so that they are envisioned at once from both within and outside the protagonists. We learn, for instance, not just whether Oskar Gassner in "The German Refugee" masters English sufficiently to deliver his lecture, but also the turmoil of self-doubt, which accompanies this effort. Similarly in *The Flood* we witness how the Hoffmans negotiate their relationships with their neighbors in Topeka, Kansas, as well as their inner conflicts about their assimilation into or resistance to this community. In *Latecomers* we watch Hartmann and Fibich growing up and becoming outwardly established in London, yet not without constant awareness of the psychological struggles intrinsic to that process—the struggle to forget and live exclusively in the present—on Hartmann's part and the converse need on Fibich's side to remember. And in *To the City* we see how Joe Beech's consummate campaign to pass for British collapses, hollowed out by the intrusion of memories and feelings he had thought to have vanquished and banned from his life together with Josef Buchsbaum.

The fictions therefore concede the malaise, the sense of distance and apartness from their second homes, which persists for many escapees, caught as they are a bit in the middle of nowhere. The fictions suggest that the malaise is more pervasive than had generally been acknowledged. They depict those who suffered no overt brutalities, yet whose lives were permanently shaped inwardly as much as outwardly by their radical dislocation from their anticipated paths. Often they seem to have adjusted quite well to their random destinations, building lives that are to all appearances pretty normal. But at some deeper level they remain distanced from, often ambivalent toward, or perhaps even alien to their new "home." While nothing ghastly befell the escapees (compared to the concentration camp survivors or to those in hiding) their involuntary relocation still had far-reaching consequences in the psychological as well as in the economic sphere, sometimes leading to a crisis later in life as they finally come to confront memories long repressed and regrets long denied. Beneath the surface of a sincerely attempted assimilation the escapee is shown to be distinctively "other," haunted by the underground presence of absence, the shadow of irreparable losses.

Through its aptitude for penetrating into the minds of its figures the fictional portrayals offer a richer, more differentiated (though admittedly more disturbing) picture than the sociological investigations. The two are ultimately complementary, each conveying its own kind of truth. While the sociological studies provide much valuable information about escapees' outer, public paths, the fictions allow revealing insights into the scars on the souls of these "shards from the explosion."

late in life?
escape vulnerable?

NOTES

To the Reader

1. Hirsch, *Last Dance at the Hotel Kempinski*, 4.
2. Furst and Furst, *Home is Somewhere Else*, 2.
3. Eppel in Hölbling and Wagnleitner, *European Emigrant Experience*, 27.
4. Ilie, *Literature and Inner Exile*, 14.
5. My mother would say "we were driven out of paradise" in recalling life in Vienna before Hitler, but she would not set foot in Austria after the war, and winced at hearing the Viennese accent.
6. Hölbling and Wagnleitner, *European Emigrant Experience*, 11.
7. Quoted in Witek and Safrian, *Und Keiner war Dabei*, 299.
8. Snowman, *Hitler Emigrés*, xx.
9. Arad, *America, Its Jews, and the Rise of Nazism*, 13.
10. Hartman, *Longest Shadow*, 10.

Introduction: "Shards from the Explosion"

1. Segev, *Seventh Million*, 33.
2. Laqueur, *Generation Exodus*, 215.
3. Ibid., 18.
4. Ambrose, *Hitler's Loss*, 22.
5. Kent, *Refugee Intellectual*, 12.
6. We were able to assemble all the documents because an official at the Viennese city hall, a patient of my father's, broke the law by making them valid for two months.
7. See Cowan and Schwartz, *Our Parents' Lives*, especially pp. 26–35.
8. Wasserstein, *Britain and the Jews of Europe*, 45.
9. Arad, *America, Its Jews, and the Rise of Nazism*, 203.
10. Ibid., 192.
11. Ibid., 199.
12. Snowman, *Hitler Emigrés*, 10.
13. Malet and Grenville, *Changing Countries*, 174. Wolff became librarian at the Weiner Library in London.
14. Gay, "Weimar Culture: The Outsider as Insider," 47.
15. Desai, *Baumgartner's Bombay*, 54–5.
16. Arad, *America, Its Jews, and the Rise of Nazism*.
17. The sole exception was a large temporary camp on the island of Mauritius. See Laqueur, *Generation Exodus*, 233–6, and Wasserstein, *Britain and the Jews of Europe*, 63.
18. Ibid., 227.
19. Spitzer, *Hotel Bolivia*, xiv and xv.
20. No relation to the author of *Hotel Bolivia*.

21. For information on emigrants to Turkey, see Levin, "Two Romanisten in America." The absence of a library prompted Auerbach to write his remarkable work, *Mimesis* using solely books in his personal possession and completely devoid of the usual critical apparatus of references to previous scholarship. I draw too on a talk by Professor Eugen Merzbacher in Durham, NC, March 15, 2001; his family had been one of those in Turkey, and he himself was educated there before going after the war to graduate school in this country.

22. Segev, *Seventh Million*, 35–46.

23. See "Sealing the Escape Routes," Wasserstein, *Britain and the Jews of Europe*, 40–80.

24. Rabinowitz tells of the concentration camp survivors who were resettled in the small town of Brownsville, Texas, where they were kindly received, but in response to questions about the food in the camp they were asked whether they had never been given dessert! (*New Lives*, 147).

25. Schwarz, *Imagining the Holocaust*, 7.

26. Wiesel, *A Jew Today*, 220.

27. For example, Friedlander (ed.) *Probing the Limits of Representation*; Hartman, *Rememberance* and *Longest Shadow*; Lang, *Holocaust Representation* and *The Future of the Holocaust*; and Langer, *Holocaust Testimonies*.

28. Hartman, *Longest Shadow*, 1.

29. Kent, *Refugee Intellectual*, 95–6.

30. See Melton, *Faces of Exile*.

31. Laqueur, *Generation Exodus*, cites the example of the distinguished Harvard historian John Clive who suddenly in the 1980s revealed his original name in Berlin and his parents' fate in an article on St. Pancras railway station in London (153). I have several friends, either themselves escapees or children of escapees, who had shed their ethnicity and later in life have returned to it.

32. For example, Hass, *Shadow of the Holocaust* and *Aftermath*; Helmreich, *Against All Odds*; and the work of the psychiatrist William C. Niederland.

33. For example, Salamon, *White Lies* (1987); Finkelstein, *Summer Long-A-Coming* (1987); Buket, *After* (1996); Rosenbaum, *Elijah Visible* (1996); Sucher, *The Rescue of Memory* (1997).

34. Moser, "Continental Britons," 2.

35. Grunberger, "Max Perutz," 10.

36. Hirsch, *Family Frames*, 23.

37. Langer, *Holocaust and the Literary Imagination*, 94.

38. Cohn, *Distinction of Fiction*, vii–viii, and 18.

39. Langer, *Holocaust and the Literary Imagination*, 8. Alongside Langer, Hartman in *Longest Shadow* and Lang in *Holocaust Representation* reach the same conclusion.

40. See "Let's Pretend," Furst, *All is True*, 28–47.

41. Langer, *Holocaust and the Literary Imagination*, 91.

42. Schwarz, *Imagining the Holocaust*, 4.

43. Bernard-Donals, "Beyond the Question of Authenticity," 1305.

2   "The Hidden Abyss": Gillian Tindall, *To the City* (1987)

1. Hass, *Aftermath*, 74 and 79.

2. Hirsch, *Family Frames*, 22.

3. Ibid., 243.

3   A "SUCCESS STORY": RUTH PRAWER JHABVALA, "A BIRTHDAY IN LONDON" (1963)

1. See Kushner, "An Alien Occupation," 569ff.
2. See London, "British Immigration Control Procedures." The arriving refugees were not aware of this. When my father was admitted to study in a British dental school and to take the final examinations after six months, we naturally believed this was a preliminary to permanent settlement in Great Britain. Yet our landing permit, issued in Dover on March 1, 1939 states "**SIX MONTHS ONLY**" (capitalized and three times underscored). This restriction always puzzled me until I learnt recently that the forty Austrian dentists were destined to go to the Colonies, specifically some to British Guiana. The outbreak of war in September 1939 intervened, and we stayed until our voluntary re-emigration in 1971.
3. London, *Whitehall and the Jews*, 233–66; Grenville, "Were the Refugees to be Repatriated?"
4. See London, "British Immigration Control Procedures."
5. Kushner, "An Alien Occupation."
6. See Berghahn, *German–Jewish Refugees in England* for the attitudes of escapees toward British Jews in regard to culture.
7. See Malet and Grenville, *Changing Countries*, 178–9 and 181.
8. Shepherd, "Fascism in Hampstead," 4.
9. Perry, "Idioms for the Unrepresentable," 112.

4   "TRY TO FORGET": MAUREEN DUFFY, *CHANGE* (1987)

1. For information on this topic see Kushner, "An Alien Occupation."
2. On the ill-treatment experienced by many of the domestics, see Malet and Grenville, *Changing Countries*, 91–3.
3. The Red Cross provided lists of survivors after the war, which were anxiously scrutinized by escapees in search of relatives and friends.
4. Elkan, "Anglo-Jewry and the Refugees," 5.

5   "TO SERVE UNDER THE CHIMNEY": W.G. SEBALD, "MAX FERBER," *THE EMIGRANTS* (1992)

1. I have worked from the German text, but cited from the English translation for the sake of uniformity and accessibility.
2. To anyone coming from Europe even as late as the mid-1960s Manchester would likely have appeared to be in a catastrophic decline since its center had been destroyed by bombing and its traditional industries, notably the cotton mills, were suffering in the wake of newer synthetic materials.

6   "THE GREAT LOSS": BERNARD MALAMUD, "THE GERMAN REFUGEE" (1963)

1. Kaplan, "On the Language Memoir," 63.
2. Berger, *Children of Job*, 38.
3. Kent, *Refugee Intellectual*, 89 and 101.

4. Ibid., 117.
5. Bilik, *Immigrant–Survivors*, 13–14; Dinnerstein, *America and the Survivors of the Holocaust*, 2–3; Arad, *America, Its Jews, and the Rise of Nazism*, 187–99. Dinnerstein, *America and the Survivors of the Holocaust*, 2–3; Arad, *America, Its Jews, and the Rise of Nazism*, 187–99.
6. Berger, *Crisis and Covenant*, 95.
7. Grinberg and Grinberg, *Psychoanalytic Perspectives on Migration*.

8   "A Bizarre Double Game": Isaac Bashevis Singer, *Shadows on the Hudson* (1998)

1. The description of the building is modeled on the West Eighty-Sixth Street house where Singer (and my uncle) used to live.
2. 1 Kings 19: 9–13.

9   "Can You Harmonize?": Carol Ascher, *The Flood* (1987)

1. "My Intentions in Writing *The Flood* by Carol Ascher," http://www.connix.com/curbston/whyflood.
2. "Brown v. Board of Education," Gunther, *Cases and Materials*, 757–61.
3. "The 'Separate but Equal Doctrine,' " Gunther, *Cases and Materials*, 754–7.
4. Grant, "Defiance: The Southern Manifesto," *Black Protest*, 268–72.
5. Kent, *Refugee Intellectual*, 130.
6. Friedman, *Menninger*, 115.
7. Ibid., 116.
8. Ibid., 182.
9. Ibid., 182–3.
10. Ascher herself married a non-Jew.
11. Friedman, *Menninger*, 180.

11   "Accepting—but not Accepted": Anita Desai, *Baumgartner's Bombay* (1988)

1. Laqueur, *Generation Exodus*, 232.
2. This complaint recalls the story (joke?) about the commander of a British internment camp who is said to have voiced his surprise that there were so many Jews among the Nazis!

12   The "Hanger-On": Ruth Prawer Jhabvala, "An Indian Citizen" (1968)

1. Malet and Grenville, *Changing Countries*, 199.
2. See Grinberg and Grinberg, *Psychoanalytic Perspectives on Migration*.
3. In Great Britain naturalized citizens were sometimes referred to as "foreigners with British passports," or more recently as "Continental Britons."
4. Another aspect never mentioned is the problem of language. In what language does Dr. Ernst communicate with Lily? Presumably in her native English. With Mrs. Chawla? What language do Maiska and her friends speak?

CONCLUSION: "A BIT IN THE MIDDLE OF NOWHERE"

1. Malet and Grenville, *Changing Countries*, 173.
2. Ibid., 242.
3. Hass, *Aftermath*, 192.
4. Cited by Snowman, *Hitler Emigrés*, 142.
5. Laqueur, *Generation Exodus*, 198–201.
6. Ibid., 284.
7. Ibid.
8. Hartman, *Longest Shadow*, 19.
9. Malet and Grenville, *Changing Countries*, 248.
10. The idea of the lack of overlap between "community" and "locality" is taken from Massey's "Double Articulation."
11. Heilbut, *Exiled in Paradise*, 29.

BIBLIOGRAPHY

PRIMARY SOURCES

Ascher, Carol. *The Flood.* CA: Crossing Press, 1987.
Begley, Louis. *The Man Who Was Late* (1992). New York: Ballantine, 1994.
Bellow, Saul. *Mr. Sammler's Planet* (1969). New York: Vintage, 1973.
Brookner, Anita. *The Latecomers* (1988). New York: Vintage, 1990.
———. *The Next Big Thing.* London: Vintage, 2002.
Buket, Melvin Jules. *After.* New York: St. Martin's Press, 1996.
Chabon, Michael. *The Amazing Adventures of Kavalier and Clay.* New York: Random House, 2000.
Delbanco, Nicolas. *What Remains.* New York: Warner Books, 2000.
Desai, Anita. *Baumgartner's Bombay* (1988). Boston: Houghton Mifflin, 2000.
Drabble, Margaret. *The Radiant Way.* London: Weidenfeld & Nicolson, 1987.
Duffy, Maureen. *Change.* London: Methuen, 1987.
Finkelstein, Barbara. *Summer Long-A-Coming.* New York: Harper & Row, 1987.
Furst, Desider and Lilian R. Furst. *Home is Somewhere Else.* Albany, NY: State University of New York Press, 1994.
Goodman, Allegra. "Fannie Mae" in *The Family Markowitz.* New York: Washington Square Press, 1997, 3–27.
Gstrein, Norbert. *Die englischen Jahre.* Frankfurt: Suhrkamp, 1999.
Hirsch, Robin. *Last Dance at the Hotel Kempinski. Creating a Life in the Shadow of History.* Hanover and London: New England University Press, 1995.
Jarrell, Randall. "Constance and the Rosenbaums" in *Pictures from an Institution* (1952). New York: Knopf, 1954, 131–83.
Jhabvala, Ruth Prawer. "A Birthday in London" in *Like Birds, Like Fishes* (1963). New York: W.W. Norton, 1964, 123–39.
———. "Disinheritance." *Blackwoods Magazine,* 4–14 (July 1979).
———. "An Indian Citizen" in *A Stronger Climate.* London: John Murray, 1968, 145–68.
———. *In Search of Love and Beauty* (1983). Washington: Counterpoint, 1999.
Keneally, Thomas. *Schindler's List.* New York: Simon & Schuster, 1982. Film directed by Steven Spielberg, 1993.
Larkin, Philip. *A Girl in Winter* (1947). Woodstock, NY: Overlook Press, 1976.
Malamud, Bernard. *The Fixer.* New York: Farrar, Straus & Giroux, 1966.
———. "The German Refugee." *Saturday Evening Post* 236, 36–9 (1963); rpt. in *The Complete Short Stories.* New York: Farrar, Straus & Giroux, 1997, 357–68.
———. "Take Pity" in *The Magic Barrel.* New York: Farrar, Straus & Giroux, 1958, 85–95.

Michaels, Anne. *Fugitive Pieces* (1996). New York: Vintage, 1998.

Ozick, Cynthia. *The Cannibal Galaxy.* New York: Knopf, 1983.

———. *The Shawl* (comprises "The Shawl" and "Rosa"). New York: Vintage, 1983.

Paretsky, Sara. *Bitter Medicine.* New York: Morrow & Co., 1987.

———. *Total Recall.* New York: Delacourt Press, 2001.

Rosenbaum, Thane. *Elijah Visible.* New York: St. Martin's Press, 1996.

Salamon, Julie. *White Lies.* Boston: Hill & Co., 1987.

Sebald, Winfried Georg Max. *Austerlitz.* Munich: Hanser, 2001; New York: Random House, 2001.

———. *Die Ausgewanderten.* Frankfurt: Eichhorn, 1992; *The Emigrants.* Trans. Michael Hulse. New York: New Directions, 1997.

Shaham, Nathan. *The Rosendorf Quartet* (1987). Trans. Dalya Bilu. New York: Grove Weidenfeld, 1988.

Singer, Isaac Bashevis. *Enemies: A Love Story* (1966). Trans. Eliza Shevrin and Elizabeth Shub. New York: Farrar, Straus & Giroux, 1972.

———. *Shadows on the Hudson* in *The Forward* (January 1957–January 1958). Trans. Joseph Sherman. New York: Plume, 1998.

———. "A Wedding in Brownsville" in *Short Friday.* New York: Farrar, Straus & Giroux, 1964; rpt. *American Jewish Fiction*, ed. Gerald Shapiro. Lincoln: University of Nebraska Press, 1998, 38–50.

Styron, William. *Sophie's Choice.* New York: Vintage, 1976.

Sucher, Cheryl P. *The Rescue of Memory.* New York: Berkley, 1997.

Tindall, Gillian. *To the City.* London: Dent, 1987.

Wiesel, Elie. *A Jew Today.* Trans. Marion Wiesel. New York: Viking, 1979.

Wilkomirski, Binjamin. *Fragments: Memories of a Wartime Childhood.* Trans. Carol Brown Janeway. New York: Schocken, 1996.

Zweig, Stefanie. *Nirgendwo in Afirka.* Munich: Wilhelm Heyne, 2000.

SECONDARY SOURCES

Abbey, William et. al. (eds). *Between Two Languages: German-Speaking Exiles in Great Britain, 1933–45.* Stuttgart: Dieter Verlag, 1995.

Ambrose, Tom. *Hitler's Loss: What Britain and America Gained from Europe's Cultural Exiles.* London: Peter Owen, 2001.

Arad, Gulie Ne'eman. *America, Its Jews, and the Rise of Nazism.* Bloomington, IN: Indiana University Press, 2000.

Bammer, Angelika (ed.). *Displacements.* Bloomington, IN: Indiana University Press, 1994.

Beer, Siegfried. "Exile between Assimilation and Re-Identification," in Hölbling and Wagnleitner, *The European Emigrant Experience*, 39–50.

Berger, Alan L. *Children of Job.* Albany, NY: State University of New York Press, 1997.

———. *Crisis and Covenant. The Holocaust in American Jewish Fiction.* Albany, NY: State University of New York Press, 1985.

Berghahn, Marion. *German Jewish Refugees in England.* New York: Berg, 1988.

Bergmann, Martin S. and Milton E. Jucovy. *Generations of the Holocaust.* New York: Basic, 1982.

Bernard-Donals, Michael. "Beyond the Question of Authenticity: Witness and Testimony in the *Fragments* Controversy." *PMLA* 116:5, 1302–15 (2001).

Bilik, Dorothy Seidman. *Immigrant–Survivors: Post-Holocaust Consciousness in Recent Jewish–American Fiction.* Middletown: Wesleyan University Press, 1981.

Cohn, Dorrit. *The Distinction of Fiction*. Baltimore and London: The Johns Hopkins University Press, 1998.

Cowan, Neil M. and Ruth Schwartz. *Our Parents' Lives* (1989). New Brunswick, NJ: Rutgers University Press, 1996.

Crane, Ralph J. *Ruth Prawer Jhabvala*. New York: Twayne, 1992.

Dinnerstein, Leonard. *America and the Survivors of the Holocaust*. New York: Columbia University Press, 1992.

Dove, Richard. *Journey of No Return: Five German-Speaking Literary Exiles in Britain, 1933–1945*. London: Libris, 2000.

Elkan, W. "Anglo-Jewry and the Refugees." *Association of Jewish Refugees Journal* 1:11, 5 (November 2001).

Eppel, Peter. "Exiled Austrians in the USA, 1938–1945: Immigration, Exile, Remigration, No Invitation to Return," in Hölbling and Wagnleitner, *The European Emigrant Experience*, 25–37.

Fleming, Donald and Bernard Baylin (eds). *The Intellectual Migration: Europe and America, 1093–1960*. Cambridge, MA: Harvard University Press, 1969.

Fox, John P. "British Attitudes to Jewish Refugees from Central and Eastern Europe in the Nineteenth and Twentieth Centuries," in Mosse, *Second Chance*, 465–84.

Friedlander, Saul (ed.). *Probing the Limits of Representation: Nazism and the "Final Solution."* Cambridge, MA: Harvard University Press, 1992.

Friedman, Lawrence J. *Menninger: The Family and the Clinic*. New York: Knopf, 1990.

Furst, Lilian R. *"All is True": The Claims and Strategies of Realist Fiction*. Durham, NC: Duke University Press, 1995.

Gay, Peter. "Weimar Culture: The Outsider as Insider," in Fleming and Baylin (eds), *The Intellectual Migration*, 11–93.

Gooneratne, Yasmine. *Silence, Exile and Cunning. The Fiction of Ruth Prawer Jhabvala* (1983). New Delhi: Orient Longman, 1990.

Grant, Joanne G. (ed.). *Black Protest: History, Documents, and Analyses*. New York: Fawcett World Library, 1968.

Grenville, Anthony. "Were the Refugees to be Repatriated in 1945?" *Association of Jewish Refugees Journal* 1:11, 7 (November 2001).

Grinberg, Leon and Rebeca Grinberg. *Psychoanalytic Perspectives on Migration*. New Haven: Yale University Press, 1989.

Grunberger, Richard. "Max Perutz Dies at 88." *Association of Jewish Refugees Journal* 2:4, 10 (April 2002).

Gunther, Gerald (ed.). *Cases and Materials*. Mineola, NY: Foundation Press, 1985.

Harris, Mark Jonathan and Deborah Oppenheimer. *Into the Arms of Strangers: Stories of the "Kindertransport."* London and New York: Bloomsbury, 2000.

Hartman, Geoffrey H. *The Longest Shadow: In the Aftermath of the Holocaust*. Bloomington, IN: Indiana University Press, 1996.

———. *Rememberance: The Shapes of Memory*. Cambridge: Blackwell, 1994.

Hass, Aaron. *The Aftermath. Living with the Holocaust*. New York: Cambridge University Press, 1995.

———. *In the Shadow of the Holocaust. The Second Generation*. Ithaca and London: Cornell University Press, 1990.

Heilbut, Anthony. *Exiled in Paradise: German Refugee Artists and Intellectuals in America from the 1930s to the Present* (1981). Boston: Beacon Press, 1984.

Heimreich, William B. *Against All Odds: Survivors and the Successful Lives They Made in America*. New York: Simon & Schuster, 1992.

Hirsch, Marianne. *Family Frames: Photography, Narrative, and Postmemory.* Cambridge, MA: Harvard University Press, 1997.

Hohendahl, P.U. and Egon Schwarz (eds). *Exil und innere Emigration.* Frankfurt: Athenäum, 1973.

Hölbling, Walter and Reinhold Wagnleitner (eds). *The European Emigrant Experience in the U.S.A.* Tübingen: Niemeyer, 1991.

Ilie, Paul. *Literature and Inner Exile: Authoritarian Spain, 1935–1975.* Baltimore: The Johns Hopkins University Press, 1980.

Jacobson, Colin (ed.). *Underexposed. Pictures Can Lie, Liars Use Pictures.* Vision on Publishing in Association with Getty Images, 2002.

Kaplan, Alice. "On the Language Memoir" in Bammer, *Displacements*, 59–70. Bloomington, IN: Indiana University Press, 1994.

Kent, Donald Peterson. *The Refugee Intellectual: The Americanization of the Immigrants of 1933–41.* New York: Columbia University Press, 1953.

Krystal, Henry (ed.). *Massive Psychic Trauma.* New York: International Universities Press, 1968.

Kushner, Tony. "An Alien Occupation—Jewish Refugees and Domestic Service in Great Britain, 1933–48," in Mosse, *Second Chance*, 553–78.

LaCapra, Dominick. *Representing the Holocaust: History, Theory, Trauma.* Ithaca: Cornell University Press, 1994.

Lang, Berel. *The Future of the Holocaust: Between History and Memory.* Ithaca and London: Cornell University Press, 1999.

———. *Holocaust Representation: Art Within the Limits of History and Ethics.* Baltimore: Johns Hopkins University Press, 2000.

Langer, Lawrence. *The Holocaust and the Literary Imagination.* New Haven: Yale University Press, 1976.

———. *Holocaust Testimonies: The Ruins of Memory.* New Haven: Yale University Press, 1991.

Laqueur, Walter. *Generation Exodus.* Waltham, MA: Brandeis University Press, 2001.

——— (ed.). *The Holocaust Encyclopedia.* New Haven: Yale University Press, 2001.

Leak, Andrew and George Paizis (eds). *Advancing Double Binds: The Holocaust and the Text. Speaking the Unspeakable.* New York: St. Martin's Press, 2000.

Levin, Harry T. "Two Romanisten in America," in Fleming and Baylin (eds), *The Intellectual Migration*, 463–84.

London, Louise. "British Immigration Control Procedures and Jewish Refugees, 1933–39," in Mosse, *Second Chance*, 485–517.

———. *Whitehall and the Jews: British Immigration Policy, Jewish Refugees and the Holocaust.* Cambridge: Cambridge University Press, 2001.

Malet, Marian and Anthony Grenville (eds). *Changing Countries: The Experiences and Achievements of German-Speaking Refugees from Hitler in Britain.* London: Libris, 2002.

Massey, Doreen. "Double Articulation: A Place in the World," in Bammer, *Displacements*, 110–21.

Melton, Judith. *The Faces of Exile. Autobiographical Journeys.* Iowa City: Iowa University Press, 1998.

Moser, Claus. "Continental Britons." *Association of Jewish Refugees Journal* 2:6, 2 (June 2002).

Mosse, Werner E. *Second Chance: Two Centuries of German-Speaking Jews in the United Kingdom.* Tübingen: Mohr, 1991.

Pauker, Pauline. "The Image of the German Jew in English Fiction," in Mosse, *Second Chance*, 315–33.

Perry, Anne. "Idioms for the Unrepresentable: Postwar Fiction and the Shoah" in Leak and Paizis (eds), *The Holocaust and the Text*, 109–24.

Rabinowitz, Dorothy. *New Lives*. New York: Avon, 1976.

Schlant-Bradley, Ernestine. *The Language of Silence. West German Literaure and the Holocaust*. New York: Routledge, 1999.

Schwarz, Daniel R. *Imagining the Holocaust*. New York: St. Martin's Press (Palgrave), 1999.

Segev, Tom. *The Seventh Million*. New York: Hill & Wang, 1993.

Shepherd, Catherine. "Fascism in Hampstead, 1945–1949." *Association of Jewish Refugees Journal* 2:4, 4 (April 2002).

Snowman, Daniel. *The Hitler Emigrés*. London: Chatto & Windus, 2002.

Spitzer, Leo. *Hotel Bolivia. The Culture of Memory in a Refuge from Nazism*. New York: Hill & Wang, 1998.

Timms, Edward and Ritchie Robertson (eds). *Austrian Exodus: The Creative Achievements of Refugees from National Socialism*. Edinburgh: Edinburgh University Press, 1995.

Wasserstein, Bernard. *Britain and the Jews of Europe 1939–1945*. New York: Oxford University Press, 1979.

Whitman, Dorit Bader. *The Uprooted: A Hitler Legacy*. Cambridge, MA: Perseus Books, 1993.

Wimmer, Adi. " 'Expelled and Banished': The Exile Experience of Austrian 'Anschluss' Victims in Personal Histories and Literary Documents," in Hölbling and Wagnleitner, *The European Emigrant Experience*, 51–72.

Witek, Hans and Hans Safrian (eds). *Und Keiner war Dabei: Dokumente des alltäglichen Antisemitismus in Wien 1938*. Vienna: Picus, 1988.

Index